To Betsy and Frank

CONTENTS

List of Illustrations

Section 2

Acknowledgements

When I wrote for *90 Minutes* football magazine in the mid-1990s it was one of those tacit agreements among the staff that you should never call the game 'soccer'. It was, we concluded, entirely un-British and smacked of, well, the American version of the game. When I use the word 'soccer' in this book, I do so not because I like it – I don't – but because it is the name used by most of the interviewees to describe the game in a country where 'football' is that other game played by men in helmets.

This, moreover, was never meant to be a book about the myriad reasons why the North American Soccer League collapsed or why the game of soccer failed to take its opportunity in the United States. There are several books already in print that more than adequately explain why America failed to take the rest of the world's game to their hearts. Instead, it was simply designed to chronicle the inconceivable peaks and all too predictable troughs of the phenomenon that was the Cosmos.

As ever, there are innumerable people that have gone beyond the call of duty to help out with this book. First and foremost, I would like to thank everyone at Passion Pictures, especially the Johns, Dower and Battsek, and the ever-helpful Jess Ludgrove. This, after all, is their book and I wholeheartedly recommend that you see their feature-length documentary of the Cosmos story, *Once in a Lifetime – the Extraordinary Story of the New York Cosmos*. Throughout the writing process Passion Pictures has always been on hand with a telephone number or a transcript, a contact or a clue, and I would like to thank them for giving me this incredible opportunity to work with them. It's been a pleasure. I would also like to thank Dan Davies for suggesting my name at the outset.

Thanks also to all those people on both sides of the Atlantic who agreed to be interviewed for the book. Every contribution, no matter how small, was much appreciated. Special thanks are reserved for Clive Toye who has put me straight on countless issues and re-directed me when I've been barking up the wrong tree on more occasions than I care to remember. All he has ever asked in return for all his advice is that I mention that he is a lifelong Exeter City fan and a member of the Exeter City Supporters Trust. It's a small price to pay. Thanks again Clive.

Thanks also to Phil Woosnam, Len Renery, the all-knowing Colin Jose and Jack Huckel at the National Soccer Hall of Fame, Dave Wasser at the NASL Alumni Association, George Tiedemann, James Trecker, Jay Emmett, Shep Messing and Jamie Trecker for their help.

I'm also indebted to Toby Mundy, Louisa Joyner and everyone at Atlantic Books for giving me the chance to write this book and for bearing with me at the death. Thanks also to my agent-cum-therapist, John Pawsey, whose advice has been invaluable.

Thanks to everyone at KYN, most notably Tim Southwell, Iestyn George, Phil Babb, Danny Crouch, Steve Read, Pandora George, Ben Marshall, Lee Goodall, Gerry East, Owen Blackhurst, Dan Owen, Joe Slater, Sifaeli Tesha, Shaun McGuckian and Jim Davies for their patience and understanding.

Advice and support came in many shapes and sizes and it would be remiss of me not to mention Gordon Thomson, Bill

Borrows, Ed Needham, Michael Hodges, Eleanor Levy, Andy Strickland, Graham Wray, Graeme Thomson and Alan Rutter. Paul Hawksbee, Andy Jacobs and everyone at Talk Sport also warrant a mention for their continued and much-valued support.

On the family front, I would like to thank Betty Farragher, Bernadette and Adrian Mullen for all their help over the years; and Mum, Dad and Darren for their support. Finally, I'd like to thank my wife, Ann. It is a constant source of bewilderment to me how you manage to entertain two pre-school children for all their waking hours and I don't know how you do it darling, but I'm really glad you can and you do. You are a wonderful wife and a marvellous mother. Thanks honey.

Gavin Newsham
Brighton
January 2006

BRAZIL, JUNE 1950

They called him Larry but his name was Joe Gaetjens. Everybody loved Joe. Cheery and unassuming, he was the kind of kid who had a smile for a stranger and who made friends like others made coffee.

Joe was smart too. In 1948, he won a government scholarship and left his home in the Haitian capital, Port-au-Prince, to study accountancy at Columbia University in New York but had ended up washing dishes in a German restaurant just to get by. Still, there was always soccer to fall back on.

On the field, Joe was a free spirit with an eye for goal. When he played upfront for the Brookhattan team in the little-known American Soccer League, he was the man on the end of every cross, the player in the right place at the right time. Quick and agile, he had the kind of spontaneity and ingenuity that left spectators breathless and defenders tackling thin air. He would go around people, over people, through people. Often, his team-mates would just give him the ball, safe in the knowledge that Joe would do the rest.

When Joe got called up to the United States national team for the 1950 World Cup Finals in Brazil nobody was surprised. So what if he wasn't actually an American? There were other players on the team that were in the same situation and the main thing, as far as soccer's world governing body, FIFA, was

1

concerned, was that he had every intention of one day becoming an American citizen.

On 29 June 1950, Joe Gaetjens and his 'compatriots' took to the field at the Belo Horizonte Stadium to face the soccer might of England. Going into the tournament, the Americans had lost all three of their three warm-up games, conceding eighteen goals and scoring none. Now, they were playing England, one of the most complete football machines in the world. They were legends everywhere; Billy Wright and Alf Ramsey; Stan Mortensen and Wilf Mannion. They had even given the 'Wizard of Dribble', Stanley Matthews, a day off, so confident were they of victory.

The USA, meanwhile, had just one full-time professional in their line-up, Ed McIlvenny. The rest of the squad was a hodgepodge of occupations, including a teacher, a trucker, a mechanic and a hearse driver. And if they weren't the best team in the world it didn't really matter. They'd still get their five bucks a day for food and laundry.

What no one had imagined, though, was that the American team would rise to the occasion. As half-time approached there was still no score. Receiving a throw-in from McIlvenny, midfielder Walter Bahr cut in from the wing and launched a speculative shot from some twenty-five yards out. As the ball winged its way goalwards, Joe Gaetjens threw himself at it, his header diverting it past the England goalkeeper Bert Williams and into the goal. But Joe didn't even see his goal. As the ball nestled in the net, he was face down in the dirt.

Despite a second-half onslaught from an England team stung into action, the Americans would cling to their slender lead to claim what many believe to be the greatest upset in the history of the game. As the referee blew the final whistle, the 10,000-strong crowd took to the pitch in jubilation, leaping over the fence and the security moat to carry the American players from the pitch.

When the first tele-printer reports of the result reached the world's press, there was widespread disbelief. The American scorer, the reports said, was one 'Larry Gaetjens', although the *New York Times* gave the goal to Ed Souza.

Back in England, meanwhile, the result was a cause of national shame. People who saw the result in their newspapers did a double-take, checking to see if the date was 1 April. England 0 USA 1. It was humiliating. 'It was like a bush-league team coming to the Bronx and beating the New York Yankees,' said the football writer Brian Glanville.

After the World Cup, Joe Gaetjens headed back to the States and, in the absence of any ticker tape parades or photo-opportunities with Harry S. Truman, carried on with his pot-washing, a nation of over 200 million people oblivious to what he had achieved.

Within four years, Joe would be back in Haiti, running a dry cleaning business, his day in the South American sun all but forgotten.

CHAPTER 1

REASONS TO BELIEVE

Steve Ross didn't know a goalkeeper from a zookeeper. American football was his game. Often, he would tell people that he had even played for the Cleveland Browns but a broken arm had put paid to his pro career. It was a nice line, but, as his close friend Jay Emmett (president of Warner Communications) explains, not exactly true. 'He said he did but he really never did… it was just bullshit, you know. Steve could do a lot of that,' he says. 'It was a Walter Mitty situation… in his wet dreams or whatever he played for the Cleveland Browns but he never did.'

Whatever the validity of his pro-football claims, there could be no doubting that Steve Ross was an A-grade sports nut. As a kid running the streets of Brooklyn, he had harboured dreams of playing for or maybe even one day owning the New York Giants. Later, when his business interests had taken off, he would even have discussions about buying the New York Jets, but it had come to naught. Quite what Steve Ross was doing with a soccer club, though, when soccer was one of the few sports he knew not a scintilla about was anyone's guess. Still, if Steve Ross, *the* Steve Ross, thought it was worth a punt, there had to be something in it.

If there was one thing Ross did know about, though, it was making money. As the chairman of Warner Communications he had amassed an empire that spanned cars and cosmetics, music and movie studios and all from the humble origins of a Manhattan funeral parlour.

There was no denying that Ross had the golden touch. He was a garrulous, gregarious free-wheeler, and his friends were always struck by how extraordinarily lucky he seemed to be. Rarely did his hunches prove to be folly. Rarely did his gambles fail to pay out. One friend would even joke that he had a 'hotline to God'. While many of his contemporaries regarded Ross as one of life's born winners, his good fortune, like his pro-football career, wasn't always what it appeared. Often, he would engineer his luck just to preserve his image. At charity raffles, for instance, Ross would nearly always emerge with the winning ticket, not because of some divine intervention but because he always bought the vast majority of the tickets.

Born Steven Jay Rechnitz in the Flatbush section of Brooklyn on 5 April 1927, Ross had got his grounding in money-making at an early age. The son of Jewish immigrants, he grew up in poverty after his father, Max, had lost his construction business and their impressive family house on Brooklyn's East 21st Street during the Depression. Desperate to find work, Max Rechnitz changed the family name to Ross in 1932.

Although the family continued to struggle, Max Ross nevertheless instilled in his son the entrepreneurial ethos that would stay with him throughout his career and his life. By the age of eight, Steve Ross would run errands to the super-market or the launderette for a nickel; he would borrow money from his family and walk twenty blocks to the cheapest cigarette shop in town, before returning home and selling the packs on to his father for a profit.

On his deathbed, Max Ross had called for Steven to offer him some final words of advice. As Steve listened intently, Max Ross told his son that in life there are those who work all day, those who dream all day, and those who spend an hour dreaming before setting to work to fulfil those dreams. 'Go into the third category,' his father added, 'because there's virtually no competition.' While his father would die in penury, his only inheritance would prove priceless.

Having graduated from Columbia Grammar School in 1945 – he had gained a scholarship place – Ross enlisted in the Navy, leaving in 1947 to enrol at Paul Smith, a junior college near the Saranac Lake in upstate New York. It was during his time at college that Ross broke his arm playing football, an injury that required a metal plate to be inserted in his forearm. It was this accident that lent credibility to his pro-football fantasy.

When he had completed his studies at Paul Smith, Ross headed to Manhattan, first to take up a job with a sportswear firm, H. Lissner Trousers, and then a swimsuit company called Farragut, belonging to his uncle, Al Smith. In school and the workplace, Ross impressed everyone with his affable nature and his ability to spot a commercial opportunity.

He had also impressed Carol Rosenthal, the daughter of Edward Rosenthal, a Manhattan funeral parlour owner. Charming, handsome and immaculately turned out, Steve Ross was the ideal suitor not just for Carol but for her family as well. Indeed, Edward Rosenthal was so taken with him he took him under his wing at the parlour.

In June 1954, aged twenty-six, Steve Ross married Carol and having shown his talents at the funeral parlour began to branch out into ventures of his own; one even involved using the parlour's limousines as evening hire cars. By the late 1950s, he had started Abbey Rent-A-Car with a bank loan, later merging it with the Kinney garage business. Then, soon after, Ross added an office-cleaning business and Edward Rosenthal's funeral parlour to his portfolio. In 1962, Ross's company, Kinney National, was taken public with a market valuation of $12.5 million.

With the capital and reputation to indulge himself in virtually any sector he deemed suitable, Steve Ross finally decided that the time was right to make his mark in the world of entertainment and on 8 July 1969 Kinney National Service Inc. paid $400 million for the world-famous but under-performing Warner Bros.-Seven Arts film studio. 'He was a financial genius,' insists Jay Emmett.

The key to all of Ross's success stories was his knack for finding the right people for the right job. Ross believed that his workforce was the single most important asset that Kinney and then Warner Communications (the name was changed in 1971) possessed and that it was his and the company's obligation to develop the talent they had.

Expertise in any of his company's fields of interest was not of paramount importance to Ross. He owned publishing companies but never read anything other than the bottom line. He owned record labels but rarely listened to popular music. 'He liked Crosby, Stills and Nash,' explains his son, Mark Ross, 'but had no idea who – or what – Joni Mitchell was.' As long as Ross had the right people in the right positions, he was confident that his company would prosper. And besides, he could always learn.

The trouble for Ross was that soccer had never made it in America. Throughout the twentieth century, there had been a succession of national soccer associations, both amateur and professional, all striving to take the game to the nation, but they came and went like buses, their plans often scuppered by internal bickering and external indifference. And all the while, the big three – baseball, basketball and pro-football – and the gentlemen of the press looked down their noses and laughed. Prescott Sullivan of the San Francisco *Examiner* was typical. 'In Europe, as in South America,' he wrote on 26 June 1968, 'they go raving mad over the game. Pray that it doesn't happen here. The way to beat it is constant vigilance and rigid control. If soccer shows signs of getting too big, swat it down.'

When the East Coast's American Soccer League (ASL) was formed in 1921, it had seemed as though professional soccer was finally on the verge of a breakthrough, especially when the American national team reached the semi-finals of the inaugural World Cup in 1930 with a side drawn mostly from the ASL. But while the game had once been played by well-heeled members of the Ivy League colleges in the nineteenth century, soccer was now suffering from an image problem, largely of its own making. Increasingly, the game was being perceived as an immigrant's game, awash with bad guys and brigands. In the 1920s, the nation's newspapers were full of stories of pitch battles and fisticuffs. Soccer's reputation, already tarnished, took another dent. On 20 April 1927, the *New York Times* reported 'FOUR HURT IN RIOT AT SOCCER CONTEST' when a game between Boston and Uruguay at Malden, Massachusetts, turned ugly. Then, on 13 February the following year, the same newspaper ran the story 'NIGHT-STICKS SWING FREELY', a report on a bust-up in a northern New Jersey title decider.

The Great Depression, however, would dispatch the American Soccer League. With neither the money nor the inclination to sustain the operation, it would be almost forty years before another professional soccer league emerged in the country.

Despite soccer's turbulent history in the States, there were still some prepared to persevere. One such person was Bill

Cox. The former owner of the Philadelphia Phillies baseball team – he had been banned from the game when he was caught betting on his own team – Cox was responsible for bringing a new soccer tournament, the International Soccer League (ISL), to the States in 1960.

Played at New York's Polo Grounds, the ISL featured eleven foreign teams (including England's West Ham United and Everton, and European sides such as Dukla Prague of Czechoslovakia) as well the American All-Stars. Unlike previous visits from foreign sides, when the games had been one-off exhibition matches, there was now a championship and a trophy to play for. While the event was never going to be the kind of success that would break soccer in the States, the ISL would nevertheless prove to be a sufficient pull for soccer fans to draw respectable five-figure crowds to many of the matches.

Those attendances and the public's receptive attitude to the tournament would prove decisive in persuading a number of investors that there was potential in soccer. At a time when expansion was occurring across all the major league sports in America, entrepreneurs began to view pro-soccer as the next big thing.

By 1965, there were three organizations vying to launch their own nationwide professional soccer leagues, including ones backed by millionaires such as Lamar Hunt and Jack Kent Cooke, as well as huge corporations like RKO General and Madison Square Garden. The decision to ratify any official national professional league, though, rested with the United States Soccer Football Association (USSFA), headed by Joe Barriskill. An Irish-American, Barriskill often would leave his shabby office in midtown Manhattan and spend his evenings as a part-time ticket usher at the New York Yankees' baseball games. Public relations, it seemed, was well down the list of the USSFA's priorities. Now, though, he was charged with deciding which of the pro-league proposals to sanction. He chose the United Soccer Association (USA).

By the spring of 1967, however, there would actually be two national professional leagues in America. Having lost out to the USA in the race for USSFA ratification, the National Professional Soccer League (NPSL) had decided to go ahead and launch itself as a pirate league, regardless of the consequences.

With time against them, the USA resorted to importing entire teams from around Europe and South America to play in their league under different names. The English clubs Wolverhampton Wanderers, Stoke City and Sunderland all joined for the summer season in 1967, becoming the Los Angeles Wolves, the Cleveland Stokers and the Vancouver Royals. Hibernian, Aberdeen and Dundee United left Scotland to become the Toronto City, the Washington Whips and the Dallas Tornado. Bangu of Brazil morphed into the Houston Stars, Italian side Cagliari landed in Chicago and became the Mustangs and New York got its own club too, the Skyliners, which was actually Uruguay's Cerro in disguise.

The rival National Professional Soccer League, meanwhile, had decided to actively recruit players for its franchises rather than just ship out teams for a few weeks in the summer. There would be some significant acquisitions. Dennis Violett, a survivor of the Munich aircrash in 1958 that took the lives of eight of his Manchester United team-mates (and three of the non-playing staff), signed for the Baltimore Bays, the Argentinian striker (and future World Cup winning manager) César Luis Menotti joined the New York Generals and Phil Woosnam, a Welsh international, arrived from Aston Villa as player-coach of the Atlanta Chiefs.

The problem for the NPSL, however, was that it was an outlaw league, without official sanction from the USSFA and therefore from the world governing body, FIFA. Consequently, the ten NPSL clubs could only play against each other and, moreover, any player who wanted to return to a club or league within the FIFA family would first be subjected to disciplinary action for having played in the banned NPSL.

With teams masquerading as other teams, outlaw leagues in operation and players running the risk of suspension simply for taking to the field, by the late 1960s American soccer was in a mess. What little support there was for the game had now been divided between the two leagues, to the detriment of both organizations and their franchises.

The teams, consisting almost entirely of foreign players with little or no affiliation to the club or the area, simply could not attract the kind of crowds they needed to break even, often playing in vast 80,000-capacity stadiums with just a couple of thousand fans watching the action. Moreover, the standard of play on offer was mediocre at best.

In a country where even one professional soccer league had found it difficult to succeed, it was imperative that the United Soccer Association and the National Professional Soccer League should amalgamate if there was to be any chance that the game would prosper.

In December 1967, the decision was finally taken to merge the two operations. The new league, called the North American Soccer League (NASL), would have two commissioners, Ken Macker from the NPSL and Dick Walsh – a man who once confessed, 'I hardly even know what a soccer ball looks like' – from the USA.

Now endorsed by FIFA, and with the threat of suspension lifted from those players who had turned out in the NPSL, the inaugural season of the NASL would feature seventeen of the twenty-two franchises from the NPSL and the USA. Over 350 players would make their debuts in the new league the next year, although, significantly, just thirty would be American.

While the standard of play improved markedly in 1968, culminating in Phil Woosnam's Atlanta Chiefs winning the title with a 3–0 aggregate win over the San Diego Toros, the growth in support had failed to materialize. At the outset of the campaign, the NASL's budget had been set with a break-even average crowd of 20,000 per game. It was an ambitious target and one that proved to be wishful thinking. By the end of the season, the average attendance was just 3,400. Casualties were inevitable.

When the dust settled, just five of the seventeen NASL franchises were left. The crash had been spectacular. Across the country, franchise owners bailed out and players' contracts were shredded. Even the commissioners jumped ship. With the NASL on the edge of a precipice and in the absence of any other willing candidates, it was left to Phil Woosnam, the Welshman who had coached the Atlanta Chiefs to the NASL title, to take on the mantle of NASL commissioner. Despite interest from several clubs back in England, Woosnam opted to stay in the States to salvage what he could from the wreckage of the league. 'What did we have to lose?' he says. 'I wouldn't have done it unless I thought we were going to succeed.'

CHAPTER 2

NEW YORK CITY SERENADE

Since accepting the challenge of resurrecting professional soccer in the United States, Phil Woosnam had discovered that it was going to be anything but easy. Franchises seemed to vanish overnight, attendances were sparse, and confidence, not to mention competence, was at an all-time low.

At least he wasn't alone. Alongside Woosnam, trying to convince America's 220 million people that soccer was the sport of the future, was the former general manager of the Baltimore Bays, Clive Toye. 'It seemed natural we would end up working together,' explains Toye. 'Phil felt a sense of mission and in my case it was plain bloody-mindedness, a determination to make people like soccer.'

Originally from Plymouth, England, Toye had been the chief football writer for the *Daily Express*, when the newspaper was still a broadsheet and outsold virtually every other in the world. After the World Cup Finals in 1966, he had left England in search of a new challenge, eventually becoming general manager of the National Professional Soccer League side the Baltimore Bays. When the NPSL had merged with the United Soccer Association to become the NASL, Toye was then poached by Woosnam to become the new league's director of administration and information. This made Clive Toye soccer's chief salesman in America.

Between them, Woosnam and Toye would steer the NASL through the difficulties of its early years, but as a 'professional' soccer league with designs on encroaching on the audience for baseball, basketball and pro-football, it was crucial that a veneer of professionalism was maintained throughout the organization. This was not always easy, when their office was a small corner of the visiting team's locker room in the Atlanta Fulton County stadium. 'We had no money and we got free office space and free telephone,' shrugs Clive Toye.

With their league down to five teams, Woosnam and Toye's workload was light and they would spend hours, sometimes days, trying to think of new and innovative ways to sell soccer to the States. As Paul Gardner wrote in his history of soccer, *The Simplest Game*, 'For them [Woosnam and Toye] a useful exercise for warding off the fear that the league might not last out the week was to leapfrog over the bleak present and to imagine the glittering future.'

Often, Woosnam and Toye would run through their wish list for the NASL. Some of their ideas were inspired, others less so. They agreed that they had to persuade as many American kids as they could to play the game and that they needed to improve their image if they were to secure any kind of useful media coverage. They should lobby FIFA to give the World Cup Finals to America and, they laughed, they may as well sign Pelé while they're at it. 'In retrospect, all ideas that if anyone heard of, [they] would have thought we were mad,' reflects Toye.

Crucial to the NASL's progress, though, was the re-establish-ment of a franchise in New York. Without a team since the New York Generals folded in 1968, America's economic capital was a key battleground in the drive to develop soccer on a national level. If the league was ever going to get that vital coverage in the press and on television – the major TV networks were all based in New York – they needed that 'major league' appeal that other sports enjoyed and that meant bringing football back to the Big Apple. 'In our youthful enthusiasm/arrogance, Phil and I decided early on that one of us would run the league and one of us New York,' explains Toye, who opted to handle the New York drive.

Having a soccer team in New York made sense, even after the failure of the Generals and the Skyliners. After all, here was a truly cosmopolitan city with nine million inhabitants, covering some 300 square miles. Within the city there were up to a hundred different languages being spoken and 60 per cent of its population came from outside of the United States, which, of course, meant there were a huge amount of soccer fans not being catered for. 'It's the special milieu that's created when you have the sons and daughters of every nation in the world living here and the sons and daughters of every state in the union living here or wanting to come here,' explained Ed Koch, mayor of New York from 1978 to 1989. 'That's an electricity that can't be created anywhere else.'

There was also some soccer heritage in the city too, as there was all along the eastern seaboard. At the turn of the century, there had been a flourishing amateur soccer scene in New York, New Jersey and Philadelphia, and the *New York Times* would carry regular reports on matches involving such teams as the Brooklyn Celtics, the Spanish-American FC and the Anglo-Saxons FC.

More importantly, there were few places in the world that accommodated sports fans as well as New York. There were heroes all over the city. There were Willis Reed, Dave DeBusschere and 'Dollar' Bill Bradley turning it on for the Knicks in the NBA, the Mets had won their first World Series, beating the Baltimore Orioles in 1969 and the legendary Joe Namath had led the Jets to a famous win over the Baltimore Colts in Superbowl III. Whatever your sport of choice, you could find the finest exponents of it at work in the Big Apple. As long as your sport of choice wasn't soccer, that is.

The unenviable task facing Phil Woosnam and Clive Toye, then, was that of somehow trying to shoehorn soccer into an already buoyant New York sports scene, awash with superstars and steeped in history. But if they could make it there, they figured, they could make it anywhere. 'It was imperative for us to get back into New York if we were going to have any impact,' explains Phil Woosnam. 'We just needed an opportunity.'

Woosnam and Toye's efforts to keep the NASL afloat would also be aided by the backing of Lamar Hunt, the millionaire owner of the Dallas Tornado franchise. The son of Texas oilman H. L. Hunt, Lamar Hunt had been rebuffed in his efforts to establish a National Football League franchise in the Lone Star State and, irked, had simply started his own rival organization, the American Football League, in 1959 instead.

For a sports obsessive like Hunt – he was a founding investor in the Chicago Bulls basketball team and had also founded the World Championship Tennis Circuit in 1967 – the game of soccer represented a new challenge and, certainly, he would throw his weight behind the NASL with gusto.

While a businessman with the profile of Hunt continued to lend both financial and moral support for the NASL, it was always possible that other, equally influential entrepreneurs would enter the fray, swayed by the fact that if Hunt was still keen on soccer then there must be something in this cuckoo sport after all.

Despite an uncertain future, the fact that there was clearly no money to be made in the game at least succeeded in exposing those potential new franchise holders that had jumped into soccer looking for a quick profit without any regard for the long-term viability of the professional game. 'In the early days a lot of baseball owners bought into soccer… only to see if it's going to take off. [They thought] I better be there and if it doesn't take off quickly enough for me I can kill it,' said Toye.

By the time the 1970 season came round, there was a sense that the NASL had turned a corner. Despite the closure of Clive Toye's old club, the Baltimore Bays, who had ended the 1969 season winning just two of their sixteen games and drawing only two hundred fans to their home fixtures, two new sides had emerged. Thanks to the persuasive powers of Phil Woosnam, the American Soccer League sides, the Washington Darts and the Rochester Lancers both found the $10,000 entrance fee to step up to the NASL, giving the league another shot at survival.

While Woosnam still had a league, it was, however, one with just six teams playing in it. Conscious of the need to create at least some semblance of competition, the commissioner enlisted the help of four foreign teams who would tour the States and play each of the regular sides in the NASL once, with the results counting towards the final league standings. Consequently, England's Coventry City, West Germany's Hertha Berlin and Varzim of Portugal would all play six games and Hapoel Petah Tikva of Israel would play five, their place in the game against the Dallas Tornado taken by Monterrey of Mexico because of the conflict with owner Lamar Hunt's Arab oil interests.

With the season underway and crowds creeping up, Phil Woosnam and Clive Toye were feeling quietly confident. But with a new plan to increase the number of NASL teams to eight for the 1971 season, they needed an investor of sufficient profile and wherewithal to launch a new franchise in the all-important New York area. To that end, Toye had even approached the British television broadcaster David Frost to see if he would be interested in financing a New York franchise. Although Frost, an avowed soccer fan, would decline, he had suggested that they speak to a friend of his at the media giant Warner Communications. Taking a note of the name – Nesuhi Ertegun – Toye informed Woosnam, who then headed off to Mexico to catch the last week of the World Cup Finals. It was one of the few perks of being the NASL commissioner.

After watching Pelé's rampant Brazil crush Italy 4–1 in the final and claim their third Jules Rimet trophy, Woosnam endeavoured to find Ron Greenwood, his old manager from his spell at West Ham United. Arriving at Greenwood's hotel, he was pointed in the direction of a cocktail party in a nearby reception room. He knocked on the door.

When the door swung open, Woosnam was greeted by a small man, offering his hand. 'Hello,' said the commissioner. 'I'm looking for Ron Greenwood, my name is Phil Woosnam.'

'Hello,' replied the man at the door. 'I'm Nesuhi Ertegun.'

It was a chance meeting that would change the face of soccer in the United States. Ertegun was the executive vice-president of the famous Atlantic Records label – a division of Warner Communcations – and, like his brother and his Atlantic co-founder, Ahmet, was an affirmed soccer fan. As the pair chatted, Woosnam sensed that Ertegun was taken with his idea of launching a soccer club in New York. Finally, thought Woosnam, he may have found the solution to his Big Apple dilemma. 'Ahmet and Nesuhi were Turkish and came from a football background,' he explains. 'As such, they had a passion for the game that many investors didn't.' As they left Mexico, Ertegun agreed that he and Woosnam should meet soon to discuss the idea further.

Back in Manhattan, Nesuhi Ertegun raised the idea with Ahmet Ertegun and his boss at Warner, Steve Ross. Surprisingly, the suggestion was met not with indifference, as Woosnam had suspected, but with genuine enthusiasm. 'Soccer,' Ertegun told his colleagues, 'is going to be the biggest sport. It's the biggest sport in the world [and] it's going to take over America.'

Certainly, the facts reinforced Nesuhi Ertegun's proposition. Even without a successful, high-profile professional soccer league in operation, there were still over three million kids playing the game across the country and the number was growing every year. Factor in New York's ethnically diverse make-up and the local interest in the game within the neighbourhoods, and there was every chance that they could have a major success story on their hands.

Convinced that the plan had legs, Steve Ross rounded up a group of like-minded colleagues and suggested that between them they privately meet the NASL's expansion fee of $350,000, which was levied on new clubs entering the league. In total, ten men, including Ross, the Ertegun brothers, Jay Emmett and the chairman and CEO of Warner Bros. movie studios, Ted Ashley, would all put up $35,000 apiece to launch Gotham Soccer Club Inc.

Within months, however, the team of investors would come to realize that financing a soccer club, even one as seemingly irrelevant as theirs, was a money pit, without any guarantee of even the smallest return and without the inherent kudos they would glean from owning a baseball or American football franchise. Fortunately, Jay Emmett, the president of Warner and Steve Ross's closest friend, had an idea. He went to the chairman. 'I said this is something that Warner should take, not us, because this is going to lose quite a bit of money and in order to build it up to what it ought to be and to be competitive with the other folks in the league we're going to have to get some pretty players and it's going to cost some money.'

Ross agreed. Between them, the owners hatched a new plan. They would transfer ownership of Gotham Soccer Club to Warner Communications. 'Then we sold our stake in this fledgling organization for one dollar,' adds Emmett. 'It was an entertainment vehicle, we were an entertainment company.'

But the new club needed a new name if it was going to make a splash in the NASL. Trouble was, all the good ones had already gone. The Giants, the Knicks, the Yankees – these were legendary New York names loaded with history, saturated in success. Even the new expansion baseball team, the New York Metropolitans – a.k.a. 'The Mets' – had stolen a march on the club.

Clive Toye started thinking. What the team needed was a name that was bigger than anything that had gone before in New York, a name that spoke volumes about the endless potential and glittering future this club could have. 'So I thought, what's bigger than "Metropolitan" and came up with Cosmopolitan... that fits New York. [But we] can't call them the Cosmopolitans or Cosmopolites. Suddenly it clicked – Cosmos.'

Intent on persuading the board that his idea, and not Nesuhi Ertegun's suggestion of 'New York Blues', was the most suitable, Toye contrived a competition among the city's soccer fans, with a prize of two free return flights to Zurich with Swiss Air for anyone who came up with the best name. He then sat down and wrote scores of letters purporting to be from fans of the team, all suggesting that 'Cosmos' was the name they wanted. Assured that the city's sports fans and not the general manager had spoken, the Erteguns relented and the name stuck. 'They [the Erteguns] weren't paying real close attention in those early years,' adds Toye.

On 10 December 1970, the New York Cosmos officially joined the North American Soccer League, its annual fee, a mere $25,000. With Clive Toye as the Cosmos's new general manager, Warner Communications had taken its first tentative steps into professional soccer and the NASL finally had its

New York franchise. And if it all went belly up, well, it could always be written off as a tax loss by Steve Ross.

The man charged with assembling a team worthy of such a stellar moniker would be another Englishman, Gordon Bradley. Born In Sunderland in 1938, Bradley was a coal miner's son whose promising career as a teenaged striker with Sunderland was cut short by a knee injury. After a two-year hiatus and a miserable spell down the pits at Easington Colliery, Bradley returned to competitive football with Bradford Park Avenue and Carlisle. His knee injury, however, had robbed him of the pace he once possessed, forcing a change in position to defender.

In 1963, Bradley made the move to the States, dividing his time between playing for Toronto City in Canada (alongside Stanley Matthews, Johnny Haynes and Danny Blanchflower) in the summer and New York in the winter, where he served as captain and coach of the New York Ukrainians. It was during his time with the Ukrainians that Bradley came to the attention of the new NASL franchise, the New York Generals. Impressed by his performances at the heart of the Ukrainian's defence and his coaching qualifications, they hired him as coach Freddie Goodwin's assistant.

If Bradley had ever doubted the wisdom of his conversion to a defensive role, the conclusive proof that he had made the right decision arrived in 1968 when the New York Generals played host to a visit from the Brazilian side Santos, who were on a tour of the States and boasted the world's best player, Pelé, in their team. Moreover, it was Bradley's job to mark him.

Dogged, resolute and seemingly unfazed by Pelé's reputation, Bradley stuck to him like a barnacle, barely giving the Brazilian space to breathe. Even at the half-time interval, when Pelé went to the sidelines to get a drink of water, Bradley was never more than half a yard behind him, as Pelé recalls:

'I said: "If I go to the rest room, will you come with me?"'
Legend has it that Pelé even asked his coach to be moved to
a new position just so he could be free of Bradley's limpet-
like attention.

'I was always a disciplined player, whether I played in
defence or midfield, but when I tried to mark Pelé he
threatened to run rampant,' explains Bradley. 'We couldn't
stop him but we did subdue him a bit, and ended up winning.
After the game, Pelé came into our dressing room with the
ball, which he had got the Santos team to sign, and gave it to
me. The Americans love an underdog and the headline the
next day was "Bradley Stops Pelé."'

While the New York Generals would defeat Santos 5–3 that
day in front of a record crowd of 24,000, it would be one of
the last hurrahs for the club, who, like so many other franchises
in that era, folded soon after. With no professional club in New
York to take him on, Bradley accepted the offer of an assistant
coach's role under his compatriot Gordon Jago at the Baltimore
Bays, but within a year they too would be gone.

With rent to pay and his soccer career seemingly petering
out, Bradley returned to New York and decided to put his
coaching qualifications to good use. He took a job at St
Bernard's School in Manhattan, and managed to mould a
bunch of twelve- and thirteen-year-olds that seemed more
interested in basketball into one of Central Park's most
formidable young teams. 'I don't believe we lost a game,' says
the coach.

By 1971, though, Gordon Bradley would be back in the
NASL, lured away by his old friend Clive Toye, to become
the first coach of the New York Cosmos. Clearly, somebody,
somewhere had seen what he had achieved at St Bernard's.

Hiring a coach and a general manager was all well and good
but finding a team was going to be more difficult, especially as

Toye and Bradley could only offer token salaries to potential players. Unperturbed, Gordon Bradley set about assembling his team, trawling the local leagues for promising players and calling in favours from old friends and team-mates. Soon, Bradley had the makings of his first squad. In came his compatriot Barry Mahy and the Trinidadian Jan Steadman, both former team-mates from the Generals. The brilliant Brazilian Jorge Siega arrived from Washington and an old colleague from Baltimore, the Ghanaian Wilberforce Mfum, also threw his hat in the ring. It was like Yul Brynner rounding up the Magnificent Seven, only trickier and on a tighter budget.

Within weeks, Gordon Bradley had his Cosmos. It was a testament to his boundless enthusiasm that he could create a team without the promise of enormous salaries or generous benefits packages. Moreover, it was proof that the appeal of living and working in the most vibrant city in the world more than made up for any monetary concerns the players may have had.

Despite being something of a diversion for Warner, the New York Cosmos represented an ideal route into sports ownership for Steve Ross, not least because the financial risk was all Warner's. Moreover, the fact that soccer had yet to take off in the States and shown little sign of doing so, was, in Ross's mind, a huge advantage. 'My father was a big sports fan,' says Mark Ross. 'I think the idea of developing a sport from scratch – because soccer was really nothing here – really turned him on.'

With Steve Ross on board and their place in the NASL guaranteed, Clive Toye decided to broach an idea that, if successful, had the potential to revolutionize soccer in

America. While his and Phil Woosnam's attempts to get the youth of the nation playing the game was showing real signs of progress, it had yet to translate into a wider interest in the professional game. What the Cosmos and, more importantly, the NASL needed was a legend, a player who had the kudos and the charisma to carry an entire league. It needed its own Babe or DiMaggio, its own Joe Namath or Walt Frazier. 'There was only one player in the world who could break through this crust of indifference,' says Toye; 'that was Pelé.'

Alongside the boxer Muhammad Ali, Pelé was the most famous sportsman in the world. He was even famous in America. Born Edson Arantes do Nascimento on 23 October 1940, he had won three World Cups with his native Brazil and scored over 1,000 career goals, and had emerged from an impoverished upbringing in the south-eastern Brazilian state of Minas Gerais to become the man universally regarded as the greatest player to ever take the football field.

Though fanciful, Toye's plan to poach Pelé from his club side, Santos, made sense. After all, here was a player who transcended his sport, a man so famous, so loved, that a survey had shown the name 'Pelé' ranked behind only Coca-Cola as the most popular brand in Europe. Here was a player who could keep the Shah of Iran waiting at an airport for three hours just so he could meet him; a player who when he visited Nigeria in 1967, persuaded the two sides in the ongoing civil war to agree to a forty-eight-hour ceasefire just so he could play in an exhibition game in the capital, Lagos.

Indeed, Pelé's fame, not to mention his unique ability, had, in 1961, resulted in the Brazilian Congress declaring that the then 22-year-old had been classified as a 'non-exportable national treasure', in much the same way that Britain values the Crown Jewels or France does the Mona Lisa. In short, Pelé wasn't for sale.

Still, it was worth a try. Certainly, Toye's idea found favour with Steve Ross, a man drawn inexorably to star names and super-sized personalities. For Ross, Pelé was another Sinatra or Aretha to add to his roster. He was box office and Ross knew it. '[Ross] was sophisticated and urbane enough to have travelled the world, and he knew there was this one athlete named Pelé who was a global icon equal to Ali,' says David Hirshey, who covered the Cosmos for the *New York Daily News*. 'Ross realized that the Cosmos would languish in the sleepy backwaters of soccer until it had a drawing card that would somehow galvanize the American public. There was only one man who could light that match, and it was Pelé.'

Buoyed by Ross's response, Clive Toye, NASL commissioner Phil Woosnam and the general secretary of the US Soccer Federation (formerly the USSFA), Kurt Lamb, flew to Kingston, Jamaica in February 1971 to meet with Pelé and his adviser, Professor Julio Mazzei, the Brazilian having just played a friendly for Santos there against Chelsea.

When the parties finally convened by the swimming pool of Pelé's hotel, Toye took a deep breath and launched headlong into his best sales pitch, insisting that Pelé was the only man on the planet who could sell soccer to the American masses. 'I told him that he had to come to America because he would have the chance to do something no one else could do – make soccer a major sport in the USA,' recalls Toye. 'He later admitted he had no idea what the hell I was talking about.'

On 17 April 1971, the New York Cosmos, without Pelé, took to the field at the Busch Memorial Stadium, St Louis, to play its first game in the North American Soccer League. It would be a successful debut, with their towering Bermudan striker, Randy Horton, recording their first ever NASL goal in a 2–1 victory.

In the crowd of 7,324 that day was the Warner chairman

Steve Ross, who looked around the ground, saw countless thousands of empty seats and rather than cut his losses and run back to the relative safety of the movie world, set his sights on turning the situation around. 'I didn't let it get me down,' he would say. 'Instead, I thought about the possibilities. The growth potential from ground zero was tremendous.'

'Ground zero' was an apt description for the state of the New York Cosmos. With a 'roster', or playing squad, largely made of local amateur players, only too keen to supplement their day jobs with a few extra bucks for playing, it was professional soccer in name only, both on and off the field.

From their microscopic office near Grand Central Station, Clive Toye, ably assisted by Pauline Badal, did what he could to raise the club's profile, the odds stacked against him. While Toye badgered the city's sports editors and handed out complimentary tickets, Gordon Bradley would spread the word of the Cosmos by hosting soccer clinics for school-children, all the time trying to lure them away from baseball and basketball. 'I cannot say how many clinics I gave,' says Bradley dispassionately, 'but I had to get those kids playing school soccer and so as they grow this year and next year it became their game.'

Between them, though, the Englishmen formed a formidable and persuasive partnership, talking up the club as though it were the next big thing in NYC and not some shoestring outfit offering players fifty bucks a game. Now, whenever they identified players they felt could make a difference to the squad, the full weight of the Cosmos negotiating team – i.e. Toye and Bradley – would swing into action, closing deals over the lobby payphone or over a cup of coffee at the local Chock Full O'Nuts. 'Ninety-nine per cent of the population had never heard of soccer,' laughs Toye. 'It was an absolutely barren country in terms of soccer.'

CHAPTER 3

THIS HARD LAND

The World Trade Center towers were all but finished. At 1,368ft and 1,362ft respectively, Minoru Yamasaki's 110-storey skyscrapers were now the world's tallest buildings, surpassing their near neighbour, the Empire State Building, by over a hundred feet. That said, they had also met with critical indifference, the chief complaint being that they looked like the boxes that the Chrysler Building and the Empire State came out of.

As the Manhattan skyline headed ever upward, the fortunes of the New York Cosmos were sliding inexorably in the opposite direction. Having enjoyed the plentiful facilities of Yankee Stadium, the Cosmos had relocated to Hofstra University Stadium in Hempstead, Long Island. Opened in 1963, Hofstra was ideal for student sport but hardly the kind of venue that professional athletes wanted to perform at or, indeed, be seen at.

With just two sets of wooden bleachers that faced the Long Island railroad, it was a world away from their previous home. The AstroTurf bowed in the middle and when it rained the pitch could have hosted the 100m freestyle. 'It was horrendous,' says the attacking midfielder Stan Startzell. 'It was the worst Astroturf in the country. It was like putting carpet down on the expressway and playing on that. The ball would bounce for ever and the field was crowned about eighteen inches so when you were running downhill the ball was actually running away from you.'

The locker rooms, meanwhile, were small and uncomfortable and the flaky grey paint on the ceiling snowed on the players' heads to such an extent that, according to the goalkeeper Shep Messing, 'you'd leave the place looking like the guy in the dandruff commercial who used the wrong brand.'

It was at Hofstra that the Cosmos employed some of its more unusual marketing ploys in order to get people through the gates. Plastic balls, bumper stickers and discount vouchers for Burger King were handed out, high school bands played at half-time and grown men paraded the pitch dressed as giant milk shakes, all, seemingly, to no avail. Books of tickets were given away to members of the press in the hope that they could offload them to influential people, but the reporters only ever used them as paperweights or doorstops. 'We were not welcomed with open arms by the media, that's for sure,' says Clive Toye. 'There was one guy in San Francisco who said pray God Americans never take to soccer because it's the beginning of Communist infiltration. Another guy [said] they are nothing but a bunch of Commies and fairies in short pants. That was the attitude to the game.'

With Pelé still, understandably, uninterested in joining the Cosmos ranks, and the weird assortment of marketing gimmicks failing to boost attendances, Toye and the Cosmos unveiled their next big idea – Harold the Chimp. Harold was a chimpanzee who had been living an easy life at Warner's Jungle Habitat wildlife reserve in West Milford, New Jersey, but who had been seconded to become the club's official mascot. Harold was a lively five-year-old, and it was his job to warm up what little crowds the Cosmos was drawing, by scampering out to the centre circle before the kick-off and playing with the match ball or, invariably, trying to eat it. 'Harold,' said Clive Toye, 'is a very clever player and there is no one in the league better at climbing along the crossbar and heading the ball in.'

Unfortunately, Harold also had a tendency to urinate at inopportune moments, sometimes on the pitch, sometimes on his handler and occasionally on both. Indeed, when he was first unveiled at a press conference at the Hotel Warwick in midtown Manhattan, he immediately passed comment on the club by urinating on the team's American midfielder, Stan Startzell. 'All of a sudden Startzell looked down and a warm pool was forming around his shoes,' recalls journalist David Hirshey. 'It's this sort of monkey business that characterized the Cosmos.'

Stan Startzell's misfortune was that he was good-looking, he worked in the Cosmos front office during the day, and he was one of the few players in the squad who could speak fluent English. ('I was the one that didn't have an accent,' he explains). Consequently, he would be one of the first in the firing line when Clive Toye and Gordon Bradley went looking for players to face the media at press conferences.

In that squad of nineteen players, there were twelve different nationalities and five different languages being spoken. The Scots chided the English, Trinidadians sided with the Bermudans and the Poles ignored the Germans. Factor in a Spaniard, a Czechoslovakian, an Israeli, a Ghanaian and two Brazilians, and it was the original League of Nations soccer team. 'I even learnt to swear in Polish,' laughs Startzell.

Given the absence of any translators in the Cosmos camp – that would come later – it was left to Gordon Bradley to make sense of it all. 'The players that were in the Cosmos in the early days were here basically because they loved the game and they wanted to have an experience in the United States,' adds David Hirshey.

Certainly, it wasn't the financial rewards that attracted such a disparate assembly of individuals. When Stan Startzell was drafted from the University of Pennsylvania to play for the Cosmos in 1972, for instance, he was given a $3,000 signing fee and promptly blew it on a Triumph Spitfire (in brown). But on a monthly salary of just $400, he lacked the wherewithal to park it anywhere in the lots of Manhattan. And when Harvard-educated goalkeeper Shep Messing signed for the club, he entered negotiations with coach Gordon Bradley confident of securing at least a five-figure salary. He settled for just $76 a week.

To make amends for the pitiful pay on offer, the players were permitted, and encouraged, to take second jobs. But then they had to. Brazilian winger Jorge Siega worked part-time slicing salami in a deli in Queens; the Scot Charlie McCully laid bricks and Barry Mahy took a job working the executive lounges at JFK airport. In his autobiography, *The Education of a Soccer Player*, Shep Messing revealed that his room-mate Lenny Renery drove a beer truck to make ends meet. That, though, is not exactly true. 'I was a teacher,' insists Renery. 'I never drove a beer truck in my life. I once drove a cab and there may well have been some beer in that but never a beer truck... that's just Shep bullshitting.'

The Bermudan striker Randy Horton, meanwhile, made ends meet by first taking a position in the accounts department at Atlantic Records and then taking a job at the same wildlife park where Harold the Chimp had been discovered. Horton was 6' 4", and brandished a huge, unkempt beard and an afro that added another four inches to his height. He was the kind of intimidating opponent you wouldn't want to run into in a well-lit, heavily policed alleyway, let alone a dark one. He even called himself 'the meanest nigger in Newark'.

On the pitch, Horton was a physical presence unlike any other in the NASL. Quick, strong and impossible to shake off the ball, he would win every aerial challenge and snaffle any opportunities to find the back of the net. But as one of the more prolific forwards in the league, Horton was a marked man. Rarely did a game go by without him being involved in an altercation or even a full-on punch-up. Often, it was just a matter of time before he or one of his assailants was sent off. As he would later confess, he was just one of a 'bunch of crazy fuckers who love to play soccer'.

Off the field, though, Horton was sensitivity personified. Affable and erudite, he was studying for a postgraduate degree in economics at Rutgers, the state university of New Jersey, and, in time, would go on to forge a successful career in Bermudan politics. A natural athlete, Horton had been offered a contract with Huddersfield Town in the English Football League and had also been offered terms with the English county cricket side Worcestershire but had rejected both deals. 'I had decided that I wanted some sun,' he says, 'and I wasn't going to get much of that in Huddersfield.'

Despite being drawn from all over the globe, those early Cosmos squads were typified by a rare solidarity. When the twice-weekly training was done, the players would hang out at Bill's Meadowbrook Inn, the nearest drinking den to Hofstra, sinking beers and playing poker. It was at Bill's during one post-training session that the goalkeeper Shep Messing discovered a latent talent for eating glass. Challenged by the New York Jets' Mike Battle to eat a light bulb and cajoled by his team-mate Bobby Smith, Messing duly obliged. All the goalkeeper will say now about the experience was that he 'ate it slowly'.

'We stuck together… there was a bond,' adds Messing, who was signed from Montreal as part of Warner's strategy to have somebody with an American birth certificate in the team. 'It didn't matter whether the guy spoke English or not, you know. We were all together. We had the same mission.'

Randy Horton agrees. 'It was difficult at times and sure, there were occasions when there were breakdowns in communications on the field, but for the most part soccer was a universal language.'

That year, the squad would also be bolstered by the arrival of the twenty-three-year-old defender Werner Roth. A fluent German speaker, Roth was a naturalized American who had left Yugoslavia with his family when he was just four years old and grown up in the Ridgewood section of Queens, an area that had sprung into life in the 1910s and 1920s thanks mainly to the endeavours of German immigrant builders. When he attended Brooklyn Technical High School, Roth was a member of the varsity squad and captained the soccer team in his final year, all the time wondering whether one day he would be good enough to make a bit of extra cash from playing semi-professionally.

He was. After college, he got the call from the German-Hungarian side in the local semi-professional Cosmopolitan League, earning himself the grand sum of fifty bucks a game at the Metropolitan Oval, a ground which boasted a pitch that had more dirt on it than it did grass. 'They were very low-key events – not a lot of visibility to the general public,' he recalls. 'It was only if you belonged to an ethnic community that you knew about the games. There were some ethnic publications that promoted the games… but generally no mention in the American media at all. We weren't even a blip on the American sports scene at that time.'

Any meaningful media coverage of the game would also be

lacking when Roth joined the Cosmos in 1972. Still the press regarded soccer as a sport entirely at odds with what their readership wanted. Junior reporters were dispatched to cover games, their seniors sniggering in the background, and editorial blunders were often punished with NASL assignments. Certainly, the press saw little future in the game, consigning what little coverage they offered to a couple of filler paragraphs at the end of the sports section. 'Soccer was the least important sport in the pantheon of American sports,' says Lawrie Mifflin of the *New York Daily News*.

David Hirshey, her colleague at the *News*, agrees. 'Sports editors treated soccer as if it were a leper colony, and you know partly it was out of sheer ignorance – they didn't know anything about the game – and partly it was out of fear, I guess, that it might grow to somehow threaten the hegemony of the three big American sports.'

One of the primary reasons why the game was yet to distract the media's or the public's attention was the lack of any American players operating within the NASL. Wherever you looked, virtually each team roster seemed to consist of Poles and Peruvians, Brits and Brazilians; even the US national team was made up mostly of naturalized Americans. The only team that bucked the trend was the St Louis Stars, who boasted eleven Americans in their seventeen-man squad, a consequence of their heavy reliance on student players from St Louis University.

Commissioner Phil Woosnam's solution to deflect the criticism that the NASL was ostensibly a foreigners' league was to introduce a college draft wherein the eight team coaches in the NASL (all of them foreign-born and largely ignorant of US college soccer) were instructed to pick young American players for their franchises.

With no homegrown heroes emerging and no tangible sense

that there was some latent public interest in soccer on the verge of erupting, the press continued to concentrate on the established American sports, which were also the ones their readers actually cared about. Why bother with a team who, according to Shep Messing, 'were drawing less than the skinflicks on Eighth Avenue' when you had the Knicks heading towards another NBA title or the legendary Willie Mays in the twilight of his career with the Mets? It was these time-honoured sports that were going to shift papers, not something as ephemeral as soccer.

Though few people in New York City may have known who or, indeed, what they were, the fledgling Cosmos at least proved it had the aptitude and the team spirit to play some decent football. With Gordon Bradley and his compatriot Barry Mahy marshalling the defence and the Scottish-born Canadian international John Kerr providing the ammunition for Randy Horton upfront, they not only won the NASL's Northern Division but took the championship itself, beating the St Louis Stars 2–1 in the final at Hofstra. The low-key nature of the event and the NASL itself was such, however, that Shep Messing once likened the achievement to winning 'the wrist wrestling championships at Petaluma'.

With a goal in the championship game taking his season tally to nine, Randy Horton would finish the season as the NASL's top goalscorer, and having taken the title of Rookie of the Year in his debut season, the Bermudan would be voted Most Valuable Player (MVP) by his fellow players. 'The ultimate compliment,' he calls it today.

That said, it was difficult to see just what Steve Ross saw in the New York Cosmos. Where once he had dreamed of owning the Giants or the Mets, complete with their superstars, sell-out crowds and wall-to-wall media coverage, now he would often arrive at Hofstra with his ten-year-old son, Mark, and sit in the largely empty stands and watch as the summer rain washed a quarter of a million dollars of Warner's cash down the drain every season.

That Ross sensed an opportunity was a tribute to his unquenchable desire to find the next big thing. That he had chanced upon a group of players who played the game for the sheer love of it and not for any great financial reward was a bonus.

☻

Steve Marshall was a twenty-three-year-old in need of a job. Since his childhood, he had dreamed of being the next Wilt Chamberlain but he was the wrong colour and, as he now admits, 'white men don't jump very well'. Still, there was always his old man.

Alton G. Marshall was the president of New York's Rockefeller Center (where Warner also had their offices) and was a personal friend of both Steve Ross and Jay Emmett. During a night out at Madison Square Garden, Marshall Snr mentioned that his son was on the lookout for work, at which point a small light bulb flickered into life over Jay Emmett's head.

The following day, Steve Marshall met up with Emmett and the Warner vice-president asked him what he knew of the New York Cosmos. Nothing, replied Marshall. 'If it wasn't the Yankees, the Giants, the Knicks or the Rangers I had no clue,' he reflects.

Emmett explained that the Cosmos was a professional soccer team that had just won the NASL championship and that with his help and the financial muscle of Warner, the club had the potential to be, well, a bit bigger than they were now. OK, said Marshall, where do I sign? 'I had no clue what I was getting into,' he now admits.

Though his job title said he was the assistant public relations director, Marshall's duties covered everything from stadium security to doorman on the press box, not that it really needed one. After games, Marshall would also have to call the city's various radio station phone-ins and their 'two listeners' in a desperate bid to squeeze out any publicity he could for the Cosmos. 'I felt like Jimmy Swaggart or Billy Graham,' he laughs.

The lack of exposure for soccer was just one of a glut of problems facing the NASL. While the quest to find American players of a sufficient standard was proving awkward, Phil Woosnam's efforts to grow the game were also being hampered by a lack of suitable facilities on which the NASL teams could play.

With few bespoke soccer pitches, clubs were forced to use college fields or stadiums designed for American football. Whereas soccer pitches tended to be 70 yards wide, the gridiron field was just 54 yards wide, the knock-on effect being that many teams were playing on narrow pitches which not only altered the very nature of the game, but made the position of winger virtually redundant.

Recognizing that Phil Woosnam and his league perhaps needed a helping hand, football's world governing body, FIFA, granted permission for the NASL to experiment with a modified offside rule. Now, instead of the offside law applying from the halfway line, a new line would be added to the pitch 35 yards from the goal, behind which a player couldn't be called offside. 'If you had teams playing offside traps at the halfway line then there was no way you were going to get through and that would just kill the game,' explains Woosnam. 'So we got permission from FIFA to test it and it worked.'

The Cosmos, however, had other problems – with discipline, or the lack of it, chief among them. As the player-coach Gordon Bradley largely overlooked his American players in favour of the European contingent in his squad – they were better players, after all – those left out in the cold were left to find alternative ways to occupy their time, most of which appeared to contravene the club's disciplinary code. Tardiness, breaking curfew, dress code violations; Gordon Bradley handed out fines like flyers.

Chief culprits were Shep Messing and Lenny Renery. Born and raised in Edgware, Middlesex, Renery had moved to the States with his family when he was twelve years old, leaving behind his true love. 'The biggest trauma in leaving England,' he recalls, 'was leaving Tottenham Hotspur behind.' Later, while studying at New York City's Columbia University, he had been spotted by Gordon Bradley and Clive Toye and asked to try out for the Cosmos, signing a $2,600 per season contract soon after. 'Because I had been born and brought up in England and had this love of the game of football I guess I was better placed than the average American player,' he explains.

Like many of the players in the Cosmos squad, Messing and Renery viewed the extracurricular side of professional soccer as every bit as important as the playing side. If Messing wasn't eating light bulbs, Renery would be arriving at official club functions dressed, deliberately, in gaudy suits he'd picked up on the cheap in Greenwich Village. 'Let's just say that I was never that concerned with whether a jacket matched a pair of pants,' says Renery.

Occasionally, though, Gordon Bradley would exact his revenge. The night before an away game against the Philadelphia Atoms, for example, Messing and Renery had decided that as they weren't going to be playing they might as well sample the many delights of Philly's nightlife. Sneaking out of the team hotel via the fire escape, they repaired to a local jazz club, where they drank until 6 a.m. 'I wasn't a sober youth,' says Renery.

Just two hours later, there was a knock at their room door. It was Bradley, who informed Renery that not only would he be playing that day but that he would be in the starting line-up. Throwing his team-mate into the shower, Messing first prepared an emergency Bloody Mary for Renery, followed by another, and then slapped him repeatedly until some semblance of sense returned to his speech and actions. Thanks to the keeper's impromptu first aid, Lenny Renery not only made it on to the field that day but played one of his most impressive games for the team, scoring his first goal as a professional in a 1–1 draw.

When Steve Ross and Kinney purchased Warner Bros.-Seven Arts movie studios in July 1969, he bought himself a ticket into a world that he had always admired from afar. Having his own film company now marked him out as something more than just a faceless name at the head of another huge corporation, and seeing Clint Eastwood or Dustin Hoffman walk into his office unannounced was more of a kick to him than any rosy quarterly report could ever be. 'Steve loved the stars,' says Jay Emmett. 'He was made for Hollywood.'

But as his business interests had flourished and Ross learned to love the heady social whirl of the movie world, his relationship with his wife Carol was suffering. Despite twenty of years of marriage, Ross had been having a long-standing affair with Cathy Mitchell, a woman he had met in Los Angeles, prompting Carol to leave him for the third and final time.

Soon after Carol Ross left, Ross would end his affair with Mitchell by reportedly handing $10,000 to Jay Emmett and instructing him to give it to her by way of a pay-off as he had already entered into another relationship with Courtney Sale, a Texan lady he had met at one of his many lavish parties.

At least Warner Bros. was in rude health. After the success of *Dirty Harry* in 1972, the studio had scored another huge hit with William Friedkin's story of Satanic possession, *The Exorcist*. With twelve-year-old Linda Blair's head-spinning performance gaining her overnight stardom, the film successfully terrified audiences the world over and took more money at the box office than any horror movie in history.

If Ross's directors needed any inspiration they didn't really need to look anywhere other than the Big Apple. New York City, as many film-makers were finding, was full of fantastic stories. From *Serpico*, Sidney Lumet's gritty account of an undercover cop fighting corruption in the NYPD, to *Mean Streets*, Martin Scorsese's tale of two-bit hoods in Little Italy (starring two relative unknowns by the names of Robert De Niro and Harvey Keitel), the city was awash not just with incredible tales, but with directors trying to make movies of those stories.

Even New York's kids were expressing themselves in new and vibrant ways. Across the five boroughs, an explosion in graffiti art was taking place, buoyed by the much-publicized exploits of Demetrius, a teenager from Washington Heights who had tagged virtually anything that didn't move in the city. Soon, scores of imitators would emerge and across New York, from Broadway to the Bronx, from Coney Island to Queens, taggers were painting the town red (and virtually every other colour in the spectrum).

In an increasingly vivid city, Shep Messing was one of its most colourful characters. With his Harpo Marx hair and a moustache later modelled by *Magnum P.I.*, Messing was the living embodiment of 1970s American man. Born in the Bronx and raised in Roslyn, Long Island, he had emerged unscathed from a childhood Mickey Mantle fascination and learned to embrace the game of soccer. He was clever too, although some of his behaviour suggested otherwise. During his time at Harvard, for instance, he had stood out as the crazy Jewish guy who housed a four-foot bear called Mingo in his dorm room. Later, he would keep pet boa constrictors, glider turtles and a South American iguana called Sam. If he ever made it in pro-soccer, he said, he would buy his own pet store.

While Messing had played for his country at the 1972 Olympic Games in Munich, he had been kept out of the Cosmos starting line-up by their Polish keeper Jerry Sularz, the NASL's Goalkeeper of the Year in 1973. While his place in the first XI was never guaranteed, his place among the substitutes was – although, as he would say later, 'It didn't hurt as much to nurse a hangover on the bench.'

Of all the Cosmos players, Messing had the most hectic schedule to contend with. As he lived in Stamford, Connecticut, with his wife Arden, he was faced each morning with a hundred-mile trip to his teaching job at Westbury High on Long Island. That meant rising at 5.30 a.m. to get to school for 8 a.m. Then, when classes had finished, he would train with the Cosmos before making the long trek back to Stamford, getting in at around 2 a.m. Appreciating Messing's torturous schedule, player-coach Gordon Bradley cut the keeper some slack when it came to practice. 'He let me run two miles instead of four,' says Messing.

As the man who occasionally kept goal in a court jester's outfit or an African tribal mask, Messing's celebrity stock soon rose. Lithe and good-looking, the goalkeeper filmed commercials for everything from Vidal Sassoon to Coca-Cola to Skol chewing tobacco, but in the spring of 1973, he received the most unusual request of his blossoming career.

Jim Bouton was a friend of Messing's who had once pitched for the New York Yankees. He had been approached by a women's magazine, *Viva*, to pose nude for a photo shoot but he had declined on the grounds that his throwing arm was out of shape. Messing, though, was less inhibited and began talking with the New York photographer Barbara Pfeffer about the idea, not least because there was a $5,000 fee on offer for the shoot. 'I was broke and not making any money,' he explains. 'I decided, you know, who's gonna know?' I didn't think anybody would see it.'

Shep Messing was teaching at Westbury the day *Viva* hit the newsstands. Instead of the artistic, dimly lit, semi-nude shots he had been anticipating, he discovered that the centrefold results were about as subtle as a brick through a window. Not even the staples covered his modesty. 'There I was, the goalkeeper for the Cosmos, laid out there naked, frontal,' he laughs. 'It was wild.'

As word spread of the pictures, it soon became clear that Messing's notion that nobody would ever lay eyes on the shots was woefully wide of the mark. As the schoolgirls sniggered and his fellow teachers tittered, the magazine eventually found its way into hands of Westbury's principal. 'I had been their star teacher the day before – professional athlete, on the Cosmos,' he recalls. 'He was mortified. He fired me in like thirty seconds. He said, "I got the superintendent on the phone and I have his full blessing to fire you. Get out of the building immediately."'

Unfortunately, there was also a copy of *Viva* lying in Clive Toye's wastepaper basket. 'Clive went nuts,' adds Messing. 'He said it was disgraceful, "We're trying to be role models, we're trying to sell the sport".' It mattered not that Messing had gained more exposure for the NASL in just one risqué photoshoot than they had enjoyed all year. It wasn't good enough, said Toye, who along with Gordon Bradley decided to drop Messing from the team and suspend him without pay. Soon after, the Cosmos decided to release Messing – without paying up the remainder of his contract.

With around $3,000 owed to him, Messing spoke to his father, Elias, who as an attorney had always handled his legal matters. Together, they decided they had a strong case for compensation as Messing's contract did not stipulate any issues regarding morality. They filed suit in the New York Civil Court. As Messing endeavoured to find another club, the *Viva* backlash hindering his efforts, Clive Toye, under pressure from Elias Messing, relented and settled the claim out of court.

As Messing prepared to move on, his career saved by an offer from the Boston Minutemen, he received a communication from Toye. It read, in part: 'In 17 years as a journalist and 8 years as a general manager, you were the first person to sue me… Now, we shall not sign Pelé unless he swears his father is not an attorney.'

Messing would not be the only one in trouble. Jay Emmett, Steve Ross's friend and confidant, had become involved in a controversial share issue for the Westchester Premier Theater. Located near the Tappan Zee Bridge, the Westchester had been built in 1972 with the intention of booking big-name recording artists – something Warner had in abundance – but when its public stock offering had faltered, Emmett and his assistant treasurer at Warner, Solomon Weiss, had stepped in to buy up stock, amid allegations of bribes changing hands and mob involvement. Hardly surprising, given that the theatre was owned by Richard 'Nerves' Fusco and Gregory De Palma, who as members of the Colombo and Gambino families respectively were known to the Federal authorities for their links to organized crime.

While Emmett was already implicated, along with several other Warner employees, it was Steve Ross that the FBI really wanted. Soon after, an investigation into the Westchester share issue would be launched. It would last the best part of a decade.

As the Cosmos lumbered on, the NASL expanded still further. Despite the passing of the franchises in Atlanta and Montreal, new teams sprung up in Baltimore, Boston, Denver, Los Angeles, San Jose, Seattle, Vancouver and Washington, taking the total number of teams in the NASL to fifteen. A new rule change, sanctioned by FIFA, also brought an end to tied games. Now, whenever the scores were tied at full-time, the game would go to a penalty shootout, with the victorious side receiving just three points instead of the six they would still get for a win in regulation time.

For the New York Cosmos, though, it was business as usual. The 1974 season had barely begun and Randy Horton was walking back to the locker room, sent off again. The Bermudan had taken a hefty blow to his shin from the Baltimore Colts' Peter Silvester and had retaliated by knocking the Englishman to the ground, like a cop barging down a dealer's door. Enraged, Silvester had picked himself up, grabbed Horton by his beard and headbutted him. When Horton had shown the referee his head wound and asked him whether he intended to take any action against his opponent, all the flustered official could mutter was 'play on'.

It wasn't the response Horton was seeking. Aggrieved at the lack of any disciplinary action, the striker took the law into his own hands and began pummelling the face of Silvester like a punchbag. A red card, inevitably, followed moments later. 'What can I say?' he says. 'He did something I didn't like.'

If Randy Horton's disciplinary record was a cause for concern, at least nobody noticed. Soccer, after all, was way down the list of water cooler topics, not least because the long-drawn-out Watergate scandal had reached its conclusion. At 9 p.m. on the evening of 8 August 1974, a hundred million viewers across the country tuned in not to see the latest episode of *Happy Days* but to hear President Richard Nixon deliver his resignation speech. The following morning, the disgraced president said his final goodbyes to his White House staff before sending his resignation letter to the Secretary of State – and self-confessed New York Cosmos fan – Dr Henry Kissinger.

After two years of allegations, investigations and resignations surrounding the Watergate break-ins, it was the final humiliation for Nixon. His successor would be Gerald Ford, who as the first unelected president in the history of the United States assured the nation that 'our long national nightmare is over' before pledging 'openness and candor' in all his actions. Just one month into his new job, on the same day Evel Knievel leapt over Idaho's Snake River Canyon on his motorbike, Ford would grant Richard Nixon a full pardon for any crimes he may or may not have committed during his time in office. What, after all, was a little burglary between friends?

Meanwhile, the Warner Bros. film of the saga, *All the President's Men*, starring Robert Redford and Dustin Hoffman as the *Washington Post* reporters Bob Woodward and Carl Bernstein who broke the story, would open to critical acclaim and go on to win four Academy Awards.

If the New York Cosmos could have stolen any more fans by breaking into a rival franchise's office they surely would have. Madcap keeper or not, their average attendance had slumped from a barely respectable 5,782 to just 3,578 and Steve Ross's hunch that soccer was the future of US sport looked, increasingly, like one of the few bad calls he had made in his stellar career.

Not that the players seemed unduly concerned. For many of the squad's European contingent, playing football seemed almost incidental. The Englishman Malcolm Dawes, for example, had been loaned to the Cosmos from his English club, Hartlepool for the summer months in 1973 and 1974, swapping away games at Scunthorpe and Swansea for fixtures in Miami and Montreal. A tenacious defender, Dawes had become one of the most consistent performers in the Cosmos side, playing every minute of every game in 1973 and nearly every game in 1974. When he wasn't playing soccer, though, he was intent on making the most of what New York had to offer. 'I'd never been to the States before, not even on holiday, but I went into it with an open mind,' he explains. 'I made sure I enjoyed every minute out there... I even went to see Elvis Presley and Frank Sinatra in concert – they didn't often play in Hartlepool.'

While the Cosmos clearly needed more fans, what it really needed was more fans like Corrado 'Joe' Manfredi. Brought up in Bari in southern Italy, Joe Manfredi had left his homeland with his family in 1952 in search of the good life. With an Italian's passion for cars and an ingrained love of football, he had settled in a country where one of his loves could be accommodated quite comfortably and where the other, for the most part, could not.

It didn't matter. As time passed, Manfredi would not only get a job as a trainee mechanic in Brooklyn and then purchase his first dealership, but also discover a thriving local soccer scene, with teams and leagues organized around neighbourhoods and communities, rather than on a regional or city basis. There was the German-American League, the Long Island Soccer League and the competition he would become actively involved with, the Italian-American League. He had also discovered a little local side called the New York Cosmos and used to go the games when nobody else in the entire city, it seemed, could be bothered. 'The people born in this country thought soccer was a joke,' he recalls. 'But people who came from other countries, we knew what soccer was because that's all we knew.'

A decade after he had opened his first car showroom and with his passion for football undimmed (despite his regular attendance at Cosmos games), Joe Manfredi received a call from Steve Ross's office suggesting they get together. Intrigued, Manfredi agreed and arranged a meeting with Ross and his deputy, Jay Emmett.

When they met, Ross explained that he had big plans for the New York Cosmos and that he needed Manfredi's help in realizing those dreams. He suggested a mutually beneficial deal. In return for a bundle of free tickets for his clients and the local leagues he was involved in, and some free advertising for his dealerships, Manfredi would hand over the keys to a few Toyotas every season to keep the squad happy. 'I supplied cars to most of the players and the front office,' he explains, 'because I wanted the club to be successful.'

CHAPTER 4

THE PROMISED LAND

Another season, another brainwave. With Phil Woosnam keen to create the impression that the NASL was every bit as vital as rival sports in the United States, the commissioner decided to rename the season's showpiece finale the 'Soccer Bowl'. Said swiftly, it almost sounded like the Super Bowl.

Five new franchises would also enter the fray in 1975, with soccer returning to Chicago for the first time since 1968. There would also be a glut of familiar faces joining the league, including the legendary Portuguese striker Eusebio, the Chelsea and England goalkeeper Peter Bonetti and the Manchester United winger Gordon Hill.

While the arrival of such talented players was welcome, they were still some distance from being the kind of name signings that would make the rest of the soccer world sit up and take notice of the much-maligned NASL. Despite the expansion, what the league needed more than ever was a player of genuine star quality, the kind of player who could provide an instant fillip for the league and persuade the most sceptical of sports fans to hand over their money at the weekend.

It wasn't for want of trying. Clive Toye, of course, had tried his luck with Pelé but to no avail, and with his four-year pipe-dream of signing the Brazilian legend looking less likely with each passing season, the Cosmos's general manager lined up another star performer as the man to take the Cosmos and American soccer on to new heights – George Best.

With his background in sports reporting, Toye (and most of the football world, for that matter) had followed the career of Best with interest and knew that he was one of the few genuine superstars left in soccer. With swarthy good looks and a talent rarely seen in the modern game, Best's skill was sublime, his appeal universal. He possessed an almost balletic grace and an ability to beat defenders with the ball seemingly glued to his feet. But trouble followed Best around like a puppy and while he had won most of the honours in club football and been voted the European Player of the Year in 1968, his career had been blighted by a seemingly insatiable appetite for the high life. 'I was born with a great gift,' he once said, 'and sometimes with that comes a destructive streak. Just as I wanted to outdo everyone when I played, I had to outdo everyone when we were out on the town.'

Increasingly, Best's name had moved from the back-page headlines to the front. There were scores of sordid tales of all-night drinking and gambling and he seemed to collect beauty queens as some men collected stamps. One tabloid even called him the 'Fifth Beatle'.

Inevitably, Best's availability had seen a number of English clubs battling to sign him, most notably Malcolm Allison's Manchester City and Brian Clough's Derby County. By far the most exciting offer to reach Best, however, came from Toye and the New York Cosmos. Certainly, it was a move that appealed to Best. Hounded by the British press and unable to walk down the streets in the UK without being mobbed or attacked, the Northern Ireland international viewed a move to New York, perhaps naively, as a fresh start and a way to enjoy a degree of anonymity while still maximizing what was left of his earning potential.

Best duly arrived in New York on 13 January 1975, checking into the Wessex House Hotel opposite Central Park. Over the course of a week, negotiations with Toye progressed so well that within days, the pair, flanked by NASL commissioner Phil Woosnam, appeared at a press conference together to launch the new official NASL match ball. 'We are very close,' said Best of the ongoing dialogue. 'As far as I am concerned there will be no problem.'

Toye was equally optimistic, explaining 'there is little to do now, except put all the details in writing.' Superficially at least, everything seemed to be going to plan; Manchester United and their manager Tommy Docherty were happy to let Best go (especially as he wasn't going to a rival club in England), Toye was happy with the player and his commitment and Best himself wasn't anticipating any problems. Indeed, by 26 January, Toye had reached an agreement with Manchester United to buy Best for a downpayment of £10,000 followed by an additional £10,000 for each appearance he made. All that was required now was for the player himself to agree personal terms, and the contracts could be signed and George Best unveiled as the biggest star to pull on the Cosmos jersey.

Best, however, would never put pen to paper, going what Toye calls 'walkabout' when the deal had been finalized and failing to turn up to sign the contracts.

Former ABC soccer commentator Paul Gardner was at that press conference. 'George Best [was] being charming, just enchanting everybody,' he recalls. '"I love it. I'm going to do this, I'm going to do that and we'll have another conference on Thursday and we'll see you all then" and off he went and they never heard from him again. They couldn't find him, apparently he was in Spain on the beach somewhere.'

Twenty-six years later, in his autobiography, *Blessed*, Best would reveal why he turned his back on a move to the

Cosmos. 'They wanted me to do a lot of promotional stuff, and, not unnaturally, to live in New York full time,' he wrote. 'I didn't fancy that. I think New York is a great city and I love the madness of it for a few days. I just didn't relish the prospect of living there full time.'

Best's failure to commit to the Cosmos rankled with Toye who had seen his chance of landing the genuinely high-profile recruit he craved scuppered at the eleventh hour. Years later, Toye would corner Best during a pre-season match between Best's new team, the LA Aztecs, and the Cosmos. '[The] teams were lining up for the anthem,' recalls Toye, 'so I walked up behind George, put him in a headlock and said, "So that's where you got to you little bugger" and he just smiled and said: "Hello, Clive" and that was that.'

Unperturbed, Toye's attentions returned to the player who had remained his number one choice, even throughout the negotiations with Best. For years, Toye had badgered Pelé, pursuing him around the globe as though he were a fugitive and taking every opportunity to remind him not what the Cosmos could do for him, but rather what he could do for the Cosmos and, more importantly, what he could do for soccer in the States. There had been meetings in São Paolo, Santos, Frankfurt, London and Toronto, all without the outcome Toye wanted. Crucially, though, Toye's hand had now been strengthened, not least by Pelé's retirement from the game at the age of thirty-three in the October of 1974.

Moreover, the player himself was now in need of money as a succession of bad business deals and poor legal advice had left him with substantial debts back in Brazil. His chief concern was the position of Fiolax, a company that manufactured rubber components for the motor industry. Although he owned only 6 per cent of shares in the company, Pelé had signed a guarantee for a bank loan on Fiolax's behalf. Needless to say, when the company defaulted, the banks came looking for Pelé. It would also transpire that Fiolax had contravened corporate regulations governing the importation of raw materials, and the outstanding loan repayments coupled with a hefty fine had left Pelé with a bill of over $1 million.

When Pelé flew to Brussels to play in the testimonial game of the Belgian captain Paul Van Himst in March, he was followed, as ever, by Clive Toye. 'I had pretty well decided I was either going to get a really positive response from him then or I was going to go away and commit suicide,' he says.

The following few days would make or break any deal. Toye's problem, however, was finding the time to sit down with the player to discuss any possible move. Pelé was a man in demand. There were cocktail parties and banquets, photo shoots and signing sessions, meetings with ministers and multimillionaires. Then there was the game itself. Everything, it seemed, except time for a meeting with Clive Toye. Eventually, after a stolen ten-minute conversation in the back of a Brussels taxi, the pair agreed to meet at Pelé's motel the morning after the match.

Toye arrived at the GB Motor Inn determined to secure Pelé's signature. Time was of the essence. Pelé was due to fly out to Casablanca that lunchtime for an audience with the King of Morocco and Toye was anxious to get down to business, even though his task had been complicated by emerging press reports linking some of Europe's biggest clubs to Pelé. 'Juventus and Real Madrid were nibbling at him and I said if you go there, all you can do is win another championship, if you come here, you can win a country. He and he alone could do something no one had ever done and bring it to the mainstream.'

But Toye's pioneer sales pitch – or 'pestering' as he puts it – seemed to be working. Pelé, after all, had never played his club football outside Brazil, and though extremely fit for a man in his mid-thirties, there was every chance he would be found wanting if he moved to the more demanding leagues of Italy or Spain. But as Toye began to sense that he was finally making headway, proceedings were brought to an abrupt end. '[There was a] knock on the door and then one by one, all these great players who had played this testimonial game all came in to give [Pelé] a hug and a kiss and say goodbye,' recalls Toye. 'Eusebio came in and Alan Simonsen and Van Himst, of course. Then Altafini came in.'

Jose Altafini was an abrasive centre-forward who held dual nationality for Brazil and Italy. Born in Brazil, he had played with Pelé for the national team in the 1958 World Cup finals under the name Mazola. Later, having moved to Italy and made a name for himself as the star striker in the AC Milan team of the early 1960s, he had opted to play for the *Azzurri* instead. When Altafini saw Toye talking to Pelé he knew immediately that he was trying to sign him, and decided to offer his services to the Cosmos as well. 'Under normal circumstances I would have snatched his hand off,' explains Toye, 'but I wanted him out of the bloody room because I had another hour with Pelé.

But Altafini wouldn't budge, badgering Toye to make him an offer of a contract. 'He wouldn't go,' adds Toye. 'I kept on saying "Later, Jose," he was [saying] "no no, how much you pay me?" So in the end I made him some insulting offer like $15,000 a year and he left in a huff.'

With Altafini finally gone, Toye persevered with Pelé as the player changed clothes, slipping into a pair of painfully tight white trousers. As the Englishman outlined his plans for the club and the NASL, Pelé bent over to pack his suitcase. Then, disaster. Pelé's trousers ripped and, as his other trousers were buried deep in his suitcase and he had neither the time nor the inclination to unpack again, he needed some emergency repairs. Off came the trousers, on went a towel and an increasingly exasperated Toye sent for a chambermaid. 'So in came this very respectable-looking middle-aged lady, took one look at Pelé, burst into tears and explained that her husband had been a huge fan, had never seen him play, had tickets to the game last night but had died two weeks before of a heart attack. Could she please have a photograph taken with Pelé?' laughs Toye. 'So now with twenty-five minutes to go of the rest of my life, we have to find a camera. She goes away to mend Pelé's trousers, comes back with the trousers, we take the photograph, she goes. I stand with my back to the door so no one else can come in and we get down to brass tacks and say OK, what about it then. So finally he agreed to sign to us for two years and I said OK, let's get it on a piece of paper. I still have that paper at home.'

Finally, Toye had his man, or at least he had an agreement in principle. Before he left for the airport, the pair discussed Pelé's personal demands – he wanted $3 million over two years – and they agreed to meet again in Rome in a fortnight's time to further discuss the deal.

Two weeks later, Clive Toye arrived in Italy accompanied by Warner executive Rafael de la Sierra, who in addition to having some control over the Cosmos purse strings was tagging along as Toye's impromptu interpreter. The fact he spoke Spanish and not Portuguese didn't matter. It seemed close enough.

Curiously, de la Sierra was a Cuban architect who had redesigned the new Warner offices in Manhattan as well as working on Villa Eden, the company's executive retreat near the Las Brisas resort in Mexico. During both projects, he had impressed Steve Ross so much that he brought him into the

Warner family and had rapidly gained a reputation as one of the rising stars of Rockefeller Plaza.

A meeting was convened at the Excelsior Hotel on one of Rome's most famous streets, the Via Veneto. Toye, decidedly more relaxed now he had at least gained an assurance from Pelé, arrived with de la Sierra, confident they could finally reach a more definite agreement with the player. But before the party had even sat down to dinner, yet alone begun contract negotiations, the hotel's bus boy had sprinted home to get a football for Pelé to autograph and the chef had emerged from the kitchens begging Pelé to sign his hat.

When they reached their table, one of the musicians from the house band wandered over to the table and, knowing that Pelé was an accomplished guitar player, handed him a guitar and pleaded with him to play for the diners. Ever courteous, Pelé duly obliged, but as he finished and accepted the applause of the restaurant, an official looking man, bedecked with ribbons and medals, appeared at his side. Explaining that he was a guest at a diplomatic function in a neighbouring room, he wondered whether Pelé would do him and his fellow guests the honour of sharing a glass of champagne with them. Pelé smiled and, much to Toye's chagrin, said yes. 'So we all have to traipse in while they all stand up in their glittering evening gowns and tiaras and toast Pelé,' he sighs.

When every last autograph had been signed and photo taken, the three men sat down to dinner. In their previous meetings, Clive Toye had only ever gained minor concessions from Pelé. He had, for example, offered to play the occasional exhibition game and host a handful of soccer clinics but nothing concrete. While such offers were welcome, they were only piecemeal suggestions, a world away from what Toye (or

'Clivie' as Pelé called him) really needed from his man. Now, however, Toye knew he had all but pulled off the biggest transfer coup in football history.

Back in the States, the new NASL season began on the same day the Vietnam War ended. Back-to-back defeats at home to Miami Toros and away to Eddie Firmani's Tampa Bay Rowdies had left player-coach Gordon Bradley and his team of triers fearing another season of underachievement. That said, the NASL was also fearing the worst. Only a handful of teams were capable of drawing five-figure crowds (most notably the San Jose Eathquakes, the Seattle Sounders and the Tampa Bay Rowdies) and attendances of three or four thousand were the depressing norm.

Quite why Pelé should want to join a struggling side in a league with no clear future was anyone's guess. To his credit, though, Clive Toye had persevered with a rare zeal, and but for the contracts being signed, had managed to get his man. With the deal all but done, Norman Samnick, the general counsel in Warner's Publishing and Licensing Division, was drafted in to conclude the outstanding issues.

As one of WCI's top lawyers, Samnick was in the process of drafting Dustin Hoffman's and Robert Redford's contracts for the film of the Watergate scandal, *All the President's Men*, but had been seconded by Steve Ross to work on the details of the Pelé deal. 'I got a call [from Ross],' says Samnick. '[He said] "I want you on a plane tonight to Brazil, you're going with Jim Kerridine [Warner's tax specialist] and you'll meet Rafael de la Sierra there." I had no idea what I was doing, why I was doing it, when we were doing it and with whom we were doing it.'

Samnick and Kerridine took the ten o'clock Pan-Am flight that evening to Rio de Janeiro, arriving in Brazil at eight the following morning. A taxi then took the pair of them to a local airport and on to a domestic flight to São Paolo, where they would meet de la Sierra. Over lunch, de la Sierra explained to Samnick and Kerridine that they were there to finalize the contracts with Pelé, before meeting the player at his home near Santos.

When the two parties reconvened, the discussions continued but progress proved slow. The chief concern for Pelé and his adviser, Valdemar De Brito, was that the player's salary should be tax-free and that it should be grossed up to account for his tax burden. With the deal on the verge of collapse, Samnick called Jay Emmett at his home in New York to seek guidance. It was 2 a.m. and Emmett, not surprisingly, was unimpressed. After listening to what Samnick had to say, Emmett hung up, because he 'knew there would be six or seven other calls'. Later that night, Emmett would meet with Clive Toye to try and salvage the deal.

Eventually, there was a breakthrough. 'We came up with some ingenious ideas to get more money, less taxes and a lot of licensing income [for Pelé],' explains Samnick. Pelé and his team were particularly taken with the idea of a 50 per cent cut of all endorsements and a new licensing deal, and his mind was as good as made up when, soon after, he received a communication from Henry Kissinger, the then Secretary of State and a goalkeeper in his youth. Previously, Kissinger had sent a letter to the Foreign Secretary of Brazil pleading with him to let their national treasure join the Cosmos, but now he would contact the player himself to persuade him to try his hand in NYC. 'In my dealings with the Brazilian government and with Pelé there was no huge resistance,' recalls Kissinger. 'I tried to convince them that to have Pelé play in the United

States was a tremendous asset for them and by that time he was no longer on the Brazilian national team so we were not taking him away from anything that Brazil wanted.'

Quite how much Kissinger's intervention swayed Pelé is debatable, but certainly it was another PR masterstroke from Warner. If the Secretary of State was getting involved then this really was news, even if it was about soccer. After twenty-four straight hours of drafting the final contracts, Samnick, Kerridine and de la Sierra completed the job. Elated but exhausted, the Cosmos delegation headed back to their hotel to gather their things and get a plane back to Rio, before getting an early-morning flight to New York the following day.

When Norman Samnick arrived back in New York, however, he was contacted by Steve Ross's office, and instructed to meet Ross, Toye and Jay Emmett at the airport the following morning. There, they would get the early flight to Hamilton, Bermuda to complete the formal signing of contracts at the Hamilton Princess Hotel. Bermuda was chosen for what Emmett describes as '[Pelé's] tax reasons'.

To help ease Pelé through the bothersome issues of visas and work permits (and to ensure that he paid as little tax as possible), Warner prepared a succession of contracts for him, with only one having any mention of soccer in it. Aside from the three-year playing deal, there was a ten-year deal for the world-wide marketing rights to the Pelé name and likeness and a fourteen-year PR contract for Warner Communications. One agreement even had his position within the corporation as that of a 'Recording Artist' with Atlantic Records. 'We owned him lock stock and barrel,' smiles Toye.

While it was, undeniably, a lucrative deal for Pelé, there was some confusion over the exact amount the Brazilian would be paid for his services. Initial press reports suggested Pelé would be paid $4.7 million over the course of his three-year contract – more than any other professional sportsman in the States at that time – but Norman Samnick, Jay Emmett and Clive Toye maintain that the amount he agreed to was $2.8 million. However the deal was examined, it was clear that for the next three years Pelé would earn more than he did in his entire career with Santos.

The deal also went far beyond merely lining Pelé's pockets. As well as two houses, an office suite at Rockerfella Plaza (with luxury bathroom, naturally) and guaranteed places in New York's best schools for his children, Pelé had sought and secured a number of additional assurances from Cosmos, including the establishment of exchange programmes between American and Brazilian sports coaches and a sponsorship deal for a soccer school for underprivileged children in Santos. He had also persuaded Clive Toye to take on Julio Mazzei as an assistant coach at the club.

When Clive Toye got back to Warner HQ, his four-year, 300,000-mile odyssey at an end, he called John O'Reilly into his office. When O'Reilly arrived Toye was sat with Gordon Bradley. 'They said: "We want to tell you something that has taken place,"' recalls O'Reilly. 'I wasn't sure if they were going to tell me I hadn't got a job or the club had folded, and they said, "We… we've signed Pelé." And I gave them a look of "you're both crazy". I used different words. And they said "No, we've signed Pelé."'

As Toye puffed on a celebratory cigar and Bradley sniggered at O'Reilly's bewilderment, the same words rang out again: 'We've signed Pelé.' O'Reilly was nonplussed. 'I said "I'm going home". It was 3 p.m. and I left for home, hours before the day was over because I truly didn't believe we had signed Pelé.'

On 10 June 1975 at a triumphant press conference at New York's famous 21 Club, the New York Cosmos announced the signing of the greatest player the game had ever seen. Outside the club was a scene of utter pandemonium, with 51st Street, 52nd Street, Fifth Avenue and the Avenue of the Americas all packed with people jostling to see what all the fuss was about.

Inside the club, though, it was much worse. Pelé was two hours late, there was no air-conditioning and according to the sign on the wall the capacity of the 21 Club's Hunt Room was 143 people. With proceedings threatening to get out of hand, John O'Reilly did a head count, stopping when the number topped 400. 'We had superstars in the United States, but nothing at the level of Pelé,' says O'Reilly. 'Everyone wanted to touch him, shake his hand, get a photo with him.'

Clive Toye agrees. 'Absolute chaos,' he adds, 'more photographers than I have ever seen in my life before.'

Eventually, Pelé made his entrance, flanked by his wife Rosa, Steve Ross, Jay Emmett, Clive Toye, Gordon Bradley and Julio Mazzei. 'For me it is like a dream,' he said. 'The United States is the capital of the world. Everybody has something to do in this life, a mission, a goal, and the only country in the world where soccer is not well known is the United States. I had a dream that one day the USA will know soccer and that is the main reason I am here now – to show this nation why soccer in the world is so important.'

As flashguns popped and Pelé posed, the sound of glass shattering caught his attention. As the media scrum battled to secure the best picture of the Cosmos's new recruit, two rival photographers had started fighting, turning over a glass-topped table as they grappled. Understandably, Pelé looked bewildered but, as he would soon discover, the madness had only just begun.

CHAPTER 5

LOST IN THE FLOOD

Downing Stadium was variously described by Cosmos officials as either a dump, a hellhole or a horror show. Situated under the Triborough Bridge at Randall's Island (the locals called it 'Vandal's Island'), it had long been a site for high school football and track and field meets and had served the student population well. But the ground had seen better days. Broken bottles littered the field, there was often no running water (apart from the overflow from the toilets above the locker rooms) and there was more grass on the road into Manhattan than there was on the pitch.

The problem for Clive Toye, however, was that the Cosmos had no other option. As their old home at Yankee Stadium was being redeveloped, the Yankees had gone to Flushing Meadow to share Shea Stadium with the Mets, leaving the Cosmos out in the cold. As a base for a mediocre team going nowhere Randall's Island was fine, but as a venue for the world's greatest ever player to showcase his vast array of skills it was woefully inadequate.

While Toye and the Warner team had done everything they could to convince Pelé that his immediate future lay with the Cosmos and converting an entire nation to soccer, the notion that the deal could be undone by the condition of its stadium had never really entered the equation. Indeed, before Pelé finally put pen to paper, Warner had flown him over Downing Stadium to show him the home of the Cosmos, but not before they had carried out some emergency maintenance on what passed for the pitch. 'We were at practice at Randall's Island, trying to avoid the broken glass on the field when all of a sudden we see a guy coming on the field and he starts spray painting the field green,' recalls Shep Messing. 'Then we see a helicopter flying over, and the helicopter leaves. They had flown Pelé over Randall's Island to show him the stadium and they had painted the dirt green so he'd think it was a nice soccer field.'

The trick was repeated for Pelé's first game at Randall's Island on 15 June when Lamar Hunt brought his Dallas Tornado team to town for an exhibition game. With CBS covering the event and a record crowd expected, it was imperative that the pitch at least looked good, even if it was still little more than a dirt track. At 6.30 a.m., Stan Cunningham, the stadium manager, gathered his team together and presented them each with a watering can into which he mixed green paint and water. His men were then dispatched on to the field of play to sprinkle over any suggestion that the playing surface was anything other than of a standard a three-time World Cup winner had come to expect. 'Pelé was a diamond in a rhinestone setting,' says David Hirshey of the *New York Daily News*. 'It was inconceivable that he would play his first game in a place that was essentially a bunch of dirt and rocks left over from the Palaeolithic era.'

Signing Pelé was a publicity coup without compare. When kick-off arrived, Downing Stadium, complete with cosmetically enhanced pitch, was heaving. Suddenly, from an unimpressive average attendance of around 7,000, there were now over 21,000 fans clamouring to see the team and, more specifically, their new star turn. From Astoria and Queens they came. In the bleachers, signs bearing the words 'Obrigado Brasil' ('Thank you, Brazil') were held high, while the traffic slowed on the Triborough Bridge as rubber-neckers paused to pinch a look at the commotion.

The game itself would be televised in twenty-two different countries and be covered by over three hundred journalists. Steve Marshall's press box, so long a place bereft of any passion or, indeed, expertise, was now ablaze with expectation. When Pelé finally ran out on to the pitch it was as if Jesus himself had decided to make his comeback.

Before the kick-off, Pelé and the Tornado's American skipper, Kyle Rote Jr, exchanged flags in the centre circle, and though Rote held the Brazilian flag upside down, it was, nevertheless, another gesture that brought a smile to Pelé's face.

After a low-key first half, adjusting to the demands of a game where all the players, the opposition included, seemed to be in awe of the little black guy with the mile-wide smile, Pelé trotted into the locker room, the sound of the crowd still ringing in his ears, and approached Clive Toye. With an anxious look on his face, he rolled down his sock and showed his leg to the general manager. 'He was quite concerned. He had this sort of green fungus on his leg and he thought he had caught a disease in his first forty-five minutes playing in New York,' recalls Toye, 'but all it was the green paint coming off.'

Assured that soap and water, rather than amputation, was the best course of treatment for his condition, Pelé returned for the second half and delighted the sell-out crowd with a headed equalizer ten minutes from time, earning the Cosmos a 2–2 draw. The following day, one local journalist reported that seeing Pelé play at Downing Stadium was like 'watching Nureyev dance in a Times Square honky tonk joint'.

Three days after his triumphant bow in a Cosmos shirt, Pelé returned to Randall's Island for his official North American Soccer League debut. The team was already nine games into their campaign and their form was unconvincing, having registered three wins and six defeats. By now, Pelé had participated in a couple of training sessions with his new team-mates and, ever the professional, the greatest player in the history of soccer had done as instructed by Gordon Bradley, a man whose career had taken him from Sunderland to Bradford Park Avenue and on to Carlisle United. 'It was a joy ride,' laughs Bradley. 'I remember the first practice. John Kerr kicked a cross that went behind him, behind Pelé's head, and he was running toward the goal. Pelé jumped up in the air and did a bicycle kick, and scored. The press couldn't believe it. I ended the practice right then.'

But while Bradley beamed, the Cosmos squad were having trouble adjusting to the fact that they were now sharing a pitch with Pelé. 'The biggest challenge for us,' explains Werner Roth, 'was not stopping and watching him play because he still had these incredible moves.'

It was a sense of total awe that would continue long after the games had finished. 'I remember one time in Boston when the Cosmos were having a team meal,' recalls David Hirshey. 'Pelé ordered the lobster special. The waiter went back to he kitchen and gave the order: eighteen lobster specials... whatever Pelé said they just followed along, blindly.'

In its last home game, the Cosmos had attracted a crowd of just 5,227 for the match against the NASL's perennial whipping boys, the Hartford Bicentennials. Now, they had to lock the gates when the ground reached its 22,500 capacity. 'There must have been another 50,000 turned away,' remembers Gordon Bradley.

The away fixtures were just as popular. In the days leading up to his first away game against Shep Messing's new team, the Boston Minutemen, the local papers were full of little else; one even billed it as 'The Minutemen v. Pelé', as if the Cosmos was a one-man team.

Sensing a quick buck, Boston owner John Sterge ditched the Minutemen's usual ground at Nickerson Field and rented out the University of Boston's Richardson Stadium for the game. It was a venue capable of holding 12,000 people but official records show that over 18,126 wedged themselves into the ground for the match. Such was Pelé's appeal.

Although the match would end in a Cosmos defeat, the game would be replayed as an official complaint lodged by Gordon Bradley was upheld by Phil Woosnam and the NASL. During the game, Pelé had scored a goal (later disallowed) and the crowd spilled on to the pitch to celebrate. Shep Messing estimates that there must have been 'a thousand bodies on the field, just trying to touch Pelé,' adding that 'It was a horrifying thing to see.'

Although Pelé would emerge from the incident unscathed, Bradley and the Cosmos complained that as Boston had failed to provide adequate security for the players the game should be replayed. Phil Woosnam agreed, and when the two teams met again, the Cosmos won 5–0.

Away from the field of play, Pelé soon discovered that the idea that he would be able to enjoy greater anonymity living in New York was flawed in the extreme and that his schedule was as hectic as ever. There was an appearance on Johnny Carson and a meeting with the president, Gerald Ford (both designed to publicize the New York Cosmos and attempt to explain exactly what this soccer thing was all about), and he would vie with a young New Jersey songwriter called Bruce Springsteen for the country's hippest magazine covers too.

Even when he took time out to enjoy himself there was no avoiding the city's burgeoning legion of soccer fans. On one occasion, Pelé accompanied the Cosmos promotions director, John O'Reilly, to an Elton John concert at Madison Square Garden, and as the pair rocked along to the strains of *Philadelphia Freedom*, a spotlight switched from the stage and focused on Pelé, resplendent in a white suit. '[Then] Elton John introduces the greatest soccer player in the world,' recalls O'Reilly. 'At that point I say, "We have to get the hell out of here…" otherwise we would've been crushed.'

Pelé's arrival would not only signal a wholesale reversal in the fortunes of the team itself but in the NASL as a realistic, viable alternative to the mainstays of baseball, basketball and American football. As well as publicizing a league in dire need of a fillip, Pelé had brought instant credibility to the standard of the game in the States, even if the quality of the play was still dubious. If the NASL was now good enough for Pelé, a three-time World Cup winner, scorer of over 1,000 career goals and the man known throughout the world as 'the king of soccer', how could any other player say no to playing in the States?

Suddenly, the Cosmos metamorphosized from being a club run by a handful of people from an inadequate office on Park Avenue into one struggling to cope with thousands of media requests and ticket orders each and every week.

Every facet of the club had to change. Sales staff were hired, advertising people recruited and promotions experts drafted in. Almost overnight, the Cosmos suddenly had over fifty support staff to help capitalize on the huge public interest prompted by Pelé's arrival.

Where once the Cosmos press conferences would be held in the locker room with a handful of hacks passing the time before the bars opened, now they were conducted in the 21 Club or the ballroom of the Plaza Hotel, with scores of journalists enjoying the trappings of a club heading for the big time. Even the quality of the buffet improved, as Jim Trecker, the Cosmos director of public relations, recalls. 'Before Pelé got to the Cosmos, you'd only have five or six journalists at a press conference and you'd serve a couple of finger sandwiches and maybe you'd open a couple of bottles of soda if it was really high end. After Pelé signed, the basic food was caviar and smoked salmon and champagne. There was no more finger sandwiches and no more beer.'

But being the next big thing in NYC presented a new set of problems. As the Cosmos revelled in its coup, it soon found that Randall's Island couldn't cope with a global superstar. The Island had been built in the depths of the Depression in the 1930s and was designed for pedestrians, not motorists. Where once fans would across from 125th Street or amble along from Astoria or Queens, now everyone drove everywhere, resulting in traffic chaos on match day. While the crowd could get in without much difficulty, the problems arose when the final whistle blew and 20,000 or more fans all wanted to leave at the same time. With only one road into Randall's Island from the east and another from the west, supporters were then faced with a two or three hour wait to finally extricate themselves from the jam.

With Pelé on a three-year contract at the club, it was clear that Clive Toye and the Cosmos had to find a new ground. Soon after Pelé's arrival, negotiations began with their first home, Yankee Stadium, and the yet-to-be-finished New Jersey Meadowlands stadium. 'Those days at Randall's were the best days, although maybe not from an accountant's view,' laughs Mark Ross.

But after years of doing anything and everything to persuade people to come see the Cosmos, some heavy traffic once a week was a nice problem to have. As the crowds flocked to

Randall's Island (and struggled to get out), Steve Marshall soon realized that he would no longer have to count the freeloaders watching from the Triborough Bridge as part of the official attendance and that the days of Harold the Chimp, men dressed as milk shakes and giving seats away at Burger King were history. Cosmos was cleared for take-off.

CHAPTER 6

MEETING ACROSS THE RIVER

For all his millions and his influence in the world of commerce, Steve Ross was just like any other dad when it came to his son, Mark. In the days before the Cosmos, the pair would venture out to hockey, football or basketball games together and eat the same cheap hot dogs and super-sized sodas that every other fan did. Now, with his old man as a bona fide NASL franchise owner, though, Mark Ross had been propelled into a world that most fourteen-year-old kids could only ever dream of. Thanks to his dad, Ross Junior now had unfettered access to the Cosmos locker room. He would go on the road with the Cosmos, eat with the Cosmos and, short of pulling on his boots and taking to the field, do everything the Cosmos did. Well, nearly everything.

Even when Mark was at school there was no escaping the Cosmos. Once, when he was playing soccer after class, his father had turned up to cheer him on from the touchline. But as the teams prepared to kick off, the whispering began. Then, the nudging. Then, the finger-pointing. There, next to Steve Ross on the sidelines, was Pelé. 'I was just like "Oh God, please. Why do you have to go and bring Pelé?" I'd get very embarrassed.'

Steve Ross's attentions, however, would soon be distracted by the woman who would become the second Mrs Ross – and it wasn't his girlfriend, Courtney Sale. In November 1975, the Warner boss had been persuaded by his friend, the former US ambassador to Switzerland, William vanden Heuvel, to join him and a friend for dinner. Her name was Amanda Burden.

While many women were transfixed by the combination of Steve Ross's natural charm and unnaturally healthy bank balance, Amanda Burden was one of the few women in New York City who was not going to be bowled over by the extent of Ross's assets. Burden's mother was Barbara 'Babe' Paley, the one-time fashion muse of the 1960s and the wife of the founder of the CBS network, William Paley (Amanda's stepfather), who, coincidentally, was one of Ross's business heroes. Her father, Babe's first husband, was Stanley Mortimer, the heir to the Standard Oil fortune.

The dinner date went very well. The attraction was instant, the chemistry unmistakeable. The only problem was that unbeknown to Burden, Courtney Sale was still Ross's girlfriend.

It mattered little. Sale was away on a business trip as part of her job in marketing and promotions at Warner's Jungle Habitat (a job Ross had given her). When she returned soon after, Ross and Burden were living together.

❂

The failure of the Cosmos to even reach the play-offs in 1975 would cost Gordon Bradley his job. Not even Pelé, it seemed, could guarantee Soccer Bowl success. As Bradley stood aside, taking a new position as vice-president of player personnel, Clive Toye set about securing the services of another English coach he had been tracking.

Ken Furphy was the manager of Sheffield United in the English First Division. He came from Stockton-on-Tees in the north-east: his playing career had stalled when he had failed to take his chance at Everton and had ended up playing for a succession of lower-league clubs, including Runcorn and Darlington. As player-coach at Workington Town, however, he discovered an aptitude for coaching and led the team to promotion to the Third Division in 1964. Later, as manager of Watford, he took the Second Division side to the semi-finals of the 1970 FA Cup, losing to the eventual winners, Chelsea. He would also become the coach of the England Under-23 side.

By 1975, however, Furphy's time with Sheffield United was coming to an end. Disagreements with the new chairman coupled with a poor start to the new season – they had just one win and one draw in their first eleven games – saw Furphy sacked at the beginning of October 1975, a 2–0 defeat at Birmingham City sealing his fate. It was the kind of sorry start that would render most managers unemployable, rather than sought after by a club with designs on world domination.

With a mortgage to pay, Furphy took a job scouting for Bobby Robson at Ipswich Town, but just three weeks into his new role he received a call from Clive Toye in New York. 'I had no idea who Clive was but they had just signed Pelé and there was a lot of talk about the Cosmos,' recalls Furphy. 'So Clive came across and saw me and then I flew out there and had an interview with the top dog, Steve Ross.'

During that meeting, Ross asked Furphy what he would do to make the Cosmos the best team in the world. To the Warner chief's delight, Furphy reeled off a succession of innovative ideas, including proposals to introduce a reserve team based around local talent (and not expensive imports) and an initiative to develop American youth players by taking them to a Cosmos camp in Ireland during the winter. 'He was a strange fellow,' says Furphy, 'but he offered me the job.'

On 22 January 1976, Ken Furphy was announced as the new coach of the New York Cosmos and, satisfied that his new manager had the nous to fufil his weighty expectations, Steve Ross handed over the Warner chequebook and gave Furphy his backing as he entered the transfer market. The coach's first move was to return to his former club, Sheffield United, and tempt his old captain, Keith Eddy, across the Atlantic. With a deal that doubled his money to £400 a week, Eddy, thirty-one, needed little persuasion. 'I went home to tell the wife about the offer. I'm sure she thought I said "York" and not "New York" and it took a while for it to sink in but in the end she was as keen as I was.'

Furphy would also sign a string of other British players who had impressed him during his years coaching in England. There was the combative Northern Ireland international Dave Clements, the vastly experienced full-back Charlie Aitken, the midfielder Terry Garbett, the Scottish winger Brian Tinnion and a striker who had always done well by Furphy, Tony Field. Aware that he was in real danger of simply turning the Cosmos into another of the NASL's replica English Football League sides, Furphy also brought in two South American midfielders, the Brazilian Nelsi Morais and the Peruvian international Ramón Mifflin. 'He [Mifflin] was one of the most skilful players I have ever seen,' recalls Keith Eddy. 'He could do things with a ball that defied belief – but he couldn't tackle a divot.'

Finally, Ken Furphy placated the Cosmos fans by signing arguably the two best American players in the NASL. With the Philadelphia franchise about to be signed over to a Mexican consortium, Furphy picked off the Atoms' goalkeeper, Bob Rigby, and their resolute full-back, Bobby Smith, for a combined $100,000. It was the kind of revolution in personnel that Steve Ross appreciated and that Ken Furphy needed to enact in order to create his own team. But it was a risk. Inevitably, with so many new faces in the Cosmos squad, it was going to take time for them to blend together and get accustomed to life in a city as mixed up as New York.

But while the Manhattan skyline was increasingly dominated by vast corporate superstructures and luxury apartment blocks, the extent of the deprivation in areas like Harlem and Bushwick was extreme. As the city struggled by, slashing budgets for everything from law enforcement to health care, the Housing and Development Administrator, Richard Starr, unveiled a controversial proposal to ease the financial burden on the city. Under a policy of what he termed 'planned shrinkage', Starr suggested dislodging the poorest people in New York by systematically withdrawing all the basic services from the city's most deprived areas. The idea was that without access to the police, sanitation, health and public transport, these neighbourhoods would become uninhabitable and the inhabitants would be forced to look for accommodation outside New York City.

Starr's scheme reinforced a long-held belief by many of New York's marginalized population that the authorities perceived them as nothing more than a blot on the landscape of the world's greatest city and that any opportunity to hasten the resettlement of impoverished minorities would be too good to pass up. Not surprisingly, the plan also met with widespread contempt. NYC's planning commissioner, Gordon J. Davis Jr, said he was 'deeply shocked' by the initiative, while Samuel D. Wright, chairman of the NYC Council's Puerto Rican and Black Legis Caucus, called for Starr's resignation, labelling his programme 'genocidal, racist, inhuman and irresponsible'. Even Mayor Beame, who had made great play of the fact that he never gagged any of his commissioners, distanced himself from the idea. While Starr's policy of planned shrinkage would never be ratified, the fact that such an idea could even be mooted demonstrated the extent of the city's fiscal troubles and the extreme measures some politicians were prepared to consider to find a fix.

As Starr endeavoured to become the most detested man in New York, the Cosmos was busy moving back to Yankee Stadium in the South Bronx (one of the areas that would have become a wasteland if Starr's proposals had ever been given the green light).

Yankee Stadium had undergone a massive transformation. After celebrating the venue's fiftieth anniversary season in 1973, the New York Yankees had moved out to Shea Stadium for two seasons while their home was razed and then rebuilt. The finished result was breathtaking. Cantilever stands had been built to improve the view for spectators, an extra ten rows of seats had been added to the top tier and the Yankees could now boast baseball's first 'telescreen' scoreboard, a facility that could provide action replays in what the press release announced was 'nine shades of grey'.

The return to its original home represented a shift in the fortunes of the Cosmos, after the painted pitches and the bottlenecks of Randall's Island. While Yankee Stadium had played host to attractions as diverse as Pope Paul VI and Muhammad Ali over the years, it had never had to accommodate an event as entirely alien as a soccer match. Now, whenever the Cosmos turned up to play, the pitching mounds would have to be removed and then replaced.

While the new stadium itself met with almost universal acclaim, the location of it was a cause for concern for some of the Cosmos's foreign contingent. Undoubtedly, the Bronx had seen better days. What was once home to aspirational, second-generation immigrants – it was even called a 'wonder borough' – was now an area increasingly defined by crime and poverty. For the pampered players, it was case of turn up, play your game and get out. 'It was a genuinely scary place,' explains Keith Eddy. 'The players' car park was surrounded by twelve-foot fences, like some high security compound.'

A month after his appointment, Ken Furphy took his new Cosmos squad to their pre-season training camp in Hempstead, Long Island, but it would be nearly a month later before Pelé joined his team-mates. While everyone at the club was aware of the Brazilian's trouble with time-keeping ('Pelé had a problem with punctuality,' says Clive Toye, 'cos the poor sod could never walk anywhere without being festooned with people'), being a month late for training represented tardiness on an entirely new level.

Typically, though, Pelé's absence was attributed to the kind of surreal set of circumstances in which only Pelé could find himself. With his family finally settled in their new surroundings, he had agreed to go on a world tour with one of his many sponsors, Pepsi. After visits to Japan, India and Uganda, Pelé made his way to Nigeria, the battle-scarred African nation that, on his last visit, had called a temporary truce in their civil war so that as many people as possible had the opportunity to see him.

On this occasion, Pelé found himself entangled in a military coup as dissident army officers attempted to depose the leader, Murtala Mohammed (who himself had overthrown the previous leader, General Yakubu Gowon, in July 1975). As the hostilities escalated and the crisis deepened, Pelé and his entourage were advised to stay in their hotel until such time as it was safe to fly out of Lagos. On 13 February, however, Mohammed was assassinated, leaving Nigeria teetering on the brink of another civil war.

While the coup would ultimately fail, Pelé's stay in the country would still be extended by another week as the

Nigerian authorities announced a week of mourning for Mohammed, closing the airport in the process. It would take some hasty intervention by Steve Ross and Henry Kissinger to eventually smuggle Pelé out of Nigeria. 'It shows you the power of the Cosmos,' says Ken Furphy, 'that they managed to hustle him to the airport and get him out.'

When Pelé finally returned to his day job, he met with his new coach ('He hugged me,' says Furphy. 'Where I came from you don't hug each other') and his new team-mates, including Keith Eddy. 'One minute I was captain of Sheffield United, the next I was in New York meeting Pelé,' says Eddy, who shared the same birthday with the Brazilian. 'He was a lovely, friendly bloke. Always had time for you, always willing to give you the benefit of his knowledge.'

It's a view reinforced by Lawrie Mifflin of the *New York Daily News*. 'We were at practice one day and a dozen or so journalists were standing round and talking to the players. One of the other journalists mentioned to Pelé that it was my birthday, and he said, "Oh, happy birthday", and "How nice…" and so forth and so on. I thought that was very nice of him. That night when I got home, a dozen red roses arrived at my apartment with a card that said "Happy Birthday, from Pelé." I'm sure that Pelé didn't go to the flower shop himself but the very fact that he asked someone to send flowers to me for my birthday I thought was a sign both of the kind of warm person he was and also of how seriously he took his mission in this country – to help spread the word about soccer. I'm sure that part of what went into his thinking was that I was a journalist for an important newspaper and that this was a good thing for him to do. But it just endeared him to me.'

Ken Furphy would make an inauspicious start to his reign at the Cosmos, losing two of its first three games at Yankee Stadium. His was a style that differed markedly from that of his predecessor, Gordon Bradley. While Bradley was relaxed, almost to the point of indifference, Furphy's approach was more regimented and, to the chagrin of the more inventive South American players in the squad, far less attacking.

Five games into the new season, and with the team failing to spark, Gordon Bradley was dispatched to Italy to spy on one of the top strikers in Serie A, Lazio's Giorgio Chinaglia. While Pelé was still an outstanding talent, especially by the sometimes dubious standards of the NASL, he was now thirty-four and showing signs of his age. What the Cosmos needed was a new goalscorer, a proven forward who could give fresh impetus to the front line and, obviously, widen the appeal of the club in New York.

Giorgio Chinaglia seemed to be the perfect candidate. A brooding Italian, with fast feet and even faster tongue, he was the irrepressible idol of the Lazio *tifosi* and a player who, as an Italian international, was already worshipped by New York's large Italian population, many of whom lived and worked near the Yankee Stadium in the Bronx.

Chinaglia had had an unorthodox upbringing. Born in Carrara, Tuscany, in 1947, he had moved with his family to Wales in 1955 as his father, Mario, looked for work. As a consequence he soon became bilingual, but spoke his English with a Welsh accent. Strong-willed and single-minded, the teenage Chinaglia displayed no talent for or interest in his schoolwork, preferring instead to spend his days playing football. Indeed, it would be Chinaglia's keen eye for goal that would eventually land him a month's trial at nearby Swansea City. The manager of the Third Division club, Walter Robbins, had watched Chinaglia score a hat-trick for Cardiff Schools against their Wrexham counterparts and, impressed by what he saw, offered him apprentice-professional terms. His time at Swansea, however, would come to a premature end when his appalling punctuality record, coupled with his penchant for the timeless teenage temptations of drinking, gambling and girls, had forced the club's hand. While the young Chinaglia could call himself a professional footballer, the harsh reality was that he was anything but.

With no British clubs interested in signing him, Swansea allowed Chinaglia to move to Italian Serie C side Massesse on a free transfer, where his talent would blossom. Within three years, Chinaglia would join Lazio for £140,000. Within nine, he would be a Lazio legend.

Off the field, Chinaglia had acquired a reputation for being brusque and obstreperous; a bar room brawler who wouldn't so much put his oar into an argument as rip the thing the from its lock and slap it across the face of anyone who dared to disagree with him. It was a trait that had got him into trouble not just at Swansea but at international level too. At the 1974 World Cup Final in West Germany, for example, Chinaglia had been substituted by coach Ferruccio Valcareggi during the group game against Haiti and responded with the most offensive of Italian curses, *vafanculo*. Injudicious as it was, Chinaglia's crime could have been excused as a simple act of petulance but for the fact that it had been transmitted live to a global television audience of 300 million people.

Suddenly, Giorgio Chinaglia was one of the most vilified men in Italy. Fans labelled him a traitor, he was ostracized by his team-mates and condemned by the media. Although he would apologize for his outburst, thereby avoiding an early flight home from the tournament, the incident had marked the beginning of the end of Chinaglia's time in Italy.

Increasingly, Chinaglia was looking to the NASL as a way out of Serie A and out of Rome. Loved and hated in equal measure as he was in the Eternal City, even his family were not immune from the side of the town that saw him as the devil incarnate. Once at a Lazio versus Roma game, Chinaglia's American wife, Connie, had been accosted by Roma fans, who had surrounded her and wrapped her in a Roma flag. Fearing for her life she had fled and demanded that the family up sticks and head across the Atlantic.

Certainly, Chinaglia loved the American way of life. In 1972, he had played an exhibition game with Lazio in New York and enjoyed the experience so much that he had set about house-hunting there soon after, with the intention of one day swapping the insanity of his celebrity lifestyle in Rome for a slightly less manic existence in the United States. In April 1975, Chinaglia duly purchased a twenty-room mansion in the well-heeled area of Englewood, New Jersey, right next door to the actress Gloria Swanson.

That summer, Chinaglia was approached by Guiseppe 'Peppe' Pinton, a former Classics teacher now working as a marketing consultant for the Hartford Bicenntennials. Pinton was from the city of Catanzaro in the Calabria area of Italy and knew only too well the box office appeal of the Lazio striker. He called Chinaglia at Englewood and introduced himself, explaining that he wanted him to guest-star in an exhibition game for Hartford against the Polish national side. Chinaglia was taken with the idea, especially the part involving an 'undisclosed fee'. Negotiations would continue, with Pinton even chartering a plane to fly over and personally impress upon the player just how vital he was to the fixture. Finally, Chinaglia agreed. It was done, says Pinton, 'in a shake of a hand'. With a $2 million insurance policy in place to cover Lazio and their prized asset, Chinaglia's appearance more than doubled the expected attendance. As news filtered through of Chinaglia's successful guest appearance in Connecticut, Steve Ross decided to go shopping again.

On the surface, a Chinaglia transfer to Cosmos seemed to make perfect sense, not least because New York was one of the few cities in the world large enough to accommodate the Italian's ego. The fact that the player had long been making very public overtures about playing in the States also made a move all the more likely. In addition to the forward's extraordinary goal-scoring record (he had, for example, scored twent-four goals in helping Lazio to the Italian League Championship title in 1974), the fact that he already enjoyed a high profile in certain, untapped parts of the city gave the Cosmos another lead into securing more support for the club.

Undoubtedly, as Gordon Bradley sat in the stands at the San Paolo stadium in Naples and watched Chinaglia lay waste to the opposition, scoring all the goals in Lazio's 3–0 win, he knew that here was a striker who could transform the Cosmos side. His hat-trick goal typified his eye for goal and his trademark doggedness. Chinaglia was bearing down on goal, trying to shake off his marker. As he tried to break away, the defender reached out and grabbed Chinaglia's shirt, pulling him back. Chinaglia, however, continued on his run even though his shirt had been ripped from his back. As the defender stopped and examined the shreds of cloth in his hands, Chinaglia went on and calmly slipped the ball past the advancing keeper and into the net. To this day, Bradley still regards that piece of brilliance as 'the greatest goal I've ever seen'.

Within two weeks, Giorgio Chinaglia would be a Cosmos player. 'He fell into our lap,' says Clive Toye. Despite some initial opposition from Lazio's president, Umberto Lenzini, and, intriguingly, Pelé, the clubs eventually agreed on a price of $750,000 (although Shep Messing claims the club paid just $240,000 for him). After an emotional final game against Torino, Chinaglia bade farewell to his legion of fans on Lazio's *curva nord* (north terrace) and headed straight to Genoa to

Tricks of the trade – Pelé bamboozles his new team-mates during his first practice with the Cosmos. *(Bettmann/Corbis)*

The main attraction – Pelé emerges in a Cosmos shirt for the very first time at Randall's Island. *(Bettman/Corbis)*

Master and servant – Giorgio Chinaglia is congratulated by Peppe Pinton after another goal for the Cosmos. *(Jim Trecker's private collection)*

Heroes' welcome – The Cosmos returns home triumphant from the 1977 Soccer Bowl in Portland, featuring (left to right) Franz Beckenbauer, Giorgio Chinaglia, Pelé, Werner Roth and Shep Messing. *(Bettman/Corbis)*

Star quality – (left to right) Carlos Alberto, Franz Beckenbauer, Pelé and Giorgio Chinaglia celebrate a goal in a game against a Japanese National All-Star team in Tokyo. *(Bettman/Corbis)*

Legends together – Pelé and new Cosmos signing Johan Cruyff embrace as (left to right) Rafael de la Sierra, Carlos Alberto, Franz Beckenbauer and Ahmet Ertegun look on. *(Bettman/Corbis)*

Shirt shrift – The English striker Dennis Tueart signs for the Cosmos with (left to right) Rafael de la Sierra, coach Eddie Firmani and Ahmet Ertegun in the background. *(Bettman/Corbis)*

Flying high – Jay Emmett, Pelé and friends on board the Warner jet. *(Jay Emmett)*

Dangling a carrot – Mario 'Bugs Bunny' Mariani and his wife Priscilla entertain the Cosmos crowd. *(Mario Mariani)*

Champions elect – Pelé celebrates a goal against the Rochester Lancers in the Conference Championship game in 1977. The Cosmos went on to win 4-1 to earn a place in the Soccer Bowl. *(Bettman/Corbis)*

Give us a 'P' – The Cosmos girls await the arrivial of their hero. *(EMPICS)*

Hail to the chief – Pelé gives President Gerald Ford some much-needed coaching. *(Bettman/Corbis)*

The power and the glory – Henry Kissinger and Pelé embrace in the Cosmos locker room. *(George Tiedemann)*

The Cosmos top brass – (left to right) Ahmet Ertegun, Steve Ross and
Jay Emmett. *(Jerry Liebman Studio)*

Give us a sign – The Cosmos fans take to the field for the first Cosmos
banner contest, 1980. *(Cosmos Official Yearbook 1980)*

WHEREAS, 1991 marks the 20th Anniversary of the Cosmos, the United State's most popular and famous soccer club; and

WHEREAS, the Cosmos will celebrate this momentous occasion with a Reunion Game at Giants Stadium on July 21, 1991 at 7 p.m. against the finest over-35 soccer team in the world, the Brazilain Masters; and

WHEREAS, the Reunion team will feature past Cosmos heroes such as Franz Beckenbauer, Carlos Alberto, Rick Davis, Vladislav Bogicevic, Hubert Birkenmeier, Eskandarian, and Steve Hunt just to name a few; and

WHEREAS, the world's most famous soccer player, Pele, will be honored before the game for his contributions to the sport in the United States and throughout the world; and

WHEREAS, the Cosmos were the class of American soccer in the late seventies and early eighties, thrilling capacity crowds at home and across the globe with unforgettable performances and poignant moments; and

WHEREAS, the Cosmos Reunion game will be an international event with telecasts in North America, South America, Europe and Japan; and

WHEREAS, Giants Stadium in East Rutherford, New Jersey is, was, and always shall be known as 'Cosmos Country';

NOW, THEREFORE, I, JIM FLORIO, Governor of the State of New Jersey, do hereby proclaim

JULY 21, 1991

as

in New Jersey. *COSMOS DAY*

GIVEN, under my hand and the Great Seal of the State of New Jersey, this twenty-seventh day of June in the year of Our Lord one thousand nine hundred and ninety-one and of the Independence of the United States, the two hundred and fifteenth.

GOVERNOR

BY THE GOVERNOR:

JOAN HABERLE, SECRETARY OF STATE

Friends in high places – July 21st 1991 officially becomes 'Cosmos Day' in the State of New Jersey. *(Cosmos Reunion Game Souvenir Programme 1991)* catch a flight to Paris. Initially, he had arranged to fly out of Rome on a scheduled Alitalia flight to the US but word had spread that some distraught members of his 21,000-strong fan club were going to throw themselves in front of the plane, so he headed for Paris, and then took a private plane to his new home.

Chinaglia arrived in the States to the kind of hero's welcome he had grown accustomed to back home. In the Italian neighbourhoods in the Bronx and Brooklyn, there were street parties held in his honour. There was even a 'Giorgio Chinaglia Night' held at a hotel on the banks of the Hudson River where hundreds of guests celebrated his arrival by collecting cash in black bin bags to present to their hero (who had been the highest-paid footballer in the world when he left Lazio, earning £85,000 a year). 'I have to tell you,' says Chinaglia, 'a lot of people wished me well, let's put it this way.'

Keen to portray an image of a player every bit as important as his illustrious Brazilian predecessor, Chinaglia began to assert himself in the Cosmos set-up, telling anyone who cared to listen how well he was regarded within Warner Communications ('I wasn't a normal player,' he still maintains) and how the club had laid on the same kind of star treatment for him as they had for Pelé. Not so, says Clive Toye. 'When we signed Pelé we flew him up in a private jet from Brazil to Hamilton, Bermuda, and we flew across to meet him there. Giorgio? We would have sent him a couple of economy class tickets to get on the plane like any other ordinary player. [But he] went to the trouble of hiring his own private jet and telling the media he was on the private jet.'

Certainly, Chinaglia's wages were nowhere near what Pelé was commanding. The *New York Daily News*, for example, reported that the Italian would be paid just $25,000 for eighteen games in his first season.

While Gordon Bradley and Ken Furphy needed no convincing about the worth of the striker they had signed, others at the club were less than enamoured of the new arrival, most notably Keith Eddy, who emerged from their first practice together singularly unimpressed. 'I didn't know anything about him,' he shrugs. 'And after that first session together I wondered what we'd bought because, to be honest, he didn't do anything.'

Chinaglia would make his Cosmos debut on 17 May against the Los Angeles Aztecs, a team now featuring George Best, the player Clive Toye had tried to sign in 1975. After turning his back on the Cosmos, Best had finally decided to make a clean break from the game in England and escape the 'goldfish bowl' that he felt he was living in.

The game was a mismatch. Moreover, the new strike pairing of Pelé and Chinaglia proved a potent combination, with each player doing his utmost to demonstrate (to the other as much as the management, the media and the fans) that he was the leading light of the Cosmos side. The result was an emphatic 6–0 victory, with Pelé and Chinaglia both scoring twice and Keith Eddy adding the other two, both from the penalty spot. 'This kind of rivalry is something I'd like to have for all the games,' said Pelé after the game.

Eddy, meanwhile, had come to realize just how good a player Chinaglia was. 'From that game I realized that here was a very special goalscorer,' says Eddy. 'He had this knack of shooting without taking any backlift at all. Compare that to me where the whole world knows I'm going to shoot about an hour in advance. If you gave him a ball over his right shoulder it would be in the back of the net before the goalkeeper even knew that he had a shot. He was deadly.'

Yet the demolition of George Best's Aztecs proved to be a false dawn. After a 2–1 win away at Boston (with both goals scored by Chinaglia), the team travelled to Tampa for a game against one of their keenest rivals, the Rowdies. Coached by Eddie Firmani, the Rowdies had won the 1975 Soccer Bowl at their first attempt and were a side capable of beating anyone in the NASL on their day.

While Ross may have been wavering over Furphy's position, he was, nevertheless, as supportive as ever of his pet project, attending every home game without fail, virtually every away fixture and helping out in whichever way he could. On the trip to Tampa, for example, the team were staying in the Marriott Hotel at Tampa Airport when Ross overheard one of the team complaining that the noise from the aircraft had prevented him from getting a sound night's sleep. Minutes later, the entire Cosmos party were ordered to pack their bags before being loaded on to coaches and taken to the altogether more tranquil Americana Hotel in Bal Harbour instead. His intervention did little to placate his players however. The following day, the Cosmos ran out at the Tampa Stadium and straight into what would prove to be its heaviest defeat of the season. Forced to rely on its young American goalkeeper, Kurt Kuykendall, the team slumped to a 5–1 defeat, a reverse inspired by a hat-trick from the former Chelsea striker Derek Smethurst.

After just eight games, Ken Furphy was feeling the heat. Chinaglia, too, had wasted no time in venting his spleen, maintaining that the club had 'an English Third Division mentality', a comment doubtless designed to provoke a manager who had spent years learning his trade in the lower leagues of English football and who had crammed his squad with players from back home in Britain. The state of affairs was compounded by the reaction of the supporters to the team's indifferent form (signs were appearing in the stands at Yankee Stadium asking Furphy to 'Go Home And Take Your

Boys With You') and by mounting restlessness in the
boardroom.

There was also an apparent rift developing between Giorgio
Chinaglia and Pelé. When Chinaglia had left Rome, he had
done so as the undisputed people's champion, a footballing
deity whose place in history was assured. He had arrived in
New York, however, as the second-best player in the Cosmos
squad. Clearly, it was a position that irked the Italian and his
rivalry with Pelé did not go unnoticed by the rest of the
Cosmos staff. '[The rift] wasn't visible but it was there,' says
Ken Furphy.

Clive Toye is less reticent. 'He is the only professional
player I have ever heard in my life who would make
criticism of Pelé,' he recalls. 'The man was so puffed up
with himself that I really think that he thought he was as
good as Pelé, was in the same class. Let's be sensible about
things.'

The issues were numerous. On away trips, for example, the
Italian regarded it as it wholly unjust that Pelé was afforded
a hotel suite when he and the rest of the players had to share
rooms. The fact that Pelé also needed space for his minder
was dismissed as irrelevant. He would complain that Pelé
had more shirts to hand out at the end of each game than he
did and it was a constant source of irritation that Pelé had his
own office at the Rockefeller Center to assist with the co-
ordination of his marketing and promotional activities. To
this day, though, Chinaglia maintains he too had his own
office at Rockefeller Plaza but it's an idea refuted by Clive
Toye. 'The only player who had his own office at the Cosmos
when I was there was Pelé and… I don't recall Giorgio having
an office although I am sure he would have wanted one if Pelé
had one.' Jay Emmett, meanwhile, describes Chinaglia's claims
as 'bullshit'.

Whatever the administrators felt about Chinaglia, it was clear that for the most part, the players liked having him around, irrespective of his unique ability to get under people's skins and the furtive manner in which he ingratiated himself with Ross and his acolytes (the players often joked that Chinaglia had his own elevator to the executive floor at Warner HQ). 'Sure, Giorgio was a character but you need that in a squad,' says Keith Eddy. 'He would always talk about himself in the third person. "Chinaglia thinks this", "Chinaglia thinks that" and I'd always be telling him to say "I think" but he never did – his ego always got in the way.'

Chinaglia possessed the kind of testing personality that was difficult, if not impossible, to ignore. Brash, forthright and opinionated, he quickly established a rapport with Steve Ross, who, as a sports obsessive, may have seen in Chinaglia the kind of larger-than-life superstar he always dreamed of being. Just how quickly this relationship developed was evident within months of the Italian joining the Cosmos. Having taken a significant wage cut when he signed for the club, Chinaglia cornered Clive Toye and asked for an additional $60,000 over the next three years of his contract. When Toye refused, Chinaglia went straight to Ross.

What was clear was that by the summer of 1976 Steve Ross had become so fixated with the Cosmos that his attentions were being diverted away from more pressing problems with the Warner movie studio and its stable of stars. 'Advised' by Giorgio Chinaglia, his curiosity in the machinations of each match became a regular and time-consuming exercise, even though his appreciation of the game itself was still lacking. Ross would spend hours analyzing every game, garnering opinions on everything from team tactics to debatable refereeing decisions. It was typical of his fiercely competitive nature that even days after a defeat he would still be considering ways and means by which he could have the result overturned. Ross, as any of his colleagues would testify, was man hell-bent on winning.

In her biography of Steve Ross, *Master of the Game*, Connie Bruck highlights the lengths to which he would often go just so he emerged victorious, citing a game of canasta he and Rafael de la Sierra once had on the Warner jet. As the pilot prepared to land, Ross ordered him to circle the airport over and over again just so he could have another opportunity to get his own back for a defeat de la Sierra had just handed him.

Take the defeat to Tampa on 6 June 1976. That the Cosmos lost was serious enough, but conceding five goals was almost too much for Steve Ross to bear. On their return, Clive Toye called Ken Furphy and told him that Steve Ross wanted to see him at his office, just as the coach was preparing to leave for a wedding anniversary dinner with his wife. It was 8 p.m. Having driven from his home in Long Island, the coach arrived at Rockefeller Plaza, met Clive Toye and Gordon Bradley in the foyer and took the elevator up to the twenty-ninth floor. 'I said to Clive, "What the hell is he on about?" and Clive just said, "I don't know."'

When they opened the door the trio found not just Steve Ross but the Ertegun brothers, Pelé and Professor Mazzei, the Peruvian player Ramón Mifflin, Giorgio Chinaglia and the man he had now signed as his personal assistant, Peppe Pinton.

What followed was a six-hour post-mortem as to why the team had suffered such a humiliating defeat. Ross produced a video tape of the match, demanding explanations as to why each goal was conceded, whose fault it was and what was going to be done to arrest the team's erratic form. At 1.15 a.m., the cross examination finally ended. 'He [Ross] just said, "Thanks Ken, keep up the good work."'

Furphy was livid. While he had no quarrel with explaining the team's performance to Ross, he felt that the presence of three of his players at the meeting had undermined his position as team coach, especially as Ross had repeatedly asked the opinions of Pelé, Mifflin and Chinaglia as to where the team was going wrong. 'Being brought up in the north-east [of England], I had to say something so I said, "Excuse me, but I will not come to another meeting like this when players are present... I will see you any time, anywhere, any place, but not like this."' Later, Pelé would even concede to his coach that he had not wanted to attend the conference, leaving Furphy in little doubt that it was Chinaglia who had convened the meeting. 'I did learn later on that it was him that had arranged the meetings,' says Furphy. 'Behind the scenes, he was certainly trying to influence things... and from what Clive [Toye] had told me, he was certainly trying to push his way in there and push me out.'

Soon after, Furphy received a telegram from Clive Toye. It read: 'Nil Illegitimus Carborundum', or, roughly translated, 'Don't Let The Bastards Get You Down.'

Despite unwavering support from Toye, Ken Furphy's tenure would end within a month. After a 4–1 defeat at the Chicago Sting, his beleaguered side headed to Washington to play the in-form Diplomats, who had won six of their last seven games. While Furphy had expected the game to be switched to a bigger stadium (a common ploy among smaller teams eager to maximize their gate receipts against the league's biggest draw), the Diplomats' coach, Dennis Violett opted to keep the game at the smaller Woodson Stadium, the local university ground, the idea being that the substandard American football pitch there would help negate the threat posed by Pelé and Chinaglia. Even the offer of $50,000 from Steve Ross to switch the game failed to persuade the

Diplomats. 'The grass must have been five or six inches long and they had just cut it where the lines were meant to be,' recalls Furphy.

It would be Furphy's last game in charge. During a difficult match, the Cosmos goalkeeper, Bob Rigby, collided with the Diplomats' English striker, Paul Cannell, swallowing his tongue in the process. With his first-choice keeper off the field, Furphy was once more reliant on Kurt Kuykendall and, once more, it ended in disaster. With the game poised at 2–2 and heading towards overtime, Kuykendall needlessly charged out of his penalty area to clear the ball but succeeded only in surrendering it to Cannell, who steered it back into the empty net.

Another post-match conference at Steve Ross's office was arranged. This time, however, Ken Furphy refused to attend. The following day, Furphy spoke to Clive Toye and asked to be paid up for the remainder of his contract, leaving Ross and his Cosmos to their own devices. 'I may have had the shortest reign but I was the only Cosmos coach that didn't get the sack,' says Furphy.

With Furphy gone, Ross called on Gordon Bradley to take the reins once more. 'I am looking at the boss of the biggest corporation in America, so I can hardly say no,' recalls Bradley. Almost overnight, the Cosmos reignited and the difference in the atmosphere at practice was palpable. Pelé, who had never really embraced Furphy's quintessentially English philosophy on the game, was smiling again, while the re-signing of the charismatic Shep Messing from the Boston Minutemen had addressed the goalkeeping problem that had cost the club so dearly of late.

The impact of a new coaching style, albeit in the form of a previous coach, was spectacular. Under Gordon Bradley's softly, softly style, the Cosmos claimed six consecutive wins to virtually assure their place in the end of season play-offs. While the side's return to form had allayed any fears Steve Ross may have harboured over the value of some of his expensive new signings, it was apparent that even when his team were performing at a level approaching their best, his infatuation for the team was still warping his judgement. On 14 July, for example, the Cosmos once again took on Tampa, this time at Yankee Stadium. Up on the mezzanine level, Clive Toye watched in horror as his team was run ragged by a Rowdies side, inspired by the bountiful talents of the Englishman Rodney Marsh and the predatory instincts of their Bermudan striker, Clyde Best. At half-time, they were trailing by three goals to one. That said, the Cosmos had had two goals disallowed by the referee, much to the annoyance of Ross.

As Toye sat in his chair, an exasperated Jay Emmett appeared at his side, and demanded that he come down to the locker room immediately. When he arrived downstairs, Toye found Steve Ross pacing up and down with 'fire coming from his nostrils'. Ross, it transpired, had been so incensed by the refereeing decisions that he had instructed his players to remain in the locker room and not go out for the second half. Toye pleaded with Ross not to carry out his protest, arguing that it was against the interests of team and the fans to abandon the game. Eventually, Ross relented, but only on the proviso that Toye made an announcement on the stadium's public address system informing the crowd (and the media) that the Cosmos would be not just be playing the second half under protest but the remainder of the season. An incredulous Toye agreed. 'Sillier things I have not said and I think sillier things I may not have heard, but in the second half Pelé scored a wonderful bicycle kick goal and we won 5–4 so that was the last we heard of that. But that was the kind of pressure that was coming – the pressure to do stupid things like that.'

Under Bradley, the Cosmos lost just two of its last ten games in the regular season, closing the campaign with an emphatic 8–2 win over Miami – Chinaglia scored five – and securing second place in the Eastern Division of the Atlantic Conference, behind Tampa Bay Rowdies. Ever-present in those games was Keith Eddy even though he had been struggling through games with a persistent groin injury that had deteriorated as the season went on. Even a trip to Lenox Hill Hospital on the Upper East Side (and an operation by the same surgeon who had treated the knee of New York Jets football legend Joe Namath in the 1960s) had failed to arrest the problem. 'I remember being sat at home waiting to go into hospital when this huge limo pulled up outside my house,' he recalls. 'I just assumed that the Cosmos had arranged it, but then Giorgio Chinaglia appears at the window. He was good like that.'

By the time the first round of the play-offs arrived, Eddy's injury had proved too much for him and his record of playing in every game that season came to an end. It didn't matter. The Cosmos dispatched Washington 2–0 to advance to the Eastern Division Championship final against Tampa. Once more, though, Keith Eddy's injury made his appearance in the game unlikely and it would take a personal plea from Pelé to convince him to play.

Against medical advice and his better judgement, the Englishman endured five injections of Novocaine and took to the field. It was a bad call. During the game Eddy tore the tendon away from his groin and left the field ten minutes before the final whistle, barely able to walk. The result, a 3–1 defeat, was also disappointing, not least because it quashed Pelé's dream of landing the Soccer Bowl title – for another season at least.

It would be an equally bad year for the president. Even though this was America's two-hundredth birthday, there had been precious little for Gerald Ford to celebrate. As the Bicentennial celebrations continued, the president was battling an economy in dire straits. Food prices were spiralling, electricity rates had risen by 30 per cent, the automotive industry was crumbling and unemployment was hitting levels not seen since the Second World War.

With his hangdog demeanour and a discernible stiffness before the television cameras, Ford had been ridiculed mercilessly by Chevy Chase on NBC's hit show *Saturday Night Live*. That year, he had also seen his twenty-three-year-old son Jack publicly confess to using marijuana and had to listen to his wife Betty praise the landmark US Supreme Court *Roe* v. *Wade* ruling legalizing abortion as a 'great, great decision'. By the end of the year, as if to compound his misery, he would be the target of two unsuccessful assassination attempts.

He would also be clearing his desk at the Oval Office, ousted by his Democrat challenger, the peanut farmer from Georgia, Jimmy Carter. Still, at least he could say he had met Pelé.

CHAPTER 7

GLORY DAYS

For an hour and a half, Steve Ross had been searching Disneyland for his son, Mark. The pair, along with Ross's girlfriend Amanda Burden and her two children, had taken a trip to Mark Ross's favourite place on earth but he had gone missing amid the rollercoasters and the rides, the Mickeys and the Minnies. When Ross eventually found his son, he was stood, wide-eyed, at an arcade game called 'Le Mans', shovelling quarters into it as though he were hypnotized.

Try as he might, though, Ross could not persuade him to leave the machine. When Mark finally tore himself away, Ross noted the name of the game's manufacturer – Atari. 'He said: "Oh my God, my son is locked into this, can't pull him away from it. This is what kids are going to be doing. We have to pursue it,"' explains Mark Ross. 'When we left Disneyland and returned to New York he bought Atari 'cause he thought he could make money.'

Atari was an innovative computer games company based in Sunnyvale, California. Started by a computer engineer by the name of Nolan Bushnell, it had began life in 1972 as Syzygy but changed its name to Atari soon after because it sounded more Japanese and therefore more credible. By 1976 they had already scored several hits with their arcade games, including 'Pong', 'Tank' and 'Breakout'. Crucially, Atari had also invented the groundbreaking Video Computer System (VCS) and the cartridge games to go with it, giving birth to an entirely new market in home entertainment.

Without the capital to exploit their successes, Bushnell began talks not just with Steve Ross and Warner but also with another electronics company who had expressed an interest in buying Atari. When Ross learned of the competition, he pulled out all the stops to persuade Bushnell that Atari's future lay with Warner. As Bushnell and his partner Don Valentine were about to fly to New York to meet Steve Ross, they were met at San Jose airport by one of the Warner jets. When they boarded the plane, they found Clint Eastwood and Sondra Locke already on board. The couple were en route to the location of a new movie and throughout the trip Eastwood proved the perfect host, making drinks and snacks for the awe-struck Atari executives.

When they arrived in New York, Ross first arranged for them to stay in a sumptuous suite at the Waldorf Towers. He then had his limo pick them up and take them to his apartment, where the three of them enjoyed dinner and then watched one of Eastwood's unreleased movies. That night, Bushnell agreed to sell Atari to Ross for just $28 million.

Within weeks, the Atari arcade games would be stacking up in the Ross household, much to Mark Ross's delight. As the resident Atari expert, it was his job to help his father's guests when they tried their luck on the games. 'I remember when [the then president] Jimmy Carter and his staff came to house,' recalls Mark Ross. 'I had to show him how to play the games.'

Ross's pampering of Nolan Bushnell was typical of a man who believed that while money was always there to be made, it was also there to be spent, and if you did the latter part right, why, you could just make yourself a whole lot more in the process. Whether he was buying art or wine or soccer teams, Ross always wanted the very best he could get his hands on. It mattered not that he knew little about these things as he nearly always had the right people around him to make the call.

The Cosmos was a case in point. While the former coach Ken Furphy maintains that Ross 'didn't know anything about football', it was, according to Ross's son Mark, of little relevance. 'So what if he didn't know anything about soccer,' he shrugs. 'What he did was find the people that did and make the team the very best. Within a year, he certainly knew a hell of a lot about soccer.'

But all was not well at Giants Stadium. As Yankees fans drowned their sorrows, their team humbled in four games by the Cincinnati Reds in the World Series, Clive Toye could sense that changes were afoot. If Steve Ross wasn't pestering him for transfer targets or advice on the offside rule, one or both of the Erteguns were making demands of their own. In October, for example, Nesuhi Ertegun approached Toye and told him that he wanted the team to sign Erol Yasin, a Turkish international goalkeeper. It was an odd request, not least because it was October and some six months until the new season, but Ertegun was adamant that the transfer had to happen. For Toye, who had grown accustomed to making virtually all of the key decisions in the development of the Cosmos, it was the first sign that the club was slipping out of his control. Yasin would would arrive at the club soon after.

It was a mild January evening in Rome. The Lazio midfielder and friend of Giorgio Chinaglia, Luciano Re Cecconi, had decided to play a trick on a friend of his who owned a jewellery store. Pulling up his coat collar to hide his identity and wearing a fedora, the twenty-eight-year-old walked into Bruno Tabacchini's shop, with a water pistol sticking through his coat. 'Nobody move,' he shouted. 'This is a robbery!'

Failing to recognize Re Cecconi, Tabacchini reached under his counter for his handgun and proceeded to riddle the player's body with bullets until his assailant was dead. It was only when he removed Re Cecconi's hat that he realized that it was a practical joke that had gone horribly wrong.

The Lazio *tifosi* and Giorgio Chinaglia were still mourning when the Cosmos arrived in Rome soon after as part of its 1977 pre-season European tour. After games against Neuchâtel Xamax and Zurich in Switzerland, the team had taken the overnight train to Rome to play against Chinaglia's former club, Lazio. While Giorgio had bored his team-mates *ad nauseam* about the esteem in which he was still held in Rome, none of them had ever really been persuaded by his claims.

At 5 a.m., the train pulled into the Stazione Termini and to the amazement of Shep Messing there was a vast crowd already waiting for a glimpse of their hero. 'There were like twenty-five-thousand people chanting for Chinaglia and they followed us in the bus, from the bus [to the] train station to the hotel, in the streets, following George. And, I said, "George, you're the man in Rome." You know, I'm not stupid, I can figure out who I've got to hang out with in Rome.'

Keith Eddy was also taken aback, although he puts the welcoming committee at nearer two thousand. 'It was like George was the King of Italy,' he says. 'Women were holding up babies for him to kiss.' Throughout his stay in Rome, Chinaglia was welcomed almost like a messiah. Even after he had scored the first goal in the Cosmos's 2–1 win over Lazio at the Stadio Olimpico, Chinaglia's popularity in the Eternal City showed no sign of abating. After the match, Chinaglia took his team-mates to one of his favourite haunts, Jackie O's nightclub, where he was led straight to his old table, past Sophia Loren, Raquel Welch and Hubert de Givenchy and plied with complimentary Dom Perignon; they even removed his shoes and gave him slippers for the evening. Once he was settled, there was a never-ending stream of well-wishers desperate to meet their hero. 'We were sitting at a table,' recalls Shep Messing, 'and the most beautiful girl in the world came up to us at the table, and went up to Giorgio, like with tears in her eyes, and just took her shirt off. [She said,] "Giorgio will you sign these?" And Giorgio didn't bat an eye. You know, he took his pen and went like this, and Smitty and Werner and myself, we just watched… We were in shock.'

Once back in the USA, the Cosmos was forced to conduct its pre-season training without its main attraction, Pelé. Irritated that no other major signings had arrived at the club, the Brazilian had decided to skip the warm-up games, preferring instead to spend time back in Brazil, attending to his business interests.

The absence of Pelé was not the only headache for the Cosmos in the close season. On the day before a friendly game against Haiti's Victory Club, Rafael de la Sierra received a call from an exasperated Clive Toye. The Haitians, he told him, had jumped immigration and disappeared. What's more, 30,000 tickets had already been sold for the game and it was too late to cancel. Thinking on their feet, de la Sierra and Toye hatched a plan. It was a long shot and one that relied upon the average American fan's wholesale lack of soccer knowledge, but it was their only option. It was time to call in Joe Manfredi.

With the assistance of a few like-minded individuals, Manfredi set about trawling Brooklyn for a team of players who could pass for the Haitian team and on Saturday afternoon, eleven complete strangers took to the field at Giants Stadium to take on the might of the Cosmos. Ninety minutes and nine Cosmos goals later, they walked off the field, as bewildered as they were when they first set foot on it. 'It was really a total farce,' smiles de la Sierra. 'I was in the stand sitting with Steve Ross and he was saying to me, "My goodness, haven't the Cosmos improved quickly?"'

Pelé would eventually report for duty just one week before the new NASL season began, but only after he had shoehorned in a meeting with the US president Jimmy Carter and his son, Chip, at the White House on 28 March.

For the 1977 season, the NASL schedule featured just eighteen teams, the franchises at Boston and Philadelphia having both gone into receivership. Elsewhere, San Diego had relocated to Las Vegas, becoming the Quicksilver; Miami moved to Fort Lauderdale to become the Strikers; San Antonio skipped across the Pacific to Honolulu to become Team Hawaii and the NASL whipping boys, the Hartford Bicentennials, became the Connecticut Bicentennials.

Once again, the NASL had tinkered with the rules laid down by soccer's international governing body, FIFA. Now, any games that ended level after a fifteen-minute period of sudden-death overtime would be decided by a shootout instead of the established penalty shootout. This new innovation saw players in a one-on-one breakaway against the opposition goalkeeper, with the outfield player having just five seconds to run from the 35-yard line and score.

Expectation at the Cosmos, meanwhile, was high, not least because the club had moved into the new Giants Stadium at East Rutherford, New Jersey and decided to drop the 'New York' prefix in their name. Wedged between oil refineries and the spectacular skyline of Manhattan, it was a $75 million, 80,000 all-seater ground and as the new stadium's first tenants

– the New York Giants themselves would not move in until the American football season started in the autumn – the Cosmos now had a base to try and exploit the creeping interest in soccer in the States.

Initially, though, the move to Meadowlands did little to reassure Ross and Emmett that the fortunes of their team were heading in the right direction. Off the field, attendances stalled at an unsatisfactory average of just over 20,000, leaving huge swathes of empty seats at the Giants Stadium. On the field, meanwhile, the team were struggling to mount any semblance of a challenge, despite the notable additions to the squad of the Brazilian defender Rildo and the perky young English winger Steve Hunt.

Hunt's career with Aston Villa in the English First Division had reached an impasse. Having played six first-team games, he had found himself back in the reserves and was unsure whether he still had a future with the club. 'I didn't even know they were playing soccer in America at the time,' says Hunt. 'I got pulled out of training and I was told there was a guy who made an offer to buy me for the New York Cosmos. You know I didn't have a clue what it was all about but having spoken to him and realizing people like Pelé were playing obviously you take notice… it's my opportunity to play with the best guy, the best footballer that's ever walked the planet and that's what persuaded me to go and he didn't disappoint both as a player or as a person. It was a fantastic experience to be part of a team with him in it.'

As soon as he had signed for the club, however, Hunt knew he had made the right decision. 'My first encounter with the Cosmos was pre-season training and it was in Bermuda… I'd been running up hills in Birmingham and this pre-season was Bermuda. [Then] [o]ur first two games on the road [were] Las Vegas and Hawaii. You know, it's not bad when you've been playing at Halifax and Preston North End [and] all of a sudden you're in Hawaii and Las Vegas.'

Pelé, meanwhile, was in the final playing year of his contract and showing only occasional glimpses of the talent that had made him famous, while Giorgio Chinaglia had yet to regain the sparkling form he had shown in 1976. By the end of May, the Cosmos had won just five of its nine games. Fortunately, as twelve of the eighteen teams in the NASL would qualify for the play-offs in 1977, there was still little doubt that the Cosmos would still be involved in the Championship games in August.

Determined to eradicate the apparent stagnation filtering through the club, Steve Ross appointed Rafael de la Sierra to oversee a new marketing drive. Ross had always been impressed with the Cuban architect's guile and imagination, not to mention his easy-going nature, and it mattered not that his field of expertise lay in structures, not soccer. 'You'll do whatever I do,' Ross had told him. Moreover, Ross regarded de la Sierra as the team's lucky charm and insisted that whenever possible he and his entire family attended the games. Once, when the Cosmos played a game in Toronto, Ross even sent the company helicopter to pick up de la Sierra's daughter from her boarding school in Connecticut.

De la Sierra's remit was to prepare a strategy to enhance the match day experience of the supporters and, in doing so, spread the word about the Cosmos and attract new fans to the games. His plan featured a raft of ideas that borrowed heavily from the strategies employed in the more mainstream sports in the States. Some were inspired, others less so. The players would now have their names on their Ralph Lauren-designed shirts ('Everybody copied us,' shrugs Chinaglia); a band would now play during the half-time interval; scores of new cheerleaders would be recruited to be Cosmos Girls;

an in-house touchline artist, Leroy Neiman, would be drafted in, although his work wasn't always popular. Once, he painted Giorgio Chinaglia resplendent in his silk robe in the Cosmos locker room. 'I'd buy it just to have a bonfire,' says Jay Emmett.

They also hired Mario Mariani, a jobbing Manhattan actor, whose role was to dress up as Bugs Bunny (another Warner product) and patrol the pitch perimeter handing out fresh carrots to an all-too receptive crowd. 'Bugs Bunny appealed to me the most [as] he is kind of a charismatic guy, a ladies kinda guy, a conman,' explains Mariani. 'I thought that I could really sort of lend something to the character so I jumped into costume one day... after a while you become the personality of the character.'

Once in character, Mario, or rather Bugs, would lead the Cosmos out on to the Astroturf and as the game progressed he would amuse the fans. 'I had a jumbo carrot that opened,' he recalls. 'It was maybe six feet... made of padded hard vinyl with green material that stuck out the top. There were things inside that I'd pull out like a rubber chicken I'd step on and then throw at the referee. They were silly things, but when Bugs Bunny did it it would be in a very large broad pantomime fashion. It was entertaining and somehow it got across. It worked.'

Cartoon legend or not, not everyone was enamoured of Bugs Bunny. 'I didn't like Bugs Bunny. I hated him,' says Jim Trecker. 'Why the fuck do we have to have Bugs Bunny on the field? I was probably too much of a purist and probably too much of a guy who didn't see the future, [but] this is what cross-marketing is all about and they [Warner] knew it long before a lot of us did.'

The cross-promotion of their products was just a small part of a wider Warner tactic designed to make the Cosmos the hottest ticket in town. Taking a leaf out of the New York Yankees' book, Steve Ross identified marketing as the key to winning over a still largely sceptical public. Increasing the club's promotional budget, he enlisted the help of a clutch of his company's contracted celebrities and studio stars, such as Mick Jagger, Robert Redford and Barbra Streisand, to turn up at games, dragging hordes of paparazzi with them. Inevitably, the following day's press would be awash with news of the Cosmos and even if it wasn't column inch after column inch of glowing testimony to the quality of the football, at least people were still talking about the Cosmos. Conversely, it also helped to keep their most bankable assets – their actors and recording artists – right where he wanted them, in the public eye.

Steve Hunt recalls those post-match brushes with celebrity. 'Some people thought that winning the championship was the highlight of the year. It wasn't, it was meeting Mick Jagger,' he insists. 'I'm a big rock and roll fan and in walks Mick Jagger and asks to see me! All he wanted to talk about is the game and all I wanted to talk about is his music.'

It was a masterstroke. By tapping into Warner's vast well of talent, Cosmos games soon grew into events on a par with glitzy film premieres or awards ceremonies and while the club was still not making any money for their parent company – Ross was predicting that the Cosmos would be in the black by 1978 – they were achieving the kind of cultural visibility that no amount of advertising could buy. 'It was a real perfect storm of corporate power,' says Jim Trecker. 'They left absolutely no stone unturned to make sure that it was a successful product.'

Giorgio Chinaglia agrees. 'We were always in the press. *The New York Times*, the *Daily News*, the *Post*. Always Warner Communications – the owner of the Cosmos, Warner

Communications,' he says. 'I figured it was at least $150,000 a week in advertisements that we saved for the company.'

According to Clive Toye, though, the notion that the fans came to see Robert Redford or Barbra Streisand sat in the mezzanine level and not Pelé performing on the pitch was 'horse manure' and nothing else.

While matters off the field were progressing, it was evident that if the Cosmos was going to maximize its commercial and playing potential it would need another of soccer's superstars on the field if it was to fill the void that Pelé would inevitably leave when he retired at the end of the season. For Clive Toye, that meant enlisting someone now, rather than wait for the end of the campaign and gamble on getting a big name replacement then.

Confident that the upturn in the club's fortunes coupled with the financial muscle of Warner could now persuade any player to join the team, Toye and de la Sierra headed to Munich intent on capturing the next-biggest name in world football – Bayern Munich's Franz Beckenbauer.

Dubbed 'The Kaiser', Beckenbauer was the complete footballer and the finest exponent of the *libero* position in the modern game. Confident and unruffled, he had led West Germany to a World Cup win in 1974 against the Netherlands and had taken his all-conquering Bayern Munich side to three consecutive European Cup triumphs.

Clive Toye had been making tentative approaches to Beckenbauer for nearly two years and viewed him as the logical choice to assume Pelé's mantle. But Beckenbauer was in the prime of his career and was reluctant to leave a country where he was regarded as a living god. And while the arrival of Pelé had certainly stirred an interest in a move to the States, Beckenbauer had decided to delay any transfer until after the 1978 World Cup Finals in Argentina.

But even though he had yet to sign any contract with the Cosmos (or any other club, for that matter), the very fact that he had even entertained the idea of leaving Bayern represented a betrayal so grave that Munich fans were already up in arms about the situation. With his life in Germany becoming insufferable – he said he couldn't even visit restaurants 'without the papers reporting my main course' – Beckenbauer called his manager, Robert Schwan, and instructed him to begin negotiations with the Cosmos. Five days later, the pair arrived in New York and met with Clive Toye and Steve Ross. 'They made a very, very clever step,' recalls Beckenbauer. 'They showed me Warner Communications, the Cosmos office… and they took me in the helicopter and we flew through Manhattan and go to Meadowlands to see the Giants Stadium and I was very impressed. I sat in the helicopter during the flight and said "OK, I come."'

Back in Munich, Beckenbauer informed the Bayern president, Wilhelm Neudecker, of the $2.8 million, four-year contract offer from the Cosmos. Within hours, counter-contracts were pushed in front of him (he would even be offered the job of assistant manager to the national team). But Beckenbauer's mind was made up – he was going to New York.

The news that he was leaving was met with a combination of grief and anger. Some supporters labelled him a traitor, others felt he was entirely justified in seeking a new challenge, especially after the treatment he had been subjected to in the press.

On Tuesday 25 May, Franz Beckenbauer became a Cosmos player. As he stepped off the plane at JFK, a crowd of kids had gathered at the airport. They were holding banners welcoming him to New York. It was a touching gesture and one that Beckenbauer appreciated, even it if had been stage-managed by Clive Toye with the assistance of some local youth teams. Then, when he made it through customs, Beckenbauer and his wife Brigitte were confronted by the kind of frenzied media presence that he was seeking to leave behind in Germany.

While he undoubtedly knew the missionary nature of his signing, Beckenbauer realized that his presence was always going to take second billing to a certain other member of the Cosmos squad. 'Pelé is the most perfect man I know,' he suggested. 'I don't think I'll be able to do for soccer in this country what he did. Pelé has no equal.'

Although the Warner board, the team management and the Cosmos fans were elated with their latest high-profile recruit, not everybody was convinced of the need for another star player. 'I can still remember Giorgio's reaction when we signed Franz Beckenbauer,' laughs Keith Eddy. 'He wasn't happy. You could tell that he saw it as yet more competition for him.'

Beckenbauer's debut would come against the Cosmos's biggest rival, the Tampa Bay Rowdies. Coached by Eddie Firmani, the Rowdies had been a constant thorn in the side of the Cosmos and, yet again, they would emerge victorious. Despite scoring a goal on his debut, Beckenbauer was helpless in trying to keep the likes of Rodney Marsh and Derek Smethurst at bay, and with Shep Messing taken to hospital with a gashed eye, the Cosmos floundered, losing 4–2.

Two days after that defeat, the Cosmos squad were midway through another practice session at Giants Stadium when a helicopter flew over the ground. Moments later, a grey-haired figure emerged through the tunnel. It was Steve Ross. Gathering the players together, Ross let rip, informing them that no longer would he tolerate the mediocrity he was witnessing and that if any player wasn't prepared to give it everything they were free to leave. The message was clear. Shape up or ship out.

❂

As the Cosmos brand expanded, so too did the size of the organization itself. Clive Toye, now president of the club, acceded to Steve Ross's suggestion of hiring a new general manager and met with his chosen candidate, Allie Sherman. As the coach of the New York Giants football team, Sherman had built up a friendship with the Warner chairman in the early 1960s when Ross, a rabid gridiron fan, had employed him to coach intermural games at his Kinney Car Rental division, as well as giving Giants team members jobs through the off-season. Toye, however, wasn't impressed. 'I talked to Allie Sherman and thought, to put it politely, that he was without value and made the mistake of telling Steve Ross that I thought he was over-qualified for the job,' says Toye. 'Talk about saying stupid things? So as he was over-qualified for general manager, Steve gave him a job as an executive of Warner liaising between myself and Steve Ross instead.'

When Sherman arrived he brought with him with a distinctly American view of precisely how the Cosmos experience could be enhanced and it was one of his more novel ideas that made Clive Toye realize that the team that had begun life as a rag-tag assembly of has-beens and wannabes was fast turning into the biggest circus in the world of sport. 'He [Sherman] said, "We are gonna liven up the kick-off, so what we will do is the eleven starting players will go into the starting circle and Pelé will start. He will juggle the ball for two minutes and then Beckenbauer will juggle the ball for two minutes and then all the others will juggle the ball for two minutes each."'

Toye was aghast. 'I said, "Well, there is only one problem with that. I am not going to humiliate them [Pelé and Beckenbauer] by asking them to be like the Harlem bloody Globetrotters juggling the ball and the other nine couldn't juggle the ball for two minutes if you bloody well paid them."'

Allie Sherman's intervention was increasingly typical of a club with no clear demarcation of power and where executives without a background in the sport felt it only right to tell the likes of Clive Toye and Gordon Bradley precisely how a soccer team should be run. As crowds edged up, everybody wanted a say in how the club operated, if only to impress upon Steve Ross just how much they shared his vision for the team. Clive Toye's position as president was becoming increasingly untenable.

Bradley too was finding it hard to do his job. Never the most voluble of coaches, he had sat by as this disparate legion of gifted individuals played their own games, ignoring his demands to adopt his tried and trusted tactic of lumping long balls forward in favour of more adventurous and attractive plays. The squad, drawn from all over the world, from nations as distant as Peru and Turkey was undoubtedly talented but lacked the cohesion that any team needed to succeed. 'The Cosmos had over $8 million worth of world class talent,' says Shep Messing, 'but we were bankrupt when it came to team spirit.'

More worrying, however, was the growing sense of dissatisfaction in sections of the Cosmos squad. On the pitch, the South American players, Brazil's Nelsi Morais and Peru's Ramón Mifflin, had a marked tendency to pass to Pelé and few others, while the two new Yugoslav imports, Jadranko Topic and Vitomir Dimitrijevic, kept themselves to themselves, both on and off the field. But it was the team's three American players – captain Werner Roth, goalkeeper Shep Messing and

defender Bobby Smith – who were fast becoming disil-
lusioned, not merely with the underachievement of the team
and the level of their salaries compared to the rest of the squad,
but the perceived influence within the organization of what
Messing calls 'the British Mafia'.

Keith Eddy dismisses the idea. 'Sure, there was a lot of
British players at the club but there wasn't a British mafia as
far as I could see. You know, the players had different
backgrounds, different cultures and that's bound to reflect
itself in the way you play the game.'

A rift had also developed between Pelé and Giorgio
Chinaglia. Despite being the NASL's top scorer in his first
season, Chinaglia had soon come to realize that as long as
Pelé was still playing for the Cosmos, he could score ten goals
a game on one leg and wearing a blindfold and still not be the
star of the show. With petty jealousies developing and egos
clashing, a team meeting was convened in the locker room.
Forthright as ever, Chinaglia weighed in first, accusing Pelé
of failing to provide him with the service he needed to score
goals. Then, to the astonishment of everyone in the room,
Pelé, a man as mild-mannered as a librarian, countered,
criticizing the Italian for his selfishness in the penalty box.
'You shoot from no fucking angle,' he raged.

Never one to back away from a quarrel, Chinaglia jumped
off his stool. 'I am Chinaglia,' he screamed, as if nobody knew.
'If I shoot from some place it's because Chinaglia can score
from that place.'

On the verge of tears, Pelé turned, shook his head and
walked out of the room. 'I remember Franz Beckenbauer said
that he couldn't imagine that he would ever come to America
and see Pelé cry,' recalls David Hirshey.

Pelé wasn't the only one on the Chinaglia hitlist. Wherever
he went, the Italian seemed capable of making friends and

enemies in equal measure. Awkward and abrasive, he once punched his young team-mate Steve Hunt in a training session after the Englishman had called him 'lazy'. 'Next thing you know he's put a right-hander on my chin,' recalls Hunt. 'So obviously I went back for him, there was a big melee… but I must say from then on we sat down and talked about that and we got on great… There wasn't a problem.'

Chinaglia had also once run into the stands at the Giants ground and waded into a gang of stadium workers who had had the temerity to question his ability. 'Man,' he reflects, 'they were huge those guys.'

As coach, it was Bradley's responsibility to pull these warring factions together and instill in them the same passion that Steve Ross felt for the club. Like Toye, however, Bradley found himself stymied by executive meddling. Now, before each game, Warner vice-president Rafael de la Sierra would appear in the locker room and slip a piece of paper into Bradley's hand. 'On it was the line-up that Bradley was supposed to start, as dictated by the Ertegun brothers, Nesuhi and Ahmet,' insists David Hirshey. 'And one thing was for certain – that line-up always included the Turkish goalkeeper Erol Yasin. I remember once that I wrote a story quoting Shep Messing as saying that he had been benched because he had the wrong passport, and Ahmet called me up and berated me for being anti-Turkish. I defended myself and said I wasn't anti-Turkish. I'm not anti-Turkish, Ahmet, I'm anti-corporate interference.'

The team's form may have been inconsistent but with genuine soccer superstars like Pelé and Beckenbauer in the team, there was still no shortage of people wanting to see them play. For the Father's Day game against Tampa, for example, a new NASL record crowd of 62,394 turned out to see Pelé score a hat-trick in a 3–1 win. 'That Father's Day in

1977 was the day soccer really arrived,' recalls Werner Roth, who nearly missed the game because of the crowd congestion. 'I'll never forget it… My car broke down on the Triborough Bridge and I was standing at the toll plaza trying to get a cab. Suddenly this car pulls up, an Italian family from Long Island, packed with aunts and uncles on their way to the Cosmos game.

'And this fan recognized me! He made everybody squeeze over and he drove as fast as he could over the George Washington Bridge, and about three miles from the stadium there was a traffic jam. We had never seen a traffic jam for a Cosmos game before. He drove up on the shoulder, honking his horn, weaving in and out, loving every minute of it.

'He was yelling: "Out of my way! I've got the captain of the Cosmos and he's going to be late!" He drove right though the parking tollbooth, right through the gates, let me off at the players' door. It was five minutes to game time. Gordon Bradley, our coach, said "Relax," because the game was delayed anyway because the crowd was backed up at the turnstiles. We had never seen anything like it.'

The Tampa match would also be the game where Steve Hunt, the cocksure English winger, decided it was high time he offered some advice to Pelé. After Hunt had bounded tirelessly up and down the wing without pausing for breath or thought, the ever-avuncular Pelé took him to one side and, as the world's greatest player is entitled to do, suggested the twenty-year-old take it easy. Hunt snapped. 'Fuck off!' he roared in full view of the 62,000 fans and the television cameras. 'I felt like decking him,' recalls Shep Messing. 'For me, abusing Pelé is akin to spitting on the flag.'

One relationship that was blossoming, however, was that between Giorgio Chinaglia and the Warner chairman. As the season progressed, the bond between the pair became impossible to ignore. Chinaglia would often turn up at Ross' house on Long Island, along with other players ('I'm sure I'm the only person in the world who's ended up playing two on two soccer in my back yard with myself and Pelé against Giorgio Chinaglia and Franz Beckenbauer,' says Mark Ross.) and now, whenever he scored, the Italian forward would even dodge his team-mates, sprint across the pitch and take a bow before the Warner chairman sat in the main stand.

Soon Chinaglia would also be accompanying Ross to many of his showbiz soirées. 'I remember when we went to Frank Sinatra's birthday party, he [Ross] said, "I'm gonna introduce you to one of your cronies",' recalls Chinaglia. 'I said "Who's that?" Frank Sinatra – it was really unbelievable.'

Werner Roth was there when Chinaglia and Ross first met on a flight to an away fixture. 'The impression that I had, in retrospect, was that they had similar personalities,' he suggests. 'They related right away and I think Giorgio was also the type of person that tends to focus on individuals that have a certain amount of power and befriend them and he has this natural instinct to get into a position of power. So I think it was that natural instinct and his compatibility with Steve that ultimately provided Giorgio with that platform to wield a lot of power in and around the Cosmos.'

Joe Manfredi and Clive Toye, however, view the relationship differently. 'Giorgio was very close to Steve Ross,' says Manfredi, '[and] Steve Ross got to love the guy a lot more... I tell you they were very, very close.'

Toye, meanwhile, was just as baffled by their rapport. 'When you have Jay Emmett... his [Steve Ross's] right-hand man in many respects asking me, "What was it with Steve and Giorgio?" then you have to know that he was as mystified as the rest of us as to why there was this enormously close connection.'

Even Chinaglia's locker marked him out as the man who would be king. While others slung a bottle of shampoo and a towel or two in theirs and Pelé stocked his with merchandise to give away, Chinaglia's locker was like a roped-off VIP area. There was a pristeen chrome hairdryer, a beautician's collection of lotions and potions, a personalized silk robe, handmade slippers, a crystal glass, a bottle of Chivas Regal, some cigarettes, a Dunhill lighter and an ashtray. It was, to all intents and purposes, a home from home for the Italian.

Away from Giants Stadium, the Italian also claimed to have the freedom of the Warner offices and, more importantly, Steve Ross's personal drinks cabinet. During one meeting between Gordon Bradley and Ross, Chinaglia arrived unannounced at Ross's office. 'He opens the door,' recalls Bradley. 'He walks from the door, past me, past Steve Ross's desk, goes to the cabinet, Chivas Regal, didn't ask, "do you mind"… It was 10 o'clock in the morning.'

That Ross and Chinaglia were close is irrefutable but some members of the Cosmos family cast doubt on the extent of their friendship. 'Steve and I worked eight hours a day together, went on vacation together [and] I don't remember Giorgio there,' says Jay Emmett. 'I don't remember him in my office. I don't remember him at Steve's house once.'

Before Clive Toye had signed Pelé, the Cosmos had, in his words, been 'a pissy little club' with just five staff running the entire operation. Now, with a new stadium, increasingly bigger crowds and a profile going through the roof, they had become an unstoppable and almost ungovernable force. 'Suddenly, everybody wanted to pick the fucking team,' he says.

Often, Toye would be summoned to Steve Ross's office on the twenty-ninth floor of the Rockefeller Center to explain the team's performance. Occasionally, he would be loaded into a limo, taken to the heliport and choppered across the river to Ross's house just to debate whether Shep Messing or Erol Yasin should be in goal. The Englishman eventually realized the futility of his position when Nesuhi Ertegun demanded to see a list of the players he and Gordon Bradley were looking to recruit. When Toye handed him eleven names, Ertgeun scanned the list and ticked the four he wanted. Three of them, however, were left-backs. 'I finally wrote a memo and said they either let me run the club the way I wanted, or else. They chose "or else".'

By 13 June, Toye had had enough. Announcing his resignation, Toye admitted that he had irreconcilable differences with the club's owners – he would later tell Shep Messing they were 'bloody bastards' – and that the two parties had vastly differing opinions about the direction the Cosmos should be heading. He did, however, sign a new contract to act as a special consultant to the club on an *ad hoc* basis, suggesting that the decision to move on was perhaps a mutually acceptable outcome. 'For six and a half years I could not have worked for a more supportive person [than Steve Ross],' he says. 'But then all these acolytes who had never been anywhere near the bloody place, hadn't lifted a finger, not a penny coming out of their pockets, not one decision they were making to help the Cosmos, were suddenly all "Steve wants this so Steve will get it… " Soccer is in part cowbell but at the core of it is a serious game between serious teams playing seriously for serious competitions and it was becoming a joke.'

Jay Emmett is in no doubt about the part Toye played in the Cosmos phenomenon. 'Clive Toye ran the Cosmos, Clive

Toye put this together. There were other very valuable people and quite frankly Giorgio [Chinaglia] was not in that group of valuable people,' he insists, adding, 'but I must say Clive was the only one we never overpaid. English guys – you don't have to pay them much, you know.'

It's a view reinforced by David Hirshey. 'Clive Toye was the last vestige of soccer-literate person in the Cosmos family, and when he left soccer became tangential to the whole enterprise,' he says. 'It was no longer about watching a team play the game to the best of its efforts. It was [about] being at a pop culture happening.'

Whatever Jay Emmett and other Warner executives felt, there could be no denying that, to the team at least, Giorgio Chinaglia was of huge importance. But after his dazzling debut season in New York, Chinaglia's form had stuttered, and while he was still one of the most accomplished strikers in the NASL, Gordon Bradley felt that the Italian's unsatisfactory return of eight goals from sixteen games entitled him to explore alternative striking options such as American rookie Gary Etherington or the South African Jomo Sono. With Chinaglia's strike rate decreasing and after two successive games where he had again failed to find the net, Gordon Bradley did the unthinkable – he dropped Giorgio Chinaglia for the game against the LA Aztecs.

While the Italian appeared to take the decision like a professional, Steve Ross, however, was staggered and when he passed by to make his customary pre-match visit to the locker room he was surprised to find his favourite player sat down, dressed in his everyday clothes. When Chinaglia told him of Bradley's decision, a furious Ross pulled rank on the coach and ordered the striker to get changed. To his credit, Chinaglia refused, but the incident would mark the beginning of the end for Gordon Bradley.

As if the difficulties with Chinaglia weren't enough for Bradley to deal with, he also had problems placating Bobby Smith, his able but extremely volatile full-back. In and out of the team through injury and suspension, Smith sat impassively as Bradley ran through the line-up on the locker room blackboard before the kick-off. Again, he had been left out.

Walking up to Bradley, Smith kicked out at the blackboard and then spat at it, screaming, 'That's what I think of your fucking coaching,' adding, 'It's a fucking joke, you English bastard.' He even challenged Bradley to a fight. Bradley, polite as ever, declined. As Smith stormed away, Bradley resumed his team talk, but it was clear that his days as Cosmos coach were numbered. Today, it would be said that Bradley had 'lost the dressing room'. In the world of the Cosmos, though, it was pretty much par for the course.

Behind the scenes, meanwhile, Rafael de la Sierra was doing his utmost to persuade Eddie Firmani to join the Cosmos. Earmarked by Chinaglia as the man to lead the club to the Soccer Bowl, he had been approached first by an associate of Chinaglia called Vito Bavaro – NASL rules prevented players from negotiating – and then by assorted Warner executives. There were also rumours that he had been seen out with Chinaglia the night before he resigned from his job at Tampa. 'We got Firmani in a very mysterious way,' says de la Sierra. 'We had to do it at night. We had to pick him up at the airport and take him to Steve Ross's apartment. We had meetings and we decided that we were going to hire him.'

Keith Eddy, however, remembers a slightly different version of events. 'Giorgio was so into the ownership that after my injury I had a call from him, asking, "Would you like to coach the team?" I said, "One, I don't want to and, two, you are not in a position to ask me." He said, "Oh yes I am, and if you don't do it I will get Firmani." A few days later, Eddie was in the job. Whatever Giorgio wanted, he got.'

After a 3–0 win over San Jose, Gordon Bradley decided to call it a day as the Cosmos coach, but like his friend Clive Toye before him, everyone knew he had been fired. In the games leading up to his 'resignation', Bradley had felt besieged by what he suspected was a Chinaglia-organized campaign to relieve him of his duties, and as it gathered pace he was powerless to halt it. Signs reading 'BRADLEY MUST GO' appeared in the crowd, he was booed whenever he made public appearances and the rumours persisted that he was about to leave. To this day, he knows who was responsible for his departure. 'I don't hate Giorgio – that's a terrible word to use –' says Bradley today, 'but he's a terrible pain in the neck sometimes.'

Clive Toye agrees. 'Apart from being a shithouse,' he says, 'he [Chinaglia] was a fine fellow.'

Chinaglia has no regrets about persuading Steve Ross to seek a new coach for the Cosmos. '[Bradley was a] [n]ice guy, but not an aggressive, winning coach, a coach that players will listen to,' he maintains. 'I think in their [Toye and Bradley's] little minds, they thought that they were really in charge of the club and they were more important than Steve Ross,' he says dismissively. 'I think they made their calculations… [and] I think they made mistakes in their calculations.'

On 7 July, the worst-kept secret in the NASL was confirmed when Eddie Firmani was announced as the new coach of the Cosmos with Gordon Bradley taking up the nebulous position of director of player development. 'Firmani was brought in by Steve Ross,' admits Ahmet Ertegun. 'We didn't have anything to do with that. We were told about it after the fact.'

Meeting the Cosmos press gang for the first time, Firmani was introduced to Phil Mushnik of the *New York Post*. 'The first thing he said [was] "Oh good, my watch has stopped running... can one of you [press] lads run it down the town and have it repaired for me?"'

Franz Beckenbauer, meanwhile, must have wondered what he had let himself in for. In just three weeks, he had seen the president sacked, Pelé cry, a fight in the dressing room and, finally, the coach fired. For the long-serving players, it was just another month at the Cosmos. For a player like Beckenbauer, who prided himself on application, commitment and professionalism, it was as if he'd walked on to the set of a poorly scripted soap opera.

CHAPTER 8

STREETS OF FIRE

On 13 July 1977, New York City was plunged into darkness when a series of lightning bolts between 8.30 p.m. and 9.30 p.m. disabled key high-voltage power lines into the city. When, twelve years earlier, the city had succumbed to a blackout, the population had reacted peacefully. In his memoir *POPism*, Andy Warhol had written that 'it was all like a big party... everybody was dancing around, lighting candles'.

But 1977 was a different era altogether and New York was now a city on the edge. Mayor Abe Beame's administration had overseen New York's worst-ever fiscal crisis and the parlous state of its finances had seen thousands of city workers and public sector staff laid off, wages frozen and essential capital improvements shelved indefinitely. With the city on the verge of bankruptcy, Beame had been left with no other option but to seek assistance from President Ford. His appeal fell on deaf ears, a rejection that gave rise to the famous *Daily News* headline 'Ford To City: Drop Dead'.

The economic malaise had also manifested itself in a wave of urban unrest, spiralling heroin use and an unprecedented rise in crime. That year, there would be 610,077 reported crimes in New York City. In 2004, for example, there were just 226,876, with 570 murders compared to 1,919 back in 1977.

The sense of unease felt by many New Yorkers had been compounded by the 'Son of Sam' murders, a shocking series of handgun strikes targeting young women that began with the shooting of eighteen-year-old Donna Lauria and her nineteen-year-old friend Jody Valenti on the evening of 29 July 1976. The killings had resulted in the biggest manhunt in the New York's history.

Within five minutes of the lights going out, New York's impoverished neighbourhoods, from Harlem to Jamaica in Queens, took to the streets, erupting in an opportunistic spree of looting, arson and violence. A thirty-block stretch of Brooklyn between Bedford-Stuyvesant and Bushwick was almost entirely destroyed and hundreds of stores were ransacked with everything from televisions to rifles being taken. Fifty Pontiacs were hot-wired and driven out of a Bronx dealership, and a taxidermist on Broadway was raided, leaving a trail of eyeballs and claws in the street.

By the time power was restored some twenty-five hours later, the NYPD had arrested 3,776 people, a figure that would undoubtedly have been higher if the police, their number already depleted by Beame's budget cuts, hadn't opted to turn a blind eye to some of the lesser offences being committed or handed down their own kind of impromptu justice. Robert Knightley was an officer of the 83rd Precinct in Bushwick. He was on duty during the blackout and recalls cops cracking rioters' shins or giving looters 'turbans' (hitting them until they had to wrap their head in a bandage). 'You just wanted to stop the riot, so you beat up the looters with axe handles and nightsticks,' said Knightley. 'You beat 'em up and left them in the street. You catch them looting, you just smacked them down and left them.'

Later, when order had been re-established – lawfully or otherwise – Mayor Beame called the events a 'night of terror'.

The hostile reaction to the blackout was typical of a city that was fast becoming a law unto itself, but after the hell of Vietnam and the disillusionment of Watergate, it was as if New Yorkers had finally grown tired of the endless political shenanigans and decided to do things their own way.

New York, for so long held back by bungling bureaucrats and inept administrations, was finding new and exciting ways to express itself. From the eye-catching graffiti adorning the subway cars to the Nueva Latina beat pumping through East Harlem, there was a sea change in the city's youth culture and the Cosmos style merely suited the Babylon that the city was fast becoming.

As most kids lacked the wherewithal to get inside the ropes at Manhattan's pricier clubs, though, they would instead stay out late at street parties in school yards or basketball courts, presided over by renegade DJs like Harlem's Kool Herc and MCs like Coke La Rock, Luvbug Starski and Busy Bee. The influential Herc would turn up, *ad lib*, unscrew the plate in the base of a nearby lamp post and hook an industrial-sized power cable up to his sound system, before pulverizing the blocks with his breakbeats.

In the mainstream clubs, though, disco was king and as the city reeled from one crisis to another, the Cosmos danced the night away at Studio 54, the city's hippest nightclub. Situated just off Broadway at 254 West 54th Street, it was opened on 26 April 1977 by entrepreneurs Steve Rubell and Ian Schrager and fast became the epicentre of pre-AIDS debauchery in Manhattan. Frequented by the likes of Warhol, Grace Jones, Bianca Jagger, Debbie Harry and legions of Hollywood's A-listers, it boasted a door policy so stringent that it made entrance to an Ivy League university seem straightforward. On one occasion, the singer Cher was turned away at the famous velvet ropes by the doorman, Marc Benecke. 'But I'm

Cher!' she blurted. 'I know who are you are!' replied the bouncer.

Inside was a scene of Bacchanalian excess, where coke and quaaludes and glitter and glam were *de rigueur*, and where a wholesale lack of inhibition was a prerequisite for entry. There were drugs on the dancefloor, sex in the toilets and the Cosmos in the basement. 'That club was one of the home bases for the players,' says Werner Roth. 'It was pretty standard Cosmos treatment. The mob would part, the velvet ropes come open and you'd be taken into a banquette or VIP room there, which at Studio 54 were open to us at any time. We got superstar treatment.'

As the darlings of the New York social scene, the Cosmos players were afforded the kind of deferential treatment usually reserved for über-cool socialites and hip new-wavers, not mere soccer players riding their luck. Journalist David Hirshey worked with Shep Messing on his autobiography, *The Education of an American Soccer Player*, and recalls one evening spent with the goalkeeper and his team-mate Werner Roth at the club. 'When we got there, there must have been two hundred or three hundred people massed behind the famous velvet ropes,' he explains. 'But the doorman recognized Messing and Roth and waved them forward. They were immediately whisked into the inner sanctum while I struggled to make my way to the front of the line. When I finally did the doorman looked me up and down and gave me a hard time until I uttered the four magic words: 'I'm with the Cosmos.' The words 'I'm with the Cosmos' were an all-access pass to a world where only first names were needed. Bianca, Mick, Liza, Andy and, of course, Pelé. There he was in the VIP room, flanked by two supermodels, taking it all in.'

For Hirshey, a regular fixture in the Cosmos locker room, the scene that unfolded before him wasn't that far removed from a post-match interview session, 'then I glimpsed the difference, as a naked Lady Godiva rode by on a white horse.'

It's a view endorsed by Messing himself. 'It was such a whirlwind... One day we were nobody and the next day we're playing the Giants Stadium and there are limos picking us up to take us right to Studio 54 after the game. It was a whirlwind of fun and work and pleasure. It was everything rolled into one, and I think the guys enjoyed it.'

But while Messing and Roth threw themselves into the club scene, Steve Hunt, the shy kid from the backstreets of Birmingham, discovered a side of life he had never experienced in the Midlands. 'I remember there was a lady there [at Studio 54] and she must have been eighty or ninety years old,' he says. 'I was told she was a regular and she was constantly on the dance floor... how she managed to do that at the age. She may have been on something, shall we say.'

Certainly, it was evident that in the summer of 1977, the Cosmos was *the* sports team of New York City, not so much for the quality of its play on the pitch, but the quantity of its play off it. While the front page headlines were hogged either by the city's continuing financial predicament or by another Son of Sam attack, the back pages were now reserved for the Cosmos, and newspapers such as the *New York Post* began devoting increasingly more column inches to covering the team, more even than the Giants or the Yankees. 'We transcended everything, every culture, every socio-economic boundary,' maintains Shep Messing. 'We were international, we were European, we were cool, we were Americans from the Bronx. We were everything to everybody.'

Yet the appeal of the Cosmos stretched far beyond the confines of Manhattan's social scene or the city's suburbs. Whenever the team took their talents on the road, attendances would increase significantly, a pattern that would be replicated right across the NASL. For example, the Los Angeles Aztecs, even with George Best in their ranks, would be lucky to draw 8,000 to their home games at the famous Coliseum. When the Cosmos came to town on 2 July 1977 however, over 32,000 turned up to see them defeat the visitors 4–1.

The Cosmos road show was an epic production. As well as the playing and coaching personnel, there was, inevitably, a clutch of Warner executives (and their extended families), the office staff and a glut of hangers-on with only tenuous links to the team. 'Sometimes I'd walk into the locker room and the place would be packed and I'd have no idea who these people were or where they came from,' says Keith Eddy. 'Everyone wanted to be part of the Cosmos experience, wherever we went.'

Lawrie Mifflin of the *New York Daily News* was one of the privileged press gang. 'It was like a travelling circus. Everybody speaking a different language, everybody with a different sort of personal assistant or trainer tagging along to help as a translator and to help with their various needs… it was an enormous entourage wherever you went and it was very entertaining.'

Instead of the fourteen or so he managed when he first joined the Cosmos in 1973, the club's travelling secretary, Steve Marshall, was now faced with organizing the travel arrangements for parties sometimes in excess of seventy people. 'It was like travelling with the Rolling Stones, I mean it was big,' he laughs. 'The way Warner wanted these guys treated was with kid gloves… They wanted to make a statement.'

Jim Trecker concurs. 'The only thing we lacked was roadies and two hundred guys to climb up the ropes and set the lights because the stadiums all came with lights, but we had everything else.'

On the road, the Cosmos was divided into two distinct groups: the experienced players who had played for and travelled with leading clubs before and knew how to handle the fans and the flashbulbs (especially when it came to making themselves anonymous) and the wide-eyed, impressionable players who found themselves feted wherever they went and presented with first-class flights, five-star hotels and an unlimited room service tab. For British players like Keith Eddy, who had been accustomed to the can of bitter culture of the English First Division, travelling with the Cosmos was another world. 'They certainly knew how to look after you,' he says.

Invariably, the Cosmos team bus followed a tacitly agreed seating plan with the bad boys like Messing, Chinaglia, Smith and Roth making a bee-line for the back seat, the Brazilian contingent sat just in front of them banging out rhythms on the window with anything that resembled drumsticks, and the English and Yugoslavs sat ahead of them cursing the South Americans for making such a din. And then there was Pelé, sleeping through everything. After games, the Brazilian would often disappear for a nap, taking two towels and lying on a bench with his feet up inside the locker and his head resting on the bench. Then, he would place one of the towels around his neck and the other to cover his face. Moments later, he would be asleep. 'He could sleep on a washing line,' says Steve Hunt. 'He could sleep on a plane, in the bus, towel over his head, [just] until he got there.'

At the front of the coach, meanwhile, would be the coaching staff and the rubber-necking Warner executives, eager to see just what high jinks the guys were getting up to. And when the Cosmos was in town, high jinks were only ever ninety minutes away. As the team's celebrity snowballed, each long, laborious away trip became like some travelling frat house.

'It was a team that knew how to party, knew where to party and knew with whom to party,' explains Jim Trecker. '[Partying] was certainly on everybody's to-do list in the course of the day. I don't mean just the players or the team but the whole front office, the whole group. No doubt about it, I've never been around a group that can party like that.'

With fame, fortune and a first-class lifestyle came, inevitably, those fans who wanted more than just an autograph or photo opportunity. Pelé, for instance, would have to get his bodyguard, Pedro Garay, to fend off the women who turned up at his hotel room hiding in laundry carts. 'Mr Pelé does not need towels tonight,' Pedro would tell them, 'but I might.'

But, after the champagne bottles had been drained and the management had gone to bed, there was still a selection of the Cosmos squad willing to give their fans a more personal insight into the life of a pro-soccer player. 'There were groupies at the hotel, groupies in the lobby, groupies in the stadium,' adds Trecker. 'Very aggressive groupies, they would stop at nothing.'

In a bid to limit the scope for scandal, a new system was employed so that those players keen to indulge themselves could do so safe in the knowledge that what happened on the road stayed on the road. 'There was kind of an unwritten rule [that] if your room-mate was in and there was a ketchup bottle or maybe a single coffee cup outside your door [then] you looked for another room because that player was busy,' says Steve Marshall.

Wherever they went in 1977, the Cosmos players seemed to be stalked by supporters or lusted after by the ladies. Club captain Werner Roth learned just how far the popularity of the team had spread when he embarked on the team's post-season tour to Europe. 'We were invited to some very interesting parties, one of which was at this beautiful mansion in the middle of Paris... It was a small dinner party where a few players, myself included, were guests and my dinner companion was a young French lady dressed in cellophane… I was very enthusiastic about dinner that evening. She couldn't speak English and I couldn't speak French but that didn't stop us getting to know each other quite well… I actually missed practice the next day.'

Shep Messing, a player who once received a delivery of a gift-wrapped girl while on a trip to Vancouver, summed up the lives of the players during those hedonistic times: 'Women, drinking, dancing, alcohol and back on the field the next day.'

Messing fails to mention drugs in his list. In a town increasingly consumed by drug use, some of the Cosmos players were inevitably tempted, although not Messing. 'A goalmouth collision is all the speed I need,' he once said. Others, however, were less restrained. 'The drug of choice was cocaine, there is no question about that, not widely, but significantly,' says Jim Trecker. 'I wouldn't want to say that drugs were a huge part of the NASL – that would be overstating the case – but there was more than one day when snow storms flew, that's for sure.'

In mid-July, the Cosmos once more entered the transfer market, securing the services of another legend. Flamengo's Carlos Alberto Torres had captained Brazil (and Pelé) to their third World Cup triumph in Mexico in 1970, scoring the memorable final goal in their comprehensive 4–1 demolition of Italy. With Alberto in the side, the Cosmos now boasted the captains of the previous two World Cup winning teams. Unlike the protracted negotiations that brought his compatriot Pelé to the club, the deal to sign Carlos Alberto was relatively straightforward. 'I asked them how much can you pay me, [is]

this amount ok?" he remembers. 'They made the deal and I signed it.'

Suave and stylish, the Brazilian would prove to be the catalyst for change that the Cosmos badly needed as it allowed Beckenbauer to dictate the game from the midfield while Alberto slipped neatly into the back line as sweeper. In some quarters, Alberto's arrival was viewed, in playing terms at least, as just as vital as Pelé's or Beckenbauer's. Ahmet Ertegun, for instance, regarded him as 'a class act', while Rafael de la Sierra considered him to be 'the key of the team' and 'the most significant signing the Cosmos had.'

Unquestionably, the effect that Carlos Alberto had on the team was dramatic. After four defeats in five games, the defender made his debut at home against the Portland Timbers on 17 July, helping the side to a comfortable 2–0 victory. Successive wins followed and even though they lost their final match of the regular season, their place in the twelve-team play-offs was assured.

In the first round, the Cosmos found themselves up against Tampa Bay Rowdies. During the regular season, the teams had played twice with each side winning one game. This time, however, there was added significance to the outcome. Aside from it being a play-off game and the first time Eddie Firmani had played his former team, this time, if the Cosmos lost, it would be the last NASL game Pelé would ever play for the team.

Going into the match, it was the Cosmos who was the in-form team, having won their last six home games and taken second place in the Eastern Division of the Atlantic Conference. With sixty goals, they were also the second-highest scorers in the NASL too. With momentum and, more importantly, a self-belief permeating the team, the King of Soccer rose to the occasion, and on a wet Wednesday night

Pelé scored twice in a 3–0 win. The victory set up a two-game series against Fort Lauderdale Strikers, the team that finished ahead of them in the Eastern Division but, crucially, had already lost twice to the Cosmos in the regular season.

Coached by the Englishman Ron Newman, the side was another largely British-based team, with half of their squad drawn from across the Atlantic. Perhaps their most famous player was the goalkeeper, Gordon Banks. As the man who helped England win the 1966 World Cup, Banks was widely considered to be the finest goalkeeper in the game, but after landing the English Footballer of the Year award in 1972 he had been involved in a collision with a truck and had lost the sight in his right eye. That he could still play was remarkable. That he was still better than many of his contemporaries was nothing short of miraculous.

If a turnout of nearly 58,000 at the Tampa game had impressed, then nobody was quite prepared for what would transpire against Fort Lauderdale. Soccer fever had finally gripped New York City. At the Cosmos ticket office, fans would call repeatedly, claiming that they were long-lost cousins of one or another of the team. Others would offer bribes. Some just begged.

When match day arrived, lines snaked around a wet Giants Stadium, and as the fans waited to get in kick-off was delayed by half an hour because of the congestion. To pass the time, the supporters staged impromptu parties in the parking lot, barbeques were lit and the beer flowed. 'It was obviously alien to what I'd come from [with] football hooliganism in England,' says Steve Hunt. 'Over there everybody was so friendly... [there was a] great atmosphere outside the ground long before we started the game.'

When the game eventually began, a new NASL record crowd of 77,691 people had sandwiched into the stadium, a fact flashed up on the electronic scoreboard. 'We had Pelé, Beckenbauer and a sell-out at Giants,' recalls the NASL commissioner Phil Woosnam. 'I looked at that and thought that finally we were making some headway.'

Fort Lauderdale scored three goals that night which might, ordinarily, have been sufficient to win the game. But they were facing the all-new Cosmos. Moreover, this finally was a team that was taking to the pitch. Prompted by Pelé and brimming with confidence, the Cosmos tore into the Strikers. Giorgio Chinaglia grabbed a hat-trick, Steve Hunt scored a couple and Franz Beckenbauer, Tony Field and Gary Etherington all added a goal apiece to complete an 8–3 drubbing.

In the locker room after the game, it was as if the Cosmos had already won the Soccer Bowl. Rowdy and jubilant, the place was awash with the great and the not so good of New York's glitterati. There, as usual, were Mick Jagger and Robert Redford, with the Erteguns following them round like puppies, stopping only to rub Pelé's feet or massage Beckenbauer's shoulders. 'Ahmet brought everyone who was anyone into that locker room,' explains Werner Roth. 'And every arrogant loud rock 'n' roller turned into a pontificating little boy in front of Pelé.'

Amid the high-fives and back-slapping, David Hirshey was trying to glean some quotes for his match report for the *New York Daily News* but it was proving difficult. With barely room to breathe, Hirshey headed for his friend, Shep Messing. As he neared the keeper, however, he took a shove to the back, prompting a domino effect collapse and sending the grey-haired gentleman in front of him sprawling into Messing's lap. 'I looked down and there, wallpapered on Messing, was Henry Kissinger,' he laughs. 'And Messing, who always had a quick-witted response to the occasion, said, "Hi, Henry, it's nice to meet you. I once attended a lecture of yours at Harvard but I fell asleep.'"

☙

On 16 August 1977, Elvis Presley, the King of Rock 'n' Roll, was found dead at his Memphis home, Graceland. Overweight, bloated and reliant on a bewildering cocktail of painkillers and anti-depressants as he was, his heart had finally succumbed.

While Americans mourned the passing of Presley, the other King in the States was doing his utmost to make his final season as a Cosmos player a successful one. Buoyed by the arrival of his compatriot Carlos Alberto and with a focus that had been conspicuous by its absence in the early part of the season, Pelé was a man on a mission and, for the first time in his Cosmos career, the whole team seemed to be behind him.

As a place in the Soccer Bowl edged ever closer, Steve Ross's obsession with the club reached new heights. Each match day, he and his son Mark would take a chopper to the stadium, land it in the same spot and then follow the same ritual. First, there was a trip to the locker room to meet the players, then the exact same route to their seats, then the same pre-match snack, at which point Mark would leave to walk down to pitch level to take some photographs of the action. 'He was a very superstitious guy about sports,' says Mark Ross.

While many of his executives feigned an interest in the team's progress and viewed their attendance at matches as a politic career move, Ross's enthusiasm was now beginning to get the better of him. Having defeated Fort Lauderdale on a shootout in the second game, the Cosmos players found themselves up against their New York neighbours, the Rochester Lancers. For the game, somebody had even fitted

Steve Ross's seat in the second level of Giants Stadium with a safety harness, partly for those occasions when he got over-excited and risked toppling over the ledge in front of him and partly because Ross knew the kind of press he and the team would get for such a little gesture. 'He'd be going insane. He'd be jumping up and down, screaming at the officials, yelling at us,' recalls Mark Ross. 'They were afraid he was going to fall over the railings and die. He was very involved.'

The two-game series against the Lancers would be a breeze and after two comfortable wins (2–1 and 4–1) the Cosmos found itself in the Soccer Bowl, with just the Seattle Sounders standing between it and a fairytale ending to Pelé's playing career.

Despite being on the verge of the biggest game in the club's short history, it seemed that the team were intent on exploiting their new-found popularity and wringing every last bit of fun out of their fame. Even on the charter flight to Portland for the final, when the team should have been resting, some of them still found time to party. 'I know in the back of that plane on the way out to Portland,' laughs Jim Trecker, 'there were two sex acts performed, right on the plane headed for the championship game... it certainly stunned me.'

It shouldn't have. Throughout his time with the New York Jets – he was their PR man from 1969 through to 1975 – and the Cosmos, Trecker had witnessed the kind of behaviour more commonly seen on rock tours. After all, these were young, fit men with time on their hands and sufficient funds to make the most of it. 'There was a sense of shared adventure,' he explains. 'Every day was an adventure whether it was at the stadium or the bar after work or even at the bar during work... I can't imagine there is any group of people that had a better time than the Cosmos group in the late seventies.'

Once, in Tulsa, Trecker, who would become the NASL's

director of publicity at the end of the season, had climbed the stairs at the team hotel only to catch one of the Cosmos players *in flagrante*. 'There seemed to be nothing wrong whatsoever with a player having a right good time in the stairwell on the stairs,' he laughs. 'Now, think how uncomfortable that must have been... I was one of the people who walked by and merely got nothing more than "Hey, how you going?" It was just out there. It was incredible.'

The day before the game, NASL commissioner Phil Woosnam gathered a select group of guests together at Portland's Hilton Hotel for a banquet in honour of Pelé. Whether the Cosmos won the Soccer Bowl or not, it was the very least he could do to thank him for turning his league around. 'He put his reputation on the line,' Woosnam told the guests. 'Deep down inside this man has a missionary zeal that very few people have. Tonight we would like to pay tribute to Pelé, the man who gave us credibility.'

Today, Phil Woosnam still regards Pelé's presence in the NASL as the single most important development in American soccer. 'He made all the difference to the league,' he says. 'Without him, who knows what would have happened?'

That same evening, Shep Messing called on Pelé in his hotel room and the Brazilian, so often the carefree spirit of the Cosmos side, opened his heart to the goalkeeper, confessing that the thought of working away from the football field scared him. 'Now I must remember to go the office,' he shrugged. 'I don't know how I will like this, to sign papers, to speak on the telephone, because twenty-two years of my life is soccer.'

Regardless of the outcome, the game against Seattle would be Pelé's last competitive game. Everybody in the Cosmos seemed determined to win the championship for their colleague. That said, some players were driven by motives other than comradeship. Bobby Smith, for instance, was intent on 'kicking the piss' out of Seattle's largely English side because he felt that too many American players were missing out because of those 'Limey cocksuckers'.

He had a point. Coached by the Scot Jimmy Gabriel, the Sounders were a tough, stubborn side with a heavy British influence. In a twenty-seven-man roster, there were sixteen players from Britain, including Harry Redknapp, Mel Machin and Tommy Ord, and while the Cosmos relied on South American finesse, the Seattle were known for their uncompromising approach to the game.

When the game got under way, it was Seattle that looked the more likely winners as they pegged the Cosmos back and bombarded Werner Roth and his defence with wave after wave of attacks. Nineteen minutes in, however, the Cosmos took the lead through a clever piece of opportunism by Steve Hunt. As the Seattle keeper, Tony Chursky, rolled the ball out to the edge of the area, Hunt crept up behind him, stole the ball off his toes and, despite the goalkeeper's despairing lunge, poked it into the unguarded net. As Chursky cursed, Hunt, with his surfer's hairdo and adolescent's moustache, was picked up and held aloft by Pelé, the pair grinning like madmen. Their lead was short-lived. Minutes later, the Sounders' English striker Tommy Ord deservedly levelled the score with a crisp drive into the corner of the net.

With the rain falling and the game just fourteen minutes from overtime, Steve Hunt made another of his trademark sprints down the wing. Reaching the byline, he pulled a devilish cross back into the penalty area and there, on the edge of the six-yard box was the predator himself, Giorgio Chinaglia, who glanced his header past Chursky and into the net. As Hunt and Chinaglia embraced, their spat earlier in the season forgotten, Pelé ran to collect the ball, and proceeded to boot it repeatedly into the back of the net. After a professional career spanning twenty years, over 1,000 career goals and three World Cup winner's medals, Pelé was clearly still as enthusiastic as ever about the game.

Chinaglia's goal would be enough for the Cosmos to take the title and provide Pelé with the perfect conclusion to his glorious career. As the two teams shook hands, the field was engulfed by fans and photographers, police and press men. Amid the pandemonium, Pelé sought out Seattle's young American defender and the Rookie of the Year, Jim McAllister, and gave him his shirt. As ever, it was a sharp and hugely symbolic piece of PR from the Brazilian and a move seen by many as the old guard (the old *foreign* guard) handing the baton on to a new generation of American players.

After the game and with the NASL Championship trophy finally in their possession, even the most hardened cynic had to concede that, for once, the Cosmos had risen above the hullabaloo that followed it everywhere. For once, they were bigger than the bullshit. 'We stopped dancing around the ball and just went out there and kicked ass,' said Werner Roth.

Down in the locker room, the party had already begun with the conversation drowned out by the sound of popping flashguns and popping champagne corks. On Eddie Firmani's tactics blackboard, somebody had written 'COSMOS; 1977 CHAMPS'. Moments later, as the team launched into another chant of 'PELÉ! PELÉ! PELÉ!', the words would be gone, washed off by a shower of champagne. 'I've never felt emotion like this in my life,' Shep Messing told the press. 'Right now, I don't even care that I won a championship, or that the Cosmos won a championship, but just that Pelé did. When I came in the locker room I was hugging him and crying with him for about five minutes. I kept saying, 'For you, for you,' and he kept saying, 'I love you, thank you.' It's such an honor to be part of giving him this championship.'

Pelé, meanwhile, was beside himself. 'After three World Cups, now this,' he beamed. 'I can stop now, as a champion. I can die now. I have everything I have wanted from my life in soccer.'

When a euphoric Steve Ross entered the locker room, he was greeted with all the reverence that the head of the world's biggest entertainment corporation warranted. First, he was drenched in yet more champagne, then he was lifted up by a gang of players and thrown, fully clothed, into the showers.

The soaking over, Ross changed into a pair of Cosmos sweatpants with a number nine on the side. They belonged to Giorgio Chinaglia.

CHAPTER 9

SPIRIT IN THE NIGHT

In September, the newly crowned NASL champions left for a two-week tour of the Far East, with the club set to become the first professional soccer team to play in the People's Republic of China. Arranged by Rafael de la Sierra and Clive Toye (prior to his departure), it was conceived as a farewell tour for Pelé but had quickly turned into a full-scale Warner vacation, with virtually the entire board of the corporation (and their wives) clamouring to get a seat on the plane.

The press also found it difficult. Lawrie Mifflin of the *New York Daily News* even pretended to be the sister of her namesake Ramón Mifflin (no relation) to get a place on the trip but she only got as far as Tokyo. Indeed, with spaces at a premium – de la Sierra had only twenty-three visas – the only way that Steve Ross, Jay Emmett and their partners could make the trip was if they travelled as the team's official photographers. So, loaded down with the hastily purchased camera equipment, Ross and Emmett joined the team on their excursion to the Orient.

After two sell-out games in Tokyo (a 4–2 win over Furakawa followed by a 3–1 victory over the Japanese All-Star team), the Cosmos finally extricated themselves from the world's most persistent autograph hunters and headed to China, not really knowing what to expect.

On their arrival in Peking, the Cosmos party was met first by 30,000 people and then by a full diplomatic reception. This time it was de la Sierra and the Ertegun brothers that did the meeting and greeting, Ross and Emmett having thrown themselves into their new roles as photographers, shooting everything that moved.

Despite the cultural and commercial constraints of the Communist regime, it seemed as though everybody was fully aware of who Pelé was. 'You wouldn't think they [the Chinese] read a newspaper, or saw a television set,' recalls Jay Emmett, 'but they knew Pelé, they might have not known anything else but they knew Pelé.'

Although largely unknown, the Chinese team were strong, organized and eager to prove themselves against the assembled stars of the Cosmos. In the first game in Peking on 17 September, they defended resolutely and held Pelé *et al.* to a 1–1 draw. Three days later (and the day after Steve Ross's fiftieth birthday bash), the Chinese humbled the Western millionaires, beating them 2–1 in Shanghai in front of 50,000 impeccably behaved and strangely silent fans who were told over the public address system when they could applaud.

Results aside, it had been a successful trip. Shep Messing called it 'an incredible education'. From a public relations perspective, the name of the Cosmos had been taken to places that Warner could never really have envisaged when they bought the club, and from the Great Wall of China to the grave of Mao Tse-Tung it had given the players a rare insight into an alternative way of life. 'It was one of the most unique places that I had ever been in terms of its culture, in terms of its architecture, in terms of its geography,' says Werner Roth. 'Just learning about their political system and seeing communism working from a close standpoint was pretty unique and pretty interesting.'

But while most of the players took the opportunity to experience what China had to offer, others, namely Giorgio Chinaglia, were less taken with the country – especially the cuisine. '[Giorgio] was very reluctant about the food,' laughs Rafael de la Sierra, who remembers eating sea slug soup and jellyfish on the trip. 'He even brought cans of cannelloni and ravioli with him.'

As the Cosmos passed on dessert, a new soccer league was being born back in the States. The Major Indoor Soccer League (MISL) was the brainchild of a Philadelphia lawyer, Earl Foreman, and was a six-a-side version of the game featuring six franchises: Cincinnati Kids, Cleveland Force, Houston Summit, New York Arrows, Philadelphia Fever and Pittsburgh Spirit.

It was an instant hit with those soccer fans who wanted breakneck action and more goals than the NASL. Soon, the MISL's most successful franchise, the Philadelphia Fever, would be posting attendances well over 8,000, significantly more than a number of NASL clubs could muster. 'This is the game Americans want,' insisted Foreman.

On 1 October 1977, Pelé's part-missionary, part-mercenary role in the NASL came to an end. His last match, an exhibition game between the Cosmos and his former club, Santos, had been sold out six weeks beforehand and would be covered by 650 journalists and broadcast in some thirty-eight nations. As the hottest ticket in town, the Cosmos had unintentionally oversold the game and actually took bookings for close to 100,000 tickets, despite Giants Stadium's capacity of just 77,000. With disappointed fans threatening everything from litigation to murder, the Cosmos narrowly averted an investigation by the New York Attorney General by issuing full refunds and complimentary tickets for future games to those supporters who had bought their tickets in good faith.

In the locker room prior to kick-off, Werner Roth gathered his team together and presented the Brazilian with a plaque, with all the squad's names on it and the inscription: 'To Pelé, the soccer player, and Edson do Nascimento, the man. Thank you'. In return, Pelé walked around the room, giving each player a small silver medal engraved with their name and Pelé's likeness, prompting Shep Messing, never the most reserved member of the Cosmos team, to start blubbering like a baby.

Then, came a visit from the only other sportsman on the planet to rival Pelé's renown – Muhammad Ali. Two days earlier, the world heavyweight champion had retained his title by beating Ernie Shavers at Madison Square Garden. Now he wanted to pay his respects to another sports legend. As the pair embraced in the locker room, a reporter asked Ali what he thought of Pelé. 'I don't know if he's a good player,' shrugged the boxer, 'but I'm definitely prettier than him.'

Later, however, Ali would concede Pelé his place alongside him in sporting history. 'Now,' he said, 'there are two of the greatest.'

Bobby Smith recalls the encounter. 'It was an awesome moment because... they'd never met each other, [but] they both wanted to meet each other,' he recalls. 'It was beautiful, you know.'

Muhammad Ali wasn't the only world figure heaping praise on the Brazilian. Even the president, Jimmy Carter, chipped in. 'Pelé,' he said, 'has elevated the game of soccer to heights never before attained in America and only Pelé, with his status, incomparable talent and beloved compassion, could have accomplished such a mission.'

As Pelé took to the pitch, Giants Stadium reverberated to the familiar chant of 'PELÉ, PELÉ, PELÉ' and as the main attraction circled the field, waving and, as ever, smiling, the New Jersey night was set ablaze with the glare of thousands of flash bulbs.

Finally, he addressed his crowd. 'I want to thank you all, every single one of you. I want to take this opportunity to ask you to pay attention to the young of the world, the children, the kids. We need them too much,' he urged. 'Love is more important than what we can take in life... Please say with me, three times. LOVE... LOVE... LOVE.'

Such was Pelé's hold over the fans at Giants Stadium that they gave their hero the send-off he wanted (and deserved) and joined in with gusto. 'I knew that if soccer gave me nothing else,' says Shep Messing, 'I had been a part of this moment, and maybe that would be enough.'

Pelé's final game at Giants Stadium would actually be half a game. Having played the first period for the Cosmos (and scored a thirty-yard thunderbolt), he switched sides at the interval to pull on the white shirt of the only other club side he had ever played for. As the game progressed, the heavens opened over New Jersey, drenching each and every one of the 75,000 congregation. The following day a Brazilian newspaper ran the headline: 'Even the Sky Was Crying.'

By the end of October, Gordon Bradley would also be gone. After all his efforts in guiding the club from the gutter to somewhere approaching the stars, he had found his new position in player development a world away from the day-to-day involvement of pulling on a tracksuit and coaching the team. When the Washington Diplomats offered the Englishman a three-year contract worth $175,000 a year to coach their side – more than he ever received at the Cosmos – Bradley handed in his resignation and headed to the capital.

As one face left New York, a new one arrived. Bronx-born Ed Koch was elected as the new Mayor, charged with restoring financial propriety to a town permanently in the red. 'We hadn't had a balanced budget for fifteen years,' he explains. 'The banks were no longer going to lend us money, city services had deteriorated and businesses and residents were moving out.'

In just three years, however, Koch would manage to turn things round for New York. By slashing budgets still further, boosting revenues wherever he could and making sure every dollar was accounted for, the Big Apple with Ed Koch at the helm pulled itself together. 'I did it because we had no option,' he says today. 'If you have no option, you'll do it.'

Despite the absence of Pelé, confidence in the NASL as a viable proposition was high. After the record attendances of the last season, the league roster for the 1978 season expanded again, taking the total number of teams to Phil Woosnam's desired target of twenty-four. That said, there was still concern for the financial viability of many clubs. While the Cosmos could relax, safe in the deep pockets of Warner Communications, four other franchises had fallen by the wayside, most notably the St Louis Stars, one of the NASL's founding members. Moreover, only one of the eighteen clubs that started the 1977 season – the Minnesota Kicks – actually made any money. And while the game in general was becoming increasingly popular in the suburbs (especially in California, where there were now five franchises) and among women and girls, there was still no network television deal in place, and what coverage there was came via smaller independent TV companies.

Not that anybody at the Cosmos really cared. With Steve Ross's money to burn, Eddie Firmani had set about finding some additional replacements for their dear, departed Pelé.

In came Vladislav 'Bogie' Bogicevic, a talented midfielder from Yugoslavian champions Red Star Belgrade, and Lazio's improbably named defender Giuseppe Wilson, who joined his old friend Giorgio Chinaglia once more.

Another Brit also arrived in the shape of Manchester City's English international Dennis Tueart, who rejected moves to Manchester United, Nottingham Forest and the Belgian side Anderlecht in favour of a reported £1,000-per-week deal at the Cosmos. Tueart was the type of player that New Yorkers appreciated. Once, when the tennis player Jimmy Connors was asked about the differences between the four Grand Slam tournaments, he said: 'The New York crowd loves to see you spill your guts. In Paris, they love good tennis. But really, they get behind you and want you to spill your guts like here. In Wimbledon, if you spill your guts all over the court, you get to clean it up yourself.'

In Tueart the Cosmos had bought a player with vast reservoirs of what the American military are wont to call 'intestinal fortitude'. Swift and agile, he was the kind of tireless runner that Giorgio Chinaglia could or would never be and would chase every lost cause as if his life, and not just his generous salary and luxury apartment, depended on it. 'I didn't realize at the time, but when I finally turned up to sign in the January of 1978 I realized that for the new season I would be replacing Pelé,' he recalls. 'When you follow the all-time world leader, an icon as far as football is concerned, it can be a bit daunting but I was just looking upon it as a fantastic opportunity to experience a new aspect of my football career.'

Worryingly for Shep Messing, Firmani had also been window-shopping for a new goalkeeper, despite the arrival of Erol Yasin the previous season. Press reports had linked several other keepers to the club, including the experienced Polish international Jan 'The Clown' Tomaszewski.

Messing's worst fears were confirmed when, on Wednesday, 22 February, he awoke to a scream from his wife, Arden. Flicking through that morning's *New York Times*, she had been shocked to find a story that the Cosmos had signed a new goalkeeper, the Canadian international Jack Brand. It was time for Messing to move on again.

Five days later, Messing signed a contract with the Oakland Stompers, a new franchise playing at Alameda County Stadium in Oakland, California. In his autobiography, *The Education of an American Soccer Player*, Messing revealed that the night before he put pen to paper on his new deal with Oakland, he composed a statement to read to the media and the Cosmos fans. Sadly, he never got to read it:

> I love being an American, and I love playing soccer. Until recently, the two didn't fit together very well. But things have changed. Playing with the Cosmos, I had the privilege to see new standards set in the NASL. Playing with the Cosmos, I had the privilege to know Pelé and Beckenbauer and Chinaglia and Alberto. All of it has been a great education and a great experience. Something new, special and still fragile is being born, and though some people may inadvertently stunt its growth, I'm confident American soccer will grow and flourish.

The new-look Cosmos began the new season as it finished the previous one, humiliating Fort Lauderdale yet again. This time, thanks to hat-tricks from Giorgio Chinaglia and Steve Hunt, it scored seven without reply. You had to feel for Gordon Banks. In the last three meetings between the teams, he had shipped eighteen goals.

While its form was dazzling, what was noticeable about the Pelé-less Cosmos was that it was now playing with a kind of freedom that had only really surfaced in the last few months of the Brazilian's time with the team. It was as if the weight of responsibility that came with pleasing Pelé had gone. Now, the members of the team could play their natural games, even if that just meant funnelling the ball to Chinaglia and watching him stick it in the back of the net. 'I was very demanding,' says Chinaglia. 'You had to give me the ball... I would be really pissed off if you didn't give me the ball. If there was a game [and] I didn't score a goal I would really be upset.'

Some things, however, never changed and even without his partner in crime, Shep Messing, to goad him, Bobby Smith was still getting into trouble. During the Cosmos's 1–0 win at Los Angeles, Smith responded to taunts from the home fans by issuing what *The Washington Post* later described as an 'obscene gesture'. Ordinarily, his misdemeanour would have gone unnoticed, but on this occasion the game was shown on cable TV in New York and his offending finger had not been edited out of the programme. It was seen by hundreds of thousands of viewers, one of whom just happened to be NASL commissioner Phil Woosnam.

Guilty as charged, Smith was first fined by Cosmos and then suspended by the league for ten days for 'conduct unbecoming an NASL player. Eddie Firmani wasn't happy, blaming the television company for Smith's ban. 'This could have been avoided if the television people did their job,' he suggested. 'After all, who do they work for? They should be loyal to the Cosmos.'

By the end of April, the Cosmos had won all of its five games, scoring seventeen goals and conceding just three. It had been an extraordinary signal of intent and if anyone had thought the absence of Pelé from the Cosmos line-up would open the door for the other teams in the NASL, they were off the mark. If anything, the Cosmos was now a much tougher proposition.

After a 5–2 trouncing on their its patch, the new Tampa coach Gordon Jago put the transformation down to the talents of Bogicevic, suggesting that the Yugoslav's left foot could 'unbutton your shirt'. As the season went on and his influence really began to tell, however, it became clear that not only could Bogie's left foot remove your shirt, but it could probably put your pyjamas on and tuck you into bed as well.

Bogicevic was, indeed, a revelation. He was imaginative, inventive and spontaneous, and capable of transforming a game in a single moment of brilliance. Ahmet Ertegun had been alerted to Bogicevic's availablility, not merely because his time at Red Star Belgrade was coming to an end, but because 'he was not asking for too much money'. In his time at the club, Clive Toye maintains that after Pelé and Beckenbauer not a single player was earning more than $60,000 and the Cosmos's annual payroll was just $800,000. 'From 1978, it was a different story, of course,' he says.

That said, there was still a decent living to be had from playing pro-soccer. For players like the Canadian defender Bob Iarusci, signed by the club after winning the Soccer Bowl with Toronto in 1976, the opportunity to play for the NASL's flagship was too good to pass up. 'They offered me $35,000 a year, an apartment and a car,' he recalls. 'And, of course, I couldn't say no to the opportunity to play with Pelé, Beckenbauer and Chinaglia.'

An ever-present in his debut season, Iarusci had been a candidate for the Rookie of the Year but Toronto was in debt to the Cosmos and something had to give. 'Because Pelé would go to each city and the games would sell out, the Cosmos had an agreement with the league that it would get a percentage of the gate,' he explains. 'The Toronto team owed the Cosmos something like $110,000 so the Cosmos said we'll forfeit that and take me.'

But while Iarusci was more than satisfied with his deal, Bogicevic was less than happy with his benefits package. 'He didn't like the automobile which we provided him with, he wasn't happy with the apartment, he wasn't happy with the television set,' laughs Ertegun.

Sensing a problem player in the making, Ertegun discussed the matter with Steve Ross. 'I said, "You know, Bogicevic is a fabulous player and he's doing the team a tremendous service just by being there, but he's going to be a lot of trouble because he's not happy with anything and anything we do is not enough."'

With a reassuring arm around his colleague, Ross instructed Ertegun that he would deal with the situation personally. That evening, as a 70,000-plus crowd turned up at Giants Stadium for 'Franz Beckenbauer Day' (in commemoration of the German's first year at the club) and the game against Seattle, Ross made his way down to the locker room in search of Bogicevic, who had not only scored but almost single-handedly engineered a 5–1 victory. Ahmet Ertegun takes up the story. 'Steve Ross goes in and says, "Bogie, what can I tell you. You were just sensational today. It was like poetry in motion. You are such a great player and it's so wonderful to have you on the team and, you know, you are such a terrific sportsman", and whatever. So Bogicevic is listening to what he was saying, without saying a word. And then he turns to me and he says, "Look, I played six years for Red Star and I scored more goals than anybody, even though I play midfield. I played five times in the European Cup and scored more goals than any Yugoslav player. I beat Liverpool by myself. I beat the Liverpool team alone, by myself. I beat Inter Milan by myself. I beat Benfica by myself. And now I come to New York and because Mr Chairman, he like the way I play, I suddenly become a good player."'

With Bogie's outburst at an end, Ross turned to Ertegun. 'I see what you mean,' he said.

It would be 17 May before the Cosmos suffered its first loss of the season, a 2–1 shootout defeat at the Portland Timbers. Yet, the club was in rude health and Steve Ross's predictions that the club would soon be making money no longer seemed so fanciful. With an average crowd at Giants Stadium of over 45,000 – they even drew 71,219 for the game against Seattle – it seemed as though the public, in New York City at least, had been won over.

Certainly, the atmosphere at the matches was as good, if not better, than ever, thanks not to some jobbing actor dressed as a giant rabbit, but to some undeniably attractive football and the all-singing, all-dancing Cosmos Girls. Debra Benitez and Holly Kelley were two of the thirty-six-strong troupe charged with entraining the crowd. 'We were Cosmos Girls,' insists Benitez. 'We weren't Cosmos cheerleaders.'

Like the players on the pitch, the cheerleading team had also undergone a transformation. As the name and fame of the Cosmos spread, they had been inundated with requests from wannabe Cosmos Girls. A rigorous audition programme was implemented, rehearsals took place three or four times a week and the girls now had to perform their kick-line choreography before, during and after the game, instead of just rustling their pom-poms for ten minutes prior to kick-off.

Stealing their kaleidoscope style from the famous Rockettes, and backed by music prepared by Debra's brother, the music producer John 'Jelly Bean' Benitez, the group took to the pitch in their pristine white uniforms to entertain the crowd at Giants Stadium:

'C.O.S.M.O.S. – COSMOS ARE THE VERY BEST'
(cue enthusiastic pom-pom rustling).

In time, the sterling work of the Cosmos Girls would gain wider recognition, and they would be selected for duty against international teams too. It would be their first experience of foreign football fans. 'The intensity was so great, the crowds were so loud, [and] there was always fights breaking out,' explains Holly Kelley, who now runs her own hairdressing salon. 'It was very, very intense… we would just sit there and we'd always be looking and [saying] "What's going on now?" because they were so passionate about their soccer [they would always say] "Move your pom-poms out of the way, we can't see the players!"'

Two players who were worth the entrance fee alone were Giorgio Chinaglia and Vladislav Bogicevic. Over the course of the season, the two had forged a prolific understanding and while the Italian took the plaudits for finding the net, it was Bogie that topped the assists statistics, unlocking defences with vision and an instinctive ability to deliver the killer pass, usually to the feet of Chinaglia. 'They had this almost mental telepathy,' explains Bob Iarusci. 'Giorgio would time his diagonal runs and time and time again Bogie would just slot the ball right into his path.'

Predictably, Bogicevic had his own take on their relationship. 'If Giorgio is happy, I am happy,' he said. 'If Giorgio is unhappy, I am unhappy. If Giorgio is very unhappy, I am gone.'

While the comment was meant by way of an explanation of their budding playing rapport, it also spoke volumes of the esteem, or even fear, in which Chinaglia was held at the club. When Pelé was around, there had always existed some checks on just how much Chinaglia could get away with but with Pelé gone Chinaglia, now an American citizen, had assumed the reins. Indeed, the Italian would often speak of the 'vision' he had for the Cosmos, a vision that did not include Pelé. In the Italian's mind he was the only person capable of making that dream a reality and if that meant offending a few people in the process then so be it. 'The great thing about Giorgio is he had no filters so he said what was ever on his mind no matter how politically incorrect,' says David Hirshey. 'I remember when he first came here and I interviewed him he said that Pelé was unfit and that he would have to carry him until he got in shape. So the Latin fans hated him for that. Then he said, later, that the Cosmos should buy more American players rather than Franz Beckenbauer, and the German fans hated him for that.'

Since leaving Italy, Chinaglia had immersed himself in his pursuit of the American dream. A wheeler-dealer without compare, he had quickly assembled his own business empire away from the internecine manoeuvring at the Cosmos. With Peppe Pinton doing his bidding, he had made a name for himself in the property development business and owned ten apartments across Manhattan. He had established his own Soccer Academy summer camp for local kids and, like other high-profile players, he enjoyed a clutch of money-spinning endorsements, from companies including Pony, Spalding and Chevrolet. He also had a Ferrari and a 1969 Corvette but chose to drive his sponsored Toyota.

Without doubt, Chinaglia had found a spiritual home in the land of opportunity. 'This is, I think, the only country in the world that permits you to choose what you want to do with your life,' he says. 'And it's the only country in the world where you can go broke three or four times and you can still make it again. The only country in the world where you decide your future – you want to work, you work; you don't want to work, you don't work, you starve.'

Peppe Pinton wasn't the only one trying to please Giorgio Chinaglia. The team's car supplier, Joe Manfredi, was also charged with helping the Italian. During a game against

Toronto, Chinaglia, disappointed that his touch in front of goal had briefly deserted him, sprinted over to Manfredi, pointing to the necklace he was wearing. 'I said, "What do you need Giorgio?" He said, "You see that thing you have on your neck?"'

Around Manfredi's neck was a good-luck charm in the shape of a small horn and Chinaglia wanted it. Ever compliant, Manfredi took it off and wiped it on Chinaglia's right boot. Seconds later, the ball found Chinaglia in the penalty area and, sure enough, he slotted one home with his right foot. 'All of a sudden he's shouting, going like this to me, "Hey Joe!"'

☻

Having been in the coach's seat for a little under a year, Eddie Firmani had taken the Cosmos to an entirely new level. Despite the loss of Pelé, his team had flourished and by the time it arrived in Memphis for the game against the Rogues the champions were in such imperious form that the only question remaining was which team would be lining up against them in the Soccer Bowl come 27 August.

The game at the Liberty Bowl, however, would be a turning point, not for the fortunes of the team, but for the future of their coach. With twenty minutes to go and, unusually, a goal down, Eddie Firmani decided to make a change. Concerned that his team had resorted to lifting high balls into the opposition's penalty area rather than playing to Giorgio Chinaglia's strengths, the coach instructed his American international striker Fred Grgurev, a player much more suited to the aerial game, to warm up. Then, just as Gordon Bradley sealed his fate by dropping Chinaglia for the LA Aztecs game in 1977, Firmani called in his number nine. As Chinaglia trudged off the field, his face a picture of rage, he stared intently at Firmani. As he made his way to the tunnel, he pointed at his coach and muttered, 'You've had it!' He then headed straight to the locker room to call Steve Ross.

In Mario Risoli's biography of Chinaglia, *Arrivederci Swansea*, Eddie Firmani reveals that the Italian's reaction to his decision that day soured an otherwise excellent relationship. 'What Giorgio did surprised me. It put a strain between both of us and I didn't bother with him after that... he should have asked me why I made the change. I would have talked with him and told him the reason why. But that's not the way he worked. Instead of being a man and coming to talk it over with me he behaved like a kid. Maybe I should have sat down with him and ironed it out but he wasn't that type. He was hard-headed.'

Eddie Firmani would use another substitute that day against Memphis. His name was Rick Davis and at just nineteen years old, he had already established himself in the USA national side, scoring after just six minutes of his debut against El Salvador. Having been plucked from his junior year at Santa Clara University, Davis had signed for the Cosmos at the tail end of the 1977 season and now the Denver-born midfielder, along with Gary Etherington, was benefiting from the NASL rule of each team having to play at least two North Americans (a definition that also included Canadians, naturalized citizens and resident alien green-card holders).

Although his appearances would be limited to a handful of run-outs as sub, he was already being billed as one of the brightest hopes for American soccer. 'The first time I walked into the locker room,' he remembers, 'there were nameplates on top of all the lockers. When I saw "Davis" next to so many other well-known names like Beckenbauer and Chinaglia, it was an incredible feeling.'

The long-awaited arrival of a good-looking, all-American golden boy in the locker room was also a novelty for the Cosmos Girls. 'It was like "Oh wow! You speak English!"' says Debra Benitez.

By the second week in July, the Cosmos had become an unstoppable force in the NASL, crushing anything that crossed its path with verve, flair and no small measure of arrogance. After twenty-two games, it had won eighteen, scoring an astonishing sixty-seven goals in the process. Up front, Giorgio Chinaglia still seemed capable of scoring whenever the urge took him while all of the new recruits, especially Bogicevic and Tueart, proved to be inspired signings.

But this was no time for resting on laurels and, like an art dealer trying to complete his collection, Steve Ross signed off a plan to try and land the last remaining legend in the modern game – Johan Cruyff. 'I said to Steve Ross that he had to hire Johan [because] he's the best player you can ever see,' recalls Franz Beckenbauer.

As the star of the Ajax team that had given the world the concept of 'total football', Cruyff had become the greatest player the Netherlands had ever produced. Three times he had been voted the European Player of the Year (1971, 1973 and 1974) and he had won the European Cup three times with Ajax. He had also led the Netherlands to second place in the 1974 World Cup, losing out to Franz Beckenbauer's West Germany in the final. Undoubtedly, his total of forty-eight games for the Netherlands (thirty-three goals) would have been more, but for disputes with the Dutch Football Association and his refusal to play in the 1978 World Cup, which he attributed to the unstable political situation in the host country, Argentina.

There had been talk of the Dutchman joining the Cosmos even when Pelé was still playing for the team, but now, as

Cruyff contemplated his future after a successful spell with Barcelona, he agreed to visit New York to discuss the idea of a move. This time, however, the American press was calling it 'a negotiating breakthrough'.

That Cruyff was prepared to negotiate at all was largely down to Rafael de la Sierra's persistence. The Warner vice-president had flown to Spain to meet with Cruyff and moot the idea of a move Stateside. With Pelé's legacy and the presence of one of his old adversaries, Franz Beckenbauer, in the team, de la Sierra was now in a position where no real sales pitch was needed. But like Pelé before him, de la Sierra found a player immersed in all manner of commercial ventures. 'He owned like five different businesses in Barcelona. He had an art gallery, he had a transport business, an export–import business,' recalls de la Sierra. 'He had 5,000 pigs in a farm and part of the deal that we had was to buy that for him to be able to go with us so I had to go to the pig farm with an accountant to count the 5,000 pigs they had there. He also had a rabbit farm and we had to go to see how those rabbits reproduce.'

With their target apparently convinced of the Cosmos's intentions, the two parties agreed to meet again at the end of the 1978 NASL season and, as a sign of his willingness to strike a deal, Cruyff agreed to play in a three-game exhibition series at the end of the season.

After his decision to replace Chinaglia earlier in the season, Eddie Firmani was now having trouble keeping certain members of his squad in check. Many players, realizing that the position of Cosmos coach was a transitory one, sided with Chinaglia. On away trips, the eleven o'clock curfew imposed by the management was often disregarded. Instead, those players intent on enjoying a night out would just stay in their rooms until 11.30 p.m. Then, as soon as the coach had switched out the lights, they would then change into their best togs and sneak out, safe in the knowledge that the management was tucked up in bed and they were out with Giorgio Chinaglia.

What's more, Chinaglia would always promise to pick up the tab for any fines incurred for breaking curfew. 'You know,' laughs Bobby Smith, 'Eddie [Firmani] would try and put a curfew and Bogie was going, "I smoke, I drink, I dance all night long. There is no curfew"... and I'd say, "I'm hanging with Chinaglia", because I knew, if he had that much power I'm hanging with him because if we get busted, he ain't gonna get benched. So I'm gonna be okay by coming in late with Chinaglia. I'm hanging with Chinaglia, you know.'

Phil Mushnick, Cosmos correspondent for the *New York Post*, agrees. 'If you got stuck next to Bobby Smith in a hotel you weren't going to sleep that night,' he remembers.

But if the players thought they were pulling the wool over the eyes of their bosses, they were wrong. Everyone, from Firmani to Steve Marshall, knew only too well what the more sociable players of the squad were up to, but as long as they were winning and Steve Ross was happy, they were afforded a little leeway. 'We did have a few characters who liked cocktails,' says Steve Marshall. 'These guys were getting paid big money and they liked their drink.'

The other problem facing those players intent on enjoying some extracurricular action was an ever-increasing travelling press corps trailing in their wake. While the larger media organizations refused the Cosmos's standing offer of all-expenses-paid trips in the interests of objectivity and independence, there was no shortage of reporters on smaller publications only too willing to surrender their journalistic integrity in return for a party with the players of the nation's most engaging sports side.

The thinking behind the Cosmos's generosity to apparently insignificant newspapers made sense. While any coverage the team could get in the established New York dailies was valuable, it was imperative to get the team into the local newspapers in New York and New Jersey. 'We needed the German daily language paper, we needed *El Diario* [the daily Spanish language paper in New York] to travel with us just like the big papers,' adds Marshall.

When the Cosmos finished the regular season, not only was it the runaway winners of the Eastern Division of the National Conference, but it had registered an all-time record points total (two hundred and twelve) and number of goals scored (eighty-eight). After a comfortable win over Seattle in the first play-off game, the Cosmos had to face the Minnesota Kicks in the next phase.

Nobody, however, could have predicted the outcome. Led by their gifted English striker Alan Willey, the Kicks took the game to the Cosmos and, for once, the New Yorkers were powerless to hold them back. At the final whistle, Willey had scored five in an improbable 9–2 win. 'We've been threatening to score a bunch against somebody, but I didn't think it would be against the Cosmos,' said Willey in the post-match press conference. 'It feels good, especially against the Cosmos, because they're the team to beat.'

Fortunately, the nature of the play-off system favoured the Cosmos. Had the tie been decided on goal difference, as virtually every other home and away series in world soccer was, the Cosmos would, barring a miracle, have been out of the running and that supremacy all season long would have amounted to nothing. As it was, all the Cosmos had to do was win the return game at Giants Stadium the following Wednesday to take the game to a mini-game decider. Win that and they were back on course. Understandably, the system soon came under fire from all quarters. All quarters that is, apart from the players, fans and officials of the New York Cosmos.

As the Cosmos prepared for the second leg, conscious that nothing but a victory would suffice, it received another unscheduled visit from Steve Ross. Gathering the squad together, he explained that he had been in the crowd at Minnesota along with scores of his Warner executives and had felt genuinely embarrassed by the mauling the Cosmos had received. 'Then he said, "I don't like to feel embarrassed,"' recalls Dennis Tueart. '[He said] "We are the best, we pay the best for the best, we want the best performances, if you don't want to be part of that see the coach and you can go now"… it was a fantastic, motivational speech.'

Buoyed or frightened by Ross's intervention (and by the fact that Minnesota's Alan Willey had publicly stated that 'there is no way we can get beat'), the Cosmos roared back with a vengeance in the second leg. Chinaglia and Tueart ran the Kicks ragged, sharing the goals in a resounding 4–0 win and taking the tie into a mini-game decider. When that game ended all-square, the match went down to a shootout but, predictably, the Cosmos, with lady luck riding on its coat tails, won through.

Although the records show that Franz Beckenbauer scored the winning goal in that shootout, it was Carlos Alberto's audacious effort that not only kept the Cosmos in the game but revealed the true talent of the man. Whereas most players in the shootout dribble the ball towards the goalkeeper and wait for him to commit himself to a save or a tackle, Alberto simply waited for the referee's whistle and then scooped the ball up into the air. As it bounced ahead of him, the Minnesota keeper Tino Lettieri advanced off his line, but was clearly confused by Alberto's intentions. With the keeper stranded outside his area, Alberto then calmly lobbed it up and over Lettieri's head and into the empty net. 'It was amazing what he did,' says Bob Iarusci, one of his team-mates that night. 'He was the first to ever try that and he had to score to keep us in the shootout... He was very, very special.'

The shock to the system that the Minnesota tie provided was a stark reminder of the perilous position the Cosmos was in. After a season where they had finally established themselves as the dominant team in the NASL (and gone some way to justifying Warner's $1 million annual investment) anything less than a repeat of their Soccer Bowl success of 1977 would be deemed a failure. Moreover, the Minnesota game had also served to remind the Cosmos players just how far they had come. Two or three years ago, they would have been elated to squeeze through to the next round of the play-offs, but now the victory met not with jubilation but a tangible sense of relief. They were becoming a proper soccer team.

The remainder of the play-offs would follow the script. Following a comfortable win over Portland in the National Conference final, the Cosmos progressed to the Soccer Bowl and a game against the Tampa Bay Rowdies at its own Giants Stadium. It was the overwhelming favourite, not least because just two hours before the kick off Tampa's captain and star striker, Rodney Marsh, pulled out of the season showpiece. The Englishman had gashed his shin in the Rowdies' American conference win over Fort Lauderdale and it had become infected in the days leading up to the game. It was another lucky break for the Cosmos, particularly because Marsh was one of those players who made a habit of giving the Cosmos defence a torrid time.

The match itself would be a non-event. Without Marsh, the Rowdies relied heavily on their defence in a desperate rearguard action aimed at keeping the Cosmos at bay. By half-time, and with nearly 75,000 fans urging them on, the New Yorkers were two goals to the good, courtesy of Tueart and Chinaglia, and while the Brazilian Mirandinha would pull a goal back for the Rowdies, it was left to Dennis Tueart to kill the game off with his second goal near the end. The Cosmos, without Pelé, had become the first repeat champions in NASL history.

After the game, the Rowdies coach Gordon Jago paid tribute to the Cosmos. 'They have so much firepower. You stop Hunt and Chinaglia's waiting. Stop him, there's Tueart. I think they've shown all season that they are a truly superior team.'

Six years earlier, Werner Roth had helped the Cosmos to its first NASL title when it had beaten St Louis in front of just 6,102 fans at Hofstra Stadium. That same night, he had celebrated by going out with his team-mates and having 'a couple of beers'. Now, after winning in front of a crowd over ten times the size of that in 1972, he said, 'I think I might party until morning.'

For Giorgio Chinaglia, it was a vindication of all the changes he had set in place and confirmed that his vision for the Cosmos was the right one. That he had played a huge part in the success was irrefutable. Ever-present in the side, he had benefited most from the ingenuity of Bogicevic and had plundered a league record thirty-four goals in just thirty games. He had also weighed in with eleven assists.

Strangely, Chinaglia would not be named as the season's Most Valuable Player (MVP). Instead, New England's British striker Mike Flanagan took the award, despite registering four goals and three assists fewer than the Italian. Chinaglia's reputation, it seemed, had preceded him. 'Of all the strikers

I saw in the NASL,' says NASL commissioner Phil Woosnam, 'Chinaglia was head and shoulders above them all. Give him the ball in the penalty area and nine times out of ten he'd score. Whatever anybody thought of him there was no denying that he was an incredible player.'

Not that Chinaglia was unduly concerned. As he fielded questions in the locker room, he was asked what was left for the Cosmos to achieve. 'I don't know,' he shrugged, drawing on his traditional post-match cigarette. 'Today, we did what we had to, no more. I guess all that's left now is to be the best in the world. We're certainly number one in this league.'

Their pre-eminence asserted, the Cosmos decided to strengthen its squad further. In late August, Johan Cruyff arrived from Spain to take part in a three-game exhibition series at Giants Stadium. While the object of the All-Star series was to raise money for UNICEF and the Spanish Red Cross, the matches were seen as an audition of Cruyff at what would be his new home.

After the series ended, it was widely assumed that the thirty-one-year-old would sign full-time for the Cosmos, but the deal never happened. Wary of criticism that the Cosmos was not only spending its way to success but in danger of making the NASL a pointless procession, the club backtracked on the move to sign Cruyff and the Dutchman eventually opted to join his former coach, Rinus Michels, at the Los Angeles Aztecs. Rafael de la Sierra, however, remembers it differently. 'We brought him [Cruyff] to New York and then we gave him to Los Angeles to create more competition in the league,' he admits.

While the Cosmos had earned the grudging respect of even their most hardened critics in the NASL, a better test of just how able a team it was would only come when it embarked on a month-long post-season tour to Europe, with games scheduled in West Germany, England, Italy, Spain, Greece, Yugoslavia and Turkey. In all there would be nine matches in just twenty-eight days, a gruelling schedule, especially at the end of a long, albeit successful, season.

It was a tour that Eddie Firmani neither wanted nor needed. Having played over forty games already that season, his weary team had been contemplating a well-earned break and the prospect of playing the cream of European football at a time when their bodies and minds would patently rather not didn't augur well.

Needless to say, the trip had not been devised by the playing or coaching staff. As part of Warner's relentless drive to publicize the team (and their company), each week without a Cosmos game was a missed opportunity, and the idea that the season started at the beginning of April and finished at the end of August was anathema to Steve Ross.

A month later, the Cosmos returned home with some humiliating results to mull over. While it had beaten Atletico Madrid and drawn with Chelsea, it had also lost 7–1 to Franz Beckenbauer's old team Bayern Munich, 6–1 to Stuttgart, and even succumbed to little-known German side Freiburg. Winning the NASL was one thing, but, for the meantime, world domination would have to wait.

CHAPTER 10

BLINDED BY THE LIGHT

It was the breakthrough Phil Woosnam had longed for. Hindered by the lack of any meaningful television coverage of his league and with only the Cosmos gaining any kind of international recognition, the NASL was at a pivotal point in its short history.

With Pelé's legacy in grave danger of coming to nothing, what the NASL needed now, more than ever, was a network TV deal to take its product into America's living rooms and to those armchair fans who had yet to sample soccer. Without one, the Cosmos could go on signing the biggest and best names in the world game, but whether it would have anyone to play against would be entirely another matter.

In mid-November, Woosnam proudly announced that the NASL had signed a two-year deal with ABC television that guaranteed nine live games, including the Soccer Bowl, during the 1979 and 1980 seasons. While Woosnam had wanted more games and more money, it was, at the very least, a huge leap forward for the league and for soccer in the States. 'Television was crucial,' says Woosnam. 'It had always been a thorn in our side and when we finally signed a deal with ABC it looked like we were getting somewhere.'

For ABC, it seemed to be a gamble worth taking. While there had been some limited coverage of World Cup tournaments in the States, there had been little programming devoted to domestic soccer. For the most part, the big networks had shied away, largely because of the difficulties of screening it. While established sports like baseball and American football were awash with myriad opportunities for commercials, soccer lacked natural breaks, not to mention the kind of intervals that would lend themselves to statistical analysis or interesting facts – something that sports fans in the States adored. Indeed, when CBS had tried to screen games in the old National Professional Soccer League in 1967, one referee, Peter Rhodes, admitted that of the twenty-one free-kicks he called in the game between Toronto and Pittsburgh, eleven were only awarded so commercial breaks could be shoehorned into the programme. He was even seen to hold one prostrate player down just so an ad break could be completed.

There was also the problem of soccer's low scores. While the NASL had introduced the shootout so that no league game could end in a tie, the notion that a team could win a game by just one goal to nil was at odds with American sports fans' expectations. Asking viewers to give two hours of their weekend in return for a single goal was always going to struggle to attract new fans to the game.

But with the upsurge in attendances and the perceptible rise in the game's profile, it appeared that the time was right for ABC to try their hand at soccer. Jim Spence was senior vice-president of ABC Sports at the time. 'We had hopes that it [the NASL] was going to be the next big thing,' he explains. 'The North American Soccer League had shown some real progress [and] the New York Cosmos were very popular... The league seemed like it had a real future so we wanted to get involved.'

Needing an authoritative, charismatic presence to front their coverage, ABC turned to Jim McKay, the widely respected host of their *Wide World of Sports* programme and a huge fan of the game. 'He loved soccer and he really had great hopes on a personal level that it would be successful,' adds Spence.

ABC also enlisted Paul Gardner as a colour commentator. Gardner was a Brit based in Manhattan. He had written an acclaimed history of soccer called *The Simplest Game* and was known as much for his passion for the sport as for his knowledge. 'I don't think anyone thought they were going to get a lot of money from TV because you only get that when the ratings come in,' he says, 'but in terms of publicity and in terms of joining the big guys [like] the NFL and the MBA... it was very important to the league at that stage.'

While the NASL and ABC were delighted with the agreement, not everyone was convinced that the deal would prove beneficial to the long-term prosperity of the league. Ed Bleier was the chairman of the NASL's Television Committee. 'I had a very different view of our television potential than the other team and club members,' he recalls. 'They wanted an instant network contract and I said we will go on television and fail, then they will blame soccer... I wanted us on anthology shows, like the *Wide World of Sports* with standings, players, saves, goals, player of the week to build all the intrinsics of the sport and only put the championship game on television. I was overruled. I got out-voted.'

The network TV deal would bring a new sense of purpose to the existing franchises in the NASL and encourage a glut of new signings to enter the fray. Johan Cruyff aside, the most prominent transfer was that which took the prolific West German striker Gerd Müller to the Fort Lauderdale Strikers. Nicknamed 'Der Bomber', Müller was, unquestionably, the most lethal striker of his generation. In his sixty-two appearances for West Germany he recorded an incredible sixty-eight goals, while in the World Cup Finals of 1970 and

1974 he scored a record fourteen in just thirteen games, including the winner in the 1974 final against the Netherlands.

While the rest of the NASL franchises were bolstering their squads, confident that national television exposure would lead to healthier crowds and increased revenue, the Cosmos too had been scouring the world for the best talent that Steve Ross could afford. Normally, this would have involved the coach earmarking those players he felt could improve his team, taking the names to the board and allowing them to commence negotiations. Now, though, Eddie Firmani found himself subject to the whim of the Warner management, and had to sit by as a steady stream of acquisitions, such as the Brazilian defender Francisco Marinho, the Dutchman Wim Rijsbergen and the Iranian Andranik Eskandarian, arrived at the club, all seemingly without the coach's blessing.

Firmani's crime, it appeared, was to have substituted Giorgio Chinaglia in the previous season, a decision that had not only damaged the relationship between the two men but suggested to the board that Firmani harboured opinions of his own. The one thing Warner didn't want in such an influential position, it seemed, was a free-thinking individual.

They could have no quarrel, though, with his record as coach. In his two seasons at the club, the Cosmos had won unprecedented back-to-back Soccer Bowls, and he had lost only a handful of games. He had taken a team who had lost their most charismatic, most accomplished player and made them an even stronger proposition.

In Francisco Marinho, the Cosmos, and not Firmani, had signed an undeniably talented player but one who could and would test the resolve of the most hardened coach. With a thatch of blond hair, an impossible tan and confidence that knew no bounds, Marinho was also the kind of player who got on Giorgio Chinaglia's nerves. In training, he would routinely take pot shots at goal from distances and angles not even Pelé would have considered, sending the ball yards over the crossbar and high into the upper tier of the stands. With his shooting threatening everything but the goal, he was soon nicknamed 'Mezzaninho' by his team-mates.

That said, Marinho was a Cosmos player through and through. Gifted on the pitch, he soon acclimatized to the rich social scene available off it. Indeed, within weeks of signing, he would even be suspended for breaking Eddie Firmani's curfew. On the eve of one home fixture, the Brazilian was caught in bed with two women at the Hasbrouk Heights Hilton in New Jersey when he should have been resting before the game.

Eddie Firmani's decision to suspend Marinho rankled with the Erteguns and soon after, when Firmani also dropped the goalkeeper – their goalkeeper – Erol Yasin, it seemed as though the coach had as good as signed his own resignation letter.

Certainly, Giorgio Chinaglia no longer had any time for the coach, their relationship now nothing more than perfunctory. It seemed that if you wronged Chinaglia you stayed wronged. Yet the Italian was still held in high regard by the club, if not by all of the Cosmos fans. For the game against Tulsa Roughnecks on 20 May, the Cosmos board declared that it would be 'Giorgio Chinaglia Day', in recognition of his extraordinary goalscoring record at the club. Over 46,000 people turned up for the game and were entertained by a succession of Chinaglia's friends and admirers who took to the pitch to deliver eulogies to the Italian striker. Clive Toye couldn't make it.

While the pre-match entertainment had been received warmly, Chinaglia then found himself being booed by sections of the home support during the game itself. The *Newsday* columnist Johnette Howard once wrote that the New York sports fan 'will boo his own mama if she burns the breakfast toast'. She wasn't wrong. Despite Chinaglia's scoring twice in a 3–1 Cosmos win, the crowd had taken the opportunity of his special day to voice their displeasure at what they perceived as his constant scheming behind the scenes. 'There were many occasions when he was roundly booed by the fans,' recalls Bob Iarusci. 'I think they just wanted him to be a player and nothing more.'

Not that he cared. As the archetypal pantomime villain, he revelled in the attention. 'It was because of my interference with the team,' he concludes. 'Some people they used to like I got rid of.'

One of those people was Eddie Firmani. When the Cosmos sacked him on 1 June 1979, it cited the inability of Firmani and the board of directors to agree on the direction of club. The same line had been peddled for Clive Toye's resignation and echoed the commonly cited reason for rock bands splitting: 'musical differences'.

Later, Ahmet Ertegun attempted to explain Firmani's dismissal. 'Look,' he told the press. 'I think Eddie Firmani's a terrific human being, and I think he's probably relieved that this is over. There was dissension in our locker room. I understand that we're probably going to always have dissension. Coaching the Cosmos is one of the hardest jobs in the world. We've got a lot of great players. We've also got a lot of personalities, you know, egos.'

As Eddie Firmani had discovered to his cost, not all of those egos lived in the locker room. Quizzed about his sacking, he remained tight-lipped, saying, 'I enjoyed my experience with Cosmos. I mean I enjoyed dealing with the players and with the public. It was the other facets I didn't enjoy so much that I don't wish to speak of.'

When Giorgio Chinaglia finally spoke on the subject, there was a discernible lack of sympathy for Firmani. 'It's all over now,' he said. 'The old coach is gone, the new coach is here and we're trying to play the best we can. Why talk about something when it's history?'

In the wake of Firmani's departure, the New York newspapers all ran pieces on the club's handling of the situation, with most expressing incredulity that Firmani had been sacked. It didn't end there. Throughout the NASL, the issue provoked a variety of opinions, ranging from bewilderment to resignation. Former Cosmos coach Gordon Bradley, now coach at the Washington Diplomats (and therefore free to say what he liked about the Cosmos), maintained the decision was typical of a club where wrong often passed for right, black could be mistaken for white and where the coach was coach in name only. 'One thing which is difficult is that men like Eddie and I grew up with a system, a system which allowed the coaches to choose their teams and then put those teams on the field as they saw fit. That way, if a coach chooses the right players and wins, he gets the credit. If not, he takes the blame, period. Here, though, especially with the Cosmos, a coach feels like he doesn't control his own destiny.'

Even the younger players in the squad were tiring of the incessant squabbling. 'You learn to live with the atmosphere,' said Gary Etherington, the twenty-one-year-old striker from North Virginia. 'I'm not saying that it's good or bad, but you kind of get used to it – it's a part of your life day-in and day-out.'

The man charged with taking the Cosmos on to a hat-trick of Soccer Bowls was Ray Klivecka. A former United States youth team coach, Klivecka was Firmani's assistant and had been asked to shoulder the responsibility for the remainder of the season. Within four days of his appointment, though, Pelé's old adviser, Professor Julio Mazzei, would be appointed as the interim technical director of the club, a move which effectively put Ray Klivecka straight back in his old position of assistant coach. 'We have great confidence in Professor Mazzei,' said an official club statement, 'because of all his years of experience in soccer and the respect he enjoys throughout the soccer world, both on and off the field.'

The fall-out from Eddie Firmani's sacking overshadowed the build-up to one of the most intriguing games that the Cosmos would play. With a 10–2 record behind it in the league, it had shoehorned an exhibition game against the reigning world champions, Argentina, into its schedule. It would prove to be a fascinating test of the team, and, according to press rumours, an opportunity for Ahmet Ertegun to sound out the Argentinian coach, César Louis Menotti, about taking over at the Cosmos at the end of the season. Having taken the Argentinian side to a World Cup victory in 1978, the chain-smoking Menotti (who had also played for the New York Generals in the late 1960s) certainly met Ertegun's criteria for a new coach. The Cosmos president had told the press that he wanted 'a top, world-renowned coach, who can give this team the kind of spirit and evenness of play we're looking for'.

When kick-off arrived, it was difficult to envisage anything other than a comprehensive Argentinian victory. After all, the visitors were the team that had outplayed an outstanding Dutch side in the World Cup Final and were considered to be at the height of their powers. In addition, the opposition could count on some typically slapdash preparations from the Cosmos. In short, there were all the ingredients for a mauling unlike anything the Cosmos would ever encounter in the NASL.

As it was, it was the Cosmos that surprised everyone. Performing at a level above and beyond most people's expectations, it more than held their own against the world champions (who also fielded a seventeen-year-old called Diego

Maradona in their line-up) and only lost when the visiting captain, Daniel Passarella, scored a controversial winner two minutes from time.

While still a defeat, the result was nevertheless a testament to the huge strides the Cosmos had made, and though the reaction of the 70,000 fans in Giants Stadium that night spoke volumes for the effort the team had put in, it was the response of the Argentinian coach which showed that the team was becoming a genuine force in the world game. Having kept his team in the locker room for over forty minutes after the final whistle, Menotti eventually appeared before the media and, through an interpreter, blamed the artificial turf for his team's less than convincing victory. 'We had to change our shoes at half-time because of the field. It gave us serious problems. I don't think you can say the Cosmos have a very good team until they learn to play in other places besides here, on this field.'

It was an ungracious reaction that did little to engage his American suitors. When he refused to entertain the idea of a money-spinning rematch, the possibility of Menotti taking over at the Cosmos withered on the vine.

If proof were needed of the superfluous nature of the position of Cosmos coach it materialized less than two weeks after Eddie Firmani's exit, when, despite the upheaval in the locker room and the uncertainty over the position of coach, the Cosmos signed the Dutch midfielder Johan Neeskens on a five-year, $1.6 million contract. 'We had to choose if we wanted a Neeskens type of player or a Cruyff type,' explained the Cosmos president, Ahmet Ertegun. 'Cruyff is thirty-two, and likes to run the show. We have enough of those.'

If previous coaches had issues with some of the signings that arrived at the club, none of them would have questioned the wisdom of buying a player of Neeskens's stature. At twenty-eight, he was in the prime of his career and boasted the kind of international experience and reputation for which any coach at any club would have paid a premium. He would also prove to be a more than capable deputy for the injured Franz Beckenbauer. 'Our ground was AstroTurf and at least half of the grounds in the league were AstroTurf and Johan had no fear of doing slide tackles,' says Steve Hunt. 'He would rip himself to pieces but next time he would do it again, you know. [He was] a very hard man and just crazy, an absolute lunatic. Good to have in your team though.'

If the size of the Cosmos organization had changed beyond recognition – the squad alone now had thirty players in it – the camaraderie was, for the most part, as strong as ever, even if the occasional spat, suspension or sacking threatened to spoil the party. Shep Messing, their former goalkeeper, once described life on the road with the New York Cosmos as being 'like a bad Fellini movie'. He had a point. If Bobby Smith and Giorgio Chinaglia weren't arguing the toss over the relative merits of communism and capitalism, then Steve Marshall was dancing up and down the aisle of the plane (or team bus) like a drunken uncle at Christmas, or Francisco Marinho was roaming from hotel bed to hotel bed on his own kind of workout.

It was all but impossible not to join in and the new recruit Johan Neeskens adapted to the Cosmos way of life in double-quick time. On one flight to an away fixture, the Dutchman decided to liven up proceedings by making the journey in drag. 'He had the lipstick, the dress on and then he stuck golf balls in his shirt. It was originally funny, but then it became uncomfortable. He stayed in drag the whole damn flight,' remembers Phil Mushnick of the *New York Post*.

Even Franz Beckenbauer, the epitome of Teutonic detachment, had long since ditched any pretensions he had to remain aloof from the craziness of the Cosmos roadshow. Now, after two years in the Big Apple, he was a man very much at ease. He could walk through Central Park without being mobbed, or go for dinner and actually enjoy it and, on the advice of his friend Shep Messing, had even discarded his hairdryer in favour of letting his hair dry naturally. Once, when Beckenbauer was dining with Ahmet Ertegun at Elaine's restaurant on Second Avenue, he noticed the film director Woody Allen at a neighbouring table and mentioned to Ertegun that he would like to meet him. As the man who knew everyone, Ertegun took Beckenbauer by the hand and led him to Allen's table. 'Before I could say anything,' recalls Ertegun, 'Woody Allen turns around and says "My God, Franz Beckenbauer!"'

Certainly, the Cosmos was a team brought together by a common purpose, not to traverse the States and convince the nation that it was right about soccer and America was wrong, but to secure handsome salaries, a first-class lifestyle and the opportunity to wring every last drop of fun out of New York City. In doing so, however, a rare team spirit and solidarity emerged and found a spiritual home in the locker room at Giants Stadium. 'I miss the locker room always. I've got married [and] family and all that stuff is beautiful, but that one part of a locker room, and that team,' sighs Bobby Smith, 'you don't replace that kind of an experience, you really don't. That locker room is our place, and it's beautiful, you know.'

Franz Beckenbauer agrees. 'In the New York Cosmos we had fourteen different nationalities,' explains Beckenbauer. 'Everybody was a stranger in the city and that's what kept the team together. We had much more spirit than with other teams I played [for].'

As the club's car supplier, the Brooklyn car dealer Joe Manfredi took it upon himself to ensure that the players never wanted for anything. He would routinely pick up the tab for team blowouts, scout towns for the best venues for post-match parties and hand over the keys to up to forty new cars to the players, management and front desk each season. 'When we went out and you would reach for your wallet it was like an insult to Joe,' explains Steve Marshall, 'because he felt like he wanted to be part of the family and unfortunately he felt the only way he could do that was to buy every drink.'

Surely nobody could begrudge Manfredi the good times. Having supported the club through the lean times Manfredi was finally hitching a ride with a team that was every bit as famous, in the major conurbations at least, as the Mets, the Giants or the Knicks. Indeed, Manfredi was now such a fundamental part of the Cosmos family that on match days he would travel with the squad on the coach (he called it the 'happy tank'), have use of his own locker in the locker room and then sit next to the substitutes in the dugout. Such was Manfredi's devotion to the Cosmos cause that he even missed the births of his children to be on the road with the Cosmos. 'I never saw them being born to be honest with you,' he admits. 'I'm not proud to say that, but I tell you being with the Cosmos – I think it was the right thing to do.'

Steve Marshall spent many a drunken evening with Joe Manfredi but while Manfredi maintains that life on the road was nothing but 'clean fun', Marshall remembers it differently. 'Joe would always want to go out,' he laughs. 'He liked the hotel bars but he liked to venture out to clubs… he was quite the party animal.'

At the end of the regular season, the Cosmos boasted a 24–6 record, and having retained their National Conference Eastern Division title with a total of 216 points, they had also broken their record for the number of points gained. That they were heading, inexorably, towards a third consecutive Soccer Bowl triumph seemed indisputable, especially after they breezed past Toronto in the opening tie of the play-offs. While the Tulsa Roughnecks took the Cosmos to a mini-game decider in the next round – a Chinaglia brace helping them through 3–1 – it would be the game against the Vancouver Whitecaps that would go down as one of the greatest games ever witnessed in the NASL.

The Cosmos and Vancouver had history. All season, Tony Waiters' Whitecaps had got the better of the New Yorkers, winning 4–1 at their own Empire Stadium in June and then winning again at Giants Stadium in July by four goals to two.

The latter game had been a prickly affair. When tempers flared during the second half, Vancouver's bear-like English goalkeeper, Phil Parkes, took the opportunity to offer Giorgio Chinaglia one of his choicest Anglo-Saxon insults. Rising to the bait, the Italian began throwing his weight around like a street brawler and the referee duly sent Chinaglia off.

Then, what had started out as a soccer match descended into farce. As the official brandished his red card, Chinaglia responded by ripping the card out of his hand, tearing it up in front of his face and then throwing the pieces to the ground. As he stormed off, the Cosmos fans began booing Parkes for his part in Chinaglia's dismissal while Parkes, a player who took great delight in antagonizing the opposition, turned to face them and blew them kisses.

The two games against Vancouver (three, if you include the mini-game) would have everything any soccer fan could ever want. There were suspensions and shootouts, heroes and heartache. There were flare-ups, disallowed goals, red cards and sheer exhaustion; Giorgio Chinaglia even barged the linesman.

Some three hours and forty minutes after the tie began it finally ended when the Cosmos's Nelsi Morais, taking the final shot of the second shootout of the day, scored his goal. For once, however, it wasn't the Cosmos that had won. According to the stadium clock, Morais's shot had come one second after the five-second deadline. The Whitecaps went through to the Soccer Bowl.

After the game, the Cosmos locker room, so often a scene of celebration and superstar shoulder-rubbing remained closed during the post-mortem into the end to their tenure as the NASL's champion team. As the media pack battled to get inside, one reporter demanded to know why they weren't allowed in. As he pushed his way forward, Jay Emmett instructed a nearby security guard to 'shut that door in his face'.

Later, Professor Julio Mazzei emerged from the gloom of the locker room and with a distinct lack of grace, poured scorn on the Whitecaps' victory. 'Vancouver won because the league wanted [the] team to win,' he grumbled. 'The officials were against us in the play-offs.'

The Cosmos's glorious reign had ended, not in dignified defeat but in allegations and petty squabbling. *Newsweek* perhaps summed it up best when it suggested that the Cosmos had been 'victims of their own arrogance'.

But while Vancouver's victory (and their eventual triumph over Tampa in the 1979 Soccer Bowl itself) was a surprise, it at least demonstrated to the other franchises that the Cosmos could be toppled and gave the impression that a new breeze was blowing through the NASL. On a wider scale, however, opinion varied as to whether the failure of the Cosmos to extend its sequence of Soccer Bowl victories was a good thing for the NASL. Although some semblance of genuine competition had been re-established in the league, there was still a feeling that despite the league's protestations to the

Hola! – The Cosmos team enjoy a pre-season trip to Mexico. (Standing, left to right, men in hats unidentified): Len Renery, Roby Young, Randy Horton, Joe Fink, Werner Roth, Jerry Sularz. (Squatting, left to right): Siggy Stritzl, Charlie Martinelli, Everald Cummings, Malcolm Dawes, Ralph Wright. *(Len Renery)*

Team spirit – The 1974 Cosmos team line up at Randall's Island. (Back row, left to right) Frank Donlavey, Len Renery, Randy Horton, Malcolm Dawes, Gordon Bradley, Barry Mahy. (Front row, left to right) Harold Jarman, Germy Rivera, Jerry Sularz, Jorge Siega, Joe Fink. *(Len Renery)*

The off-duty Cosmos – (left to right) Shep Messing, Giorgio Chinaglia, Werner Roth and Franz Beckenbauer. *(Shep Messing)*

Star spotting – Shep Messing and friend with Pelé and Eusebio. *(Shep Messing)*

Flag day – Prior to his debut for the Cosmos, Pelé was joined on the pitch at Downing Stadium by Dallas' Kyle Rote Jr. *(Peter Robinson/ EMPICS)*

The New York Cosmos 1976 – (front row, left to right) Trainer Joel Rosenstein, Kurt Kuykendall, Bob Rigby, Terry Garbett, Jorge Siega, Pelé, Keith Eddy, Giorgio Chinaglia, Bob Smith, Werner Roth, Charlie Aitken, Edward Edgar, Shep Messing. (Back row, left to right) Head Coach Gordon Bradley, Frank Sauer, Barry Mahy, John Russo, Dave Clements, Charlie Mitchell, Ramon Mifflin, Nelsi Morais, Tony Field, Brian Tinnion, Brian Rowan, Mike Dillon, Tony Donlic, Assistant Coach Professor Julio Mazzei, Assistant Coach Joe Mallet. *(Shep Messing)*

Happy days – Franz Beckenbauer and Carlos Alberto share a joke. *(George Tiedemann)*

Access all areas – US Secretary of State Henry Kissinger joins Franz Beckenbauer in the locker room. *(George Tiedemann)*

What's up Doc? – Bugs Bunny wows the crowd at Giants Stadium. *(George Tiedemann)*

YES! – A record crowd for the 1977 play-off game against Fort Lauderdale Strikers. *(George Tiedemann)*

Smokin' – The irrepressible Giorgio Chinaglia. *(George Tiedemann)*

Dutch master – Johan Cruyff meets the press after signing a short-term deal with the Cosmos. *(George Tiedemann)*

Dream ticket – Pelé's farewell game against Santos at Giants Stadium was a sell-out. *(Shep Messing)*

The greatest – Muhammad Ali joins Pelé on the pitch at his farewell game against Santos. "Now there are two of the greatest," said Ali. *(George Tiedemann)*

The end – Pelé says his goodbyes to Giants Stadium.
(George Tiedemann)

Turning Japanese – After his last game in New York, Pelé and the Cosmos headed off on a tour of the Far East. *(Shep Messing)*

contrary, the Cosmos was still carrying the NASL and if their support began to wane then what future was there for the other franchises?

For all Phil Woosnam's fervour – he once told ABC's Jim Spence that the NASL would be bigger than the NFL within ten years – it was becoming painfully clear that soccer was never going to gain parity with baseball, basketball or football and the ratings for ABC's live games certainly suggested that soccer was a game that had barely registered on the public's radar. Locally, the ratings in those cities where soccer had strong franchises (New York, Washington, Tampa, etc.) had been respectable, but on a national basis the sport had bombed.

Of course, the problem had been compounded by the failure of the Cosmos to reach the Soccer Bowl, and its unexpected exit in the play-offs had dented not just the attendance at the final game – just 50,699 turned up, despite claims by Phil Woosnam that over 60,000 tickets had been sold – but had hit ABC's overall ratings too. With a 2.7 rating (equivalent to approximately two million households) ABC were having difficulty finding sufficient advertising support. 'In all candour,' says Jim Spence, 'our affiliated stations around the country were not enamoured with a property that was generating those low ratings. Affiliates are selling their local spots and when you generate that kind of a rating it negatively impacts their sales effort.'

As the league sought to allay ABC's fears that their investment was misplaced, it was clear that the scheduling of the nine live games had been a major contributing factor in the disappointingly low ratings. Showing live games on a Saturday afternoon (when fans and families the nation over had better things to do) had proved folly and the feeling that the NASL had snapped ABC's hand off when the deal came along without really examining the detail was hard to avoid. 'I think we sold our souls to national television, and we've gotten very little in return,' said Jack Krumpe, the vice-president of Madison Square Garden, owners of the Washington Diplomats. 'Why should we agree to let them put games on at 2.30 p.m. on Saturday in the middle of the summer? That just isn't worth a darn, it has no dramatic impact at all. Look at the ratings, they've been abysmal.'

There was also a steadfast public perception that, for all the razzmatazz, big-name players and million-dollar salaries, soccer was still a foreigners' game. Moreover, while the Cosmos's Rick Davis had blossomed into one of the league's most consistent performers, he was still just one of only a handful of Americans who had the potential to make a name for himself. This noticeable absence of any homegrown heroes for the viewing public to follow not only quashed potential merchandising and advertising opportunities for the league but also served to reinforce the belief that soccer and Uncle Sam weren't really meant for each other.

It wasn't just the ratings. Despite a determined effort to present a soccer show every bit as professional as those they produced for the mainstream American sports, ABC had struggled to adjust to the demands of covering so unpopular a sport. Stymied by the need for commercial breaks they would often cut away to a break only to return to find that they had missed a major incident in the game, sometimes even a goal. Paul Gardner, however, maintains that given the constraints, ABC did an efficient job of televising the NASL. 'They were very, very professional those guys and they learned very quickly,' he explains. 'If you look back at those telecasts I think you will see that the quality of them was excellent... considering that this was the first time that most of these had ever done soccer.'

If the ratings for the ABC games had been dismal, the attendances at Giants Stadium were also a cause for concern for Steve Ross and Warner. Although the average turnout for a Cosmos home game had only dropped by a little over 1,000 per game, the fall to 46,690 was the first decline since the move to Meadowlands and, more worryingly, the first fall in attendances in five seasons.

There was more bad news on the horizon for the Cosmos. After a season in which he had had managed just one substitute appearance for his team, the Cosmos captain Werner Roth had been forced to retire because of a knee injury. Of the scores of players that had ever pulled on the Cosmos shirt, it was Roth, the kid from Ridgewood, who had witnessed the incredible transformation of the soccer club. He had been there when only a few hundred people had bothered to show up. He had been there when they had to paint the pitch green. And he had been there when a monkey was the main attraction. Now, as his Cosmos drew crowds of fifty, sixty and seventy thousand, he found his playing career cut short by injury. Today, Roth looks back on his years with the club with affection, concluding that 'It was the best of times and it was the worst of times.'

Keen to repay his loyalty, the Cosmos board soon gave Roth a new role as director of youth development at the club, although he was also exploring other avenues. As well as trying to establish his own Soccer Safari training schools and commentating on the radio, Roth had also been offered a leading role in *Escape to Victory*, a John Huston film about a team of Allied POWs who take on the might of Nazi Germany in a soccer game. Pelé was already in it, as were Michael Caine and Sylvester Stallone, and the producer Freddie Fields wanted Roth as one of the Allied players, 'until they found out that I could speak German and then all of a sudden I became the captain of the Germans.'

CHAPTER 11

THE LONG GOODBYE

There can be few clubs in soccer history that would consider two successive championship titles and a semi-final appearance in three seasons as a failure. But then there has never been a club like the Cosmos. Professor Julio Mazzei's and Ray Klivecka's failure to make it three titles in succession would, predictably, cost them their jobs.

Depending on your view, Hennes Weisweiler was either the perfect or the most inappropriate replacement. He had made his name as the manager behind the remarkable transformation of German side Borussia Moenchengladbach from second-division non-entities into European giants. As the coach at one of Europe's biggest clubs, Barcelona, he had acquired a reputation for being authoritarian and intransigent. But although he came highly recommended by Franz Beckenbauer, his appointment still came as a surprise. At fifty-nine, Weisweiler was in the twilight of his career and also spoke imperfect English (the same could have been said of any number of the Cosmos staff, players included). 'Throughout our history we always had at least one translator or another that had to translate the coach's directions into one of a few other languages,' says Werner Roth.

Within weeks of his appointment, however, in May 1980,

Weisweiler had the team performing better than they had in some time. The West German Hubert Birkenmeier, for example, now found himself as the first-choice goalkeeper and was repaying his coach with some outstanding displays in goal. New players like the young Paraguayan midfielder Julio César Romero and the American Angelo DiBernardo had slotted seamlessly into the side and Vladislav Bogicevic had even been transformed, miraculously some said, from mercurial talent (i.e. lazy) to the one of the most industrious players in the Cosmos squad.

With the team apparently rejuvenated, the Cosmos recorded eight straight victories in the aftermath of Weisweiler taking charge. During the run, Giorgio Chinaglia also became the league's all-time leading scorer with his 102nd goal during the away fixture at the California Surf. The only disappointment for Chinaglia and the Cosmos was that just 8,660 people were there to see the occasion. Clearly, the idea that a Vancouver or a Tampa could topple the Cosmos had done little to increase the crowds at games outside the soccer strongholds. They were even struggling in Philadelphia, once the home to a thriving franchise. For their game against the Chicago Sting, they managed to pull an official crowd of just 2,478, although journalists at the game estimated the real total was actually around 1,000. 'Kind of depressing,' was the ex-Cosmos keeper Bob Rigby's response, now playing for the Fury.

The Cosmos also picked up its first trophy under Weisweiler when it won the inaugural Trans-Atlantic Challenge Cup. It was a new four-team tournament that also included Vancouver Whitecaps from the NASL, Italy's Roma and England's Manchester City (which now featured Dennis Tueart in their line-up). Thanks to two wins, a draw and six Chinaglia goals, the Cosmos took the title.

Visible success was what Steve Ross craved and whenever he scanned the sports pages to find the Mets bagging the headlines with their record-breaking $21million franchise sale or the Yankees signing up Dave Winfield on a ten-year, $23 million deal, it irked him that the Cosmos wasn't there mixing it with them. The occasional trophy not only went some way to justifying his and Warner's investment in the club, but it marked the team – his team – out as winners. There was nothing Steve Ross loved more than a winner.

Ross's mind, however, would soon be occupied by more pressing problems. After experiencing chest pains for some time he suffered a serious heart attack in June 1980. From his hospital bed, Ross ordered that his condition be kept secret, maintaining that it would be bad for the company if the truth came out. Whenever anyone asked after him, Amanda Burden would just say he was suffering from backache. At fifty-two, though, Ross was faced with a stark choice. He could quit smoking and pass on the ice cream and fudge sauce, his doctors told him, or could he start making his funeral arrangements. Soon after, the Parliaments were kicked into touch.

His health was by no means Ross's only concern. On a personal level, his marriage to Burden was faltering. According to Connie Bruck in *Master of the Game*, Burden would often confide in friends that she found it difficult to be married to a man whose cultural tastes and whose interests away from the world of Warner were so limited. A case in point was the Cosmos trip to China in 1977, when on the lengthy flight she sat by and watched Ross and Jay Emmett play backgammon for hour after hour without even acknowledging her presence.

There were also problems with his son, Mark. Now nineteen, he, more than his sister Toni, had found his father's divorce and remarriage traumatic and began to question his father's relationship with Burden. Ever since his father had started seeing Burden, Mark Ross had found it difficult to accept; he had even slammed a chocolate pudding into her face when she had arranged a dinner for the Ross family and her children from a previous marriage, Flo-Belle and Carter.

When, in 1977, Ross had insisted that the Cosmos would soon be yet another profitable part of the Warner stable, he was, for once, talking from his heart and not his head. For all the pleasure he gleaned from the games, the team was fast turning into a headache. The financial burden of running a team with a lower profile and with fewer paying supporters than it once boasted was becoming increasingly difficult to defend. At one shareholders' meeting, Ross was asked just how much the Cosmos was costing the company. 'About two cents a share,' he quipped.

It was a typically astute response from Ross. Defusing a potentially awkward situation with humour, he had not only allayed his investors' fears but cleverly concealed the fact that two cents a share actually translated into an ugly annual loss of more than $5 million a year.

Of course, the Cosmos losses were much easier to stomach given the irrepressible success of Atari. In 1979, after licensing 'Space Invaders' from Bally for its VCS home console, the division posted an annual profit of $6 million. In 1980, it had risen to just short of $70 million, and showed no sign of abating. Commercially and culturally, Atari had far exceeded Ross's expectations. From the junior high schools to the back alley bars, everyone knew about Atari. Coin shortages were commonplace as people clamoured to play the machines and truancy levels climbed as kids skipped class to hit the arcades. Later, *Time* magazine would call the period 'The Age of Atari' while Thomas 'Tip' O'Neill, the Speaker of the House of Representatives, termed the new crop of thrusting young congressmen 'Atari Democrats'. What had started out as a speculative dabble in the world of computers for Steve Ross (albeit one that cost him $28 million) was fast turning into the biggest success story of his career.

Inevitably, the success of Atari and its new 2600 machine spawned imitators, most notably Mattel's Intellivision, which featured games such as baseball, blackjack and poker as well as boasting significantly better graphics. In 1980 as well a challenge to the hegemony of 'Space Invaders' arose in the shape of Namco's 'Pac-Man'. Originally, the game had been called 'Puck-Man' but was rapidly changed when vandals began altering the machine's lettering.

Much of the credit for Atari's rise went to Raymond Kassar. A graduate of Harvard Business School, Kassar had replaced Atari's founder, Nolan Bushnell, as the head of the division in 1978 and had brought a more regimented approach to Atari, dividing it into two distinct parts: consumer electronics (which included home computers) and coin-operated games. It gave the company much-needed structure and a better base from which it could begin to fully exploit the fervent public interest not merely in computers and computer games but in affordable technology more generally.

As the new Golden Boy of Warner, Kassar was rewarded handsomely for his endeavours, reportedly receiving a bonus of $4 million in 1980. In time, he would also be presented with a luxury apartment in Trump Tower and be given the same kind of unhindered access to Warner's private planes, helicopters and fleet of limousines that only the most cherished of executives (and Steve Ross's children) received. 'Incentive compensation,' Ross once explained, 'is the most important thing in business.'

While Warner wallowed in Atari's phenomenal success, the Cosmos carried on regardless. The problem, in terms of the NASL and its future, however, was that no other franchise had Atari as a big brother, and while the Cosmos could withstand falling crowds (they were down 21 per cent on the same time in 1979) protected by Steve Ross' patronage, other franchises were struggling to stay afloat. 'Maybe we've taken people for granted,' said Dominick Flora, the executive assistant in charge of Cosmos marketing in 1980. 'That's why we're going back to basics. We can't afford to become complacent. We've already gone back to promoting tailgating and putting Dixieland bands in the parking lots.'

Banjos aside, even ABC television was forced to concede that soccer, while not exactly a bum steer, had largely bypassed the nation's viewers. Midway through the season, the television ratings for the NASL had dropped still further from those of 1979 and this despite ABC opting to run six telecasts on consecutive Sundays. As the two parties sat down to discuss the possibility of a new deal, it was painfully obvious that real cracks were now beginning to appear in the NASL. Woosnam, somewhat unrealistically, wanted more money and more live games. ABC, meanwhile, looked at the bare facts and questioned what, if anything, it had to gain from continuing to cover a sport that had failed to capture the viewing public's imagination. 'I don't know whether it'll be back or not. All you can go by is the ratings and we haven't even seen negligible improvement this season,' said Chet Forte, director of production creative services for the network. 'I don't think soccer's really caught on yet and I'm not sure it ever will on a large scale. I don't think Americans can associate with foreign players. We're hurting on TV but I think the league overall is hurting, too. There are a lot of franchises floundering.'

The NASL, it seemed, had been guilty of believing its own press and, perhaps, believing that what had happened at Giants Stadium could still be replicated on a national level. As Woosnam and ABC broke off discussions, Forte told the press that the NASL needed to reassess its place in the hierarchy of American sports. 'I think they're living in a test tube,' he concluded. 'They think they've got the best thing in the world. Basically, they think they're more than they really are.' It was a damning comment, especially from a self-confessed fan of the game.

While not yet terminal, the downturn in interest in the NASL had inevitable implications for the rest of the game in the States. Other leagues that had sprung up, like the American Soccer League and the Cosmopolitan League, were faring even worse than the NASL, primarily because they had neither the star names nor the exposure of the NASL. Moreover, it did little to assist the case of the United States Soccer Federation (USSF), which was in the preliminary stages of attempting to bring the World Cup Finals to America. In a bid to convince the world governing body, FIFA, that they were more than capable of hosting the game's premier tournament, the USSF had announced that a youth competition involving nineteen of the twenty-three nations that comprised CONCACAF (Confederation of North, Central American and Caribbean Association Football) would be held in cities across the United States from during August. 'If we can prove to FIFA we can handle this tournament well,' said the USSF president, Gene Edwards. 'We can consider it a dry run for the Youth World Cup in 1983 or 1985 and maybe we can ask to host the big one in 1990.' It would be 1994 before the USSF finally got its chance to host the World Cup Finals.

That youth tournament would represent a chance for the new star of the Cosmos team, nineteen-year-old rookie Jeff

Durgan, to prove himself on an international stage. Having been signed in the 1979 amateur draft (coming out of Stadium High School in Tacoma, Washington), Durgan had been given his chance at centre-back just four games into the 1980 season following injuries to the Brazilian defender Oscar and the Dutchman Wim Rijsbergen. After some resilient displays, coach Weisweiler had been so impressed by his poise at the heart of the Cosmos back-line that he soon became the first choice in the position.

As the season progressed and Durgan repelled the finest strikers the NASL had to offer, including the likes of Klaus Toppmoller of Dallas and Oscar Fabbiani of Tampa Bay, he would follow in the footsteps of Randy Horton (1971) and Gary Etherington (1978) and be voted Rookie of the Year by his NASL colleagues. 'I'm honored that the other players in the league thought I was worthy of this award,' said the defender. 'I'm glad they think I have ability. I just hope I can continue to progress as much in the future as I have this season.' The question was whether anyone, not just Jeff Durgan, would have a future in the NASL.

One player who had decided he didn't have a future in America was Franz Beckenbauer. After four memorable seasons in the NASL, 'The Kaiser' announced on 1 July 1980 that he had accepted a long-standing offer of a two-year contract with the Bundesliga side SV Hamburg and would be returning home to West Germany once his contract at the Cosmos had expired in October. He would be thirty-five years old.

Certainly, it was clear that Warner Communications wanted the German international to stay and even issued a statement through executive vice-president Rafael de la Sierra. It read: 'The Cosmos are very sorry to learn of Franz Beckenbauer's decision to return to West Germany. We did everything we could to keep him here, but money was apparently not a factor in his decision.'

Yet Beckenbauer's decision wasn't entirely of his own volition. Throughout his playing career, he had benefited from a lucrative contract with the West German sporting goods giant Adidas. It was a deal that was due to expire at the end of 1985 and Adidas had reportedly instructed Beckenbauer that it would not be renewed unless he returned to West Germany. As long as he stayed and played in the States he was of little use to them. When Beckenbauer finally made his mind up to return, he informed Adidas and was promptly given a lifetime promotional contract with the company. 'I was told I always had a job with Warner Communications,' Beckenbauer said of the Cosmos's parent company, 'but as what? As Mickey Mouse? Or is it Bugs Bunny?'

Beckenbauer's decision to quit the Cosmos seemed sensible. Not only was there a tangible sense that the NASL had already peaked, but Beckenbauer now had the perfect opportunity to return home to Germany and set himself and his family up for life.

In the regular season, Giorgio Chinaglia had continued to be the forward to fear in the NASL and his return of thirty-two goals in as many games represented yet another remarkable season for the striker. It seemed that regardless of whoever had the misfortune to sit in the coach's chair, Chinaglia recognized that once he crossed that white line it was his responsibility to find the net. It was a task he performed with ruthless efficacy.

Chinaglia's tally in the regular season may have been extraordinary but it paled into insignificance compared to his

performances in the play-offs. In the eight games (including
the Soccer Bowl itself) the Italian found the net eighteen times.
In one game against Tulsa, he scored seven goals in an 8–1
win. In the NASL's fourteen years, no player had ever scored
more than five goals, a record shared by several players,
including Chinaglia, and a feat rightly recognized by everyone
who witnessed the Italian's one-man show, even Tulsa's shell-
shocked keeper Eugene DuChateau. 'The man is incredible,'
he said resignedly.

Coach Weisweiler was more lavish in his praise. In the
locker room after the game, the Cosmos trainer Joel Rosenstein
squeezed some eye drops into Weisweiler's left eye. 'You see,'
joked the coach. 'My eyes can't believe what they just saw.'

The NASL commissioner Phil Woosnam, meanwhile, told
the *New York Times* that Chinaglia was one of the great strikers
in history. 'You put him in the same category with Ferenc
Puskás, Pelé and Jimmy Greaves. They are the best finishers
of our time.'

At the press conference, Chinaglia was, understandably, a
man in demand. As he cradled the match ball, presented to
him by the referee, John Davies, he was besieged by the media
and had to battle his way through to the phone to take a
congratulatory call from Steve Ross, who was still recuperating
at home in the Hamptons. When he returned to face the press,
Chinaglia, a man of many words, found it difficult to put his
achievement into perspective. 'It was a beautiful night,' he
beamed.

As the soccer world united in acclamation of Chinaglia, it
emerged that not everyone appreciated the Italian's latest feat,
especially Mario Mariani, (a.k.a. Bugs Bunny). 'I would do a
lap around the stadium every time a goal would be scored,
that was my thing,' explains Mariani. 'I had to do seven laps
and you know, by the fifth one the fans were thinking how

the heck can this guy do [another] set of laps around the stadium in that costume in the middle of the summer here in the sweltering humidity of New Jersey.'

The Cosmos went on to a third NASL title in four seasons. Despite some initial resistance from their opponents, the Fort Lauderdale Strikers, the Soccer Bowl ended in a comprehensive 3–0 win for the New Yorkers, Giorgio Chinaglia scoring twice and taking the awards for the game's and the play-offs' Most Valuable Player. 'We had something to prove this season, something to prove today,' he said. 'I also had something to prove because unfortunately I must prove myself every game. There are many people who would like to crucify me if I make a mistake or if I fail.'

As it had for his predecessor, Pelé, Soccer Bowl had proved to be a fitting finale to Franz Beckenbauer's time with the Cosmos. As the game ended, he loped across the field at Washington's RFK Stadium, keeping himself to himself and standing at the back of the pack as the players performed a lap of honour. Unlike Pelé, though, there were no tears, precious few hugs and nobody saw fit to carry him off the field. That, apparently, was the way 'The Kaiser' wanted it.

The jubilation of another Soccer Bowl success was short-lived and not merely because of Beckenbauer's imminent departure. In playing Beckenbauer in his favoured position of sweeper in the game, coach Hennes Weisweiler had been forced to drop Carlos Alberto, the NASL's four-time defender of the year. Having paced the hotel corridors until 5 a.m. on the day of the game considering his line-up, Weisweiler made what he called 'one of the hardest decisions I have ever made in soccer', adding that 'Carlos was a true sportsman about it. He said he understood.'

Perhaps Weisweiler's explanation of his decision lost something in the translation. With ten minutes to go in the game, Weisweiler had ushered Alberto to warm up and prepare to take the field, but the chain-smoking Brazilian, clearly riled, waved him away. 'Why go in with ten minutes left?' he said later. 'I feel very bad. I have spoken with Rafael [de la Sierra] about this. I am not sure I can play for this coach again next year. I may not be back.'

Neither the result nor the fact that it had been over-shadowed by Weisweiler's wrangle with Carlos Alberto came as much of a shock. Indeed, the row was still rumbling on when, three days after the Soccer Bowl, over 71,000 – the Giants Stadium's largest crowd of the year – turned out for Franz Beckenbauer's farewell game, an exhibition match between the Cosmos and a Select Stars XI, cherry-picked from the rest of the NASL.

While it would have been entirely appropriate that so many supporters had turned out to show their appreciation for the German legend, the brutal truth was that they had actually shown up to see Pelé, who was making his first appearance in a Cosmos shirt since his retirement in 1977. Now forty and working for the Cosmos as a consultant, Pelé had agreed to make a guest appearance for Beckenbauer and in the forty-three minutes he played showed flashes of the transcendent talent that had taken him to the very peak of the world game. He even scored, although the Cosmos would go on to lose 3–2.

When he left the field just before half-time, the Brazilian turned to Beckenbauer and handed him his number ten shirt and as he walked off the pitch, waving, he received the kind of ovation that suggested it was his benefit match and not the farewell game for Franz Beckenbauer. 'When the Cosmos won the 1977 NASL championship in my last year, it was a perfect going-away present for me, and Franz Beckenbauer had a lot to do with that championship,' said Pelé. 'I hope that by playing in his farewell game, I can help in some way to make his going-away present just as memorable.'

When Beckenbauer first touched down in New York in 1977 he had doubted whether he could ever replicate the impact that Pelé had had on the game of soccer in the States. Although there was no doubt that he was one of the most influential players of his generation, Beckenbauer lacked the natural charisma and gregarious nature that Pelé possessed, and while he had given his all for the Cosmos, his quiet demeanour hadn't really endeared him to the crowd in the same way as they took to the Brazilian.

Even his perfunctory farewell speech compared badly to Pelé's. Whereas the Brazilian had demanded that the entire crowd at Giants Stadium repeat the word 'Love' three times, Beckenbauer appeared on the pitch at half-time and said: 'You are the best fans in the world. Good luck to you and good health.'

The country was buzzing. Not with the general election result that saw a sixty-nine-year-old former Hollywood actor, Ronald Reagan, chosen as the US's oldest-ever president, but with the lasting drama of who shot J. R. Ewing? CBS's hit soap *Dallas* had ended its spring series with Larry Hagman's devious oilman gunned down in his office by a mystery assailant, and everyone had an opinion as to who had carried out the attack. When the identity of the attacker was finally revealed – it was his mistress and sister-in-law Kristin – the show broke all records, registering a 53.3 rating for a 76 per cent share.

How Phil Woosnam could have done with such a cliff-hanger in the NASL. Sadly, short of engineering a plot to have

Giorgio Chinaglia gunned down at Giants Stadium there was little he could do to convince ABC to extend their coverage of his league. For the new season, only play-off games would feature on national television. 'We had to make a hard decision. And we decided not to continue,' explains Jim Spence. 'We really hoped when we got involved that the NASL would be a long-term franchise for ABC Sports... we didn't think it was going to be hugely successful, from a financial point of view or a rating point of view, but we thought it could be and hoped it would be successful enough that we would be able to continue on a long-term basis.'

Soccer, the sport of the future, was fast becoming a thing of the past. Contrary to the NASL's line, the object now was not expansion but survival. Everywhere, there were teams fighting for their existence. The Houston Hurricane, the Rochester Lancers, the Atlanta Chiefs and the Detroit Express were all on the brink of folding, and even Gordon Bradley's Washington Diplomats, a team with Johan Cruyff and a 65 per cent season increase in attendances, and which registered a 53,000 crowd for the game against the Cosmos, were battling extinction. They even mooted the idea of moving the franchise to New York but were quickly rebuffed by Warner.

The well-heeled and curious would no longer throw money at clubs in the hope that they too could find their own Pelé and magically uncover some dormant interest in the game in their area. Financiers were now realizing that buying into a franchise was not just a gamble but economic recklessness. It didn't help that changes in the tax legislation had also made investing in a franchise less attractive (if that were possible). Previously, private individuals with no association with sport could use a loss on a soccer team as a tax write-off but now only those who made their money in sports, like Warner or Madison Square Garden (owner of the Diplomats), could claim such rebates.

The difference between Warner and MSG, though, was that the Cosmos, regardless of its deficit, still performed a useful function for its owners in that whenever the team traversed the globe (as it did in the post-season tour to Europe and Egypt in October 1980) it did so with a clear objective – to help Warner break into untapped or valuable markets.

With franchises failing and television turning its back on soccer, it had become glaringly obvious that the NASL's rapid expansion from eighteen teams in 1977 to twenty-four teams the following year was the primary reason for what many saw as impending self-destruction. Twenty-four teams meant having to divide what little TV money there was an additional six ways. It also meant there were now an extra six stops in the schedule, which meant further expense. 'We had eighteen clubs, six were doing OK, six were doing great, six we had to get rid of. [Then] we added six more clubs,' recalls Clive Toye. 'So now we are six good, six OK, twelve rubbish.'

For all its good intentions, it appeared that the NASL had mistaken the boom of the Cosmos, with its sell-out crowds, celebrity-laden stands and star-studded side, for some wider upsurge in the game nationally. 'Most of the people [franchise owners] who came in late were attracted by what they saw at Giants Stadium, which was a big crowd, beautiful stadium and all these celebrities,' adds Toye. '[They said] [f]or three million bucks I can buy myself into that.'

It was apparent that for as long as Warner bankrolled the Cosmos the NASL title was theirs for the taking every season. The other franchises could chase the dream, but unless they had a sugar daddy with pockets as cavernous as Steve Ross's they were always going to be fighting a losing battle.

At the NASL's board of directors meeting at Chicago's O'Hare Hilton hotel in December, the vexatious issue of the Cosmos came up once more. Terry Hanson, vice-president of the Atlanta Chiefs, was one of the most vocal on the subject. 'A lot of people in the league followed the example of the Cosmos and spent money on players. I think that was a mistake,' he maintained. 'In Atlanta we learned that our objective was to create a sound business rather than trying to compete with the Cosmos to win the championship. I tell you, those Cosmos were the best and the worst thing that happened to this league.'

CHAPTER 12

ALL OR NOTHIN' AT ALL

After the shock of his heart attack in June 1980, Steve Ross booked a cruise on the *QE2* for him and Amanda. It was part recuperation, part reward for Amanda's efforts in helping him back to health. While his intentions were admirable, Ross couldn't have foreseen that the trip would signal the beginning of the end for their marriage. Stuck on the ship for days on end with nowhere to run or hide, Ross and Burden realized how distant they had become from each other.

Matters failed to improve when they returned to Manhattan and argued about where they were going to live. Ross had ambitious plans to redevelop his grand apartment at 740 Park Avenue and employ a large staff to help maintain it, but although she had come from an affluent background, Burden was indifferent to the trappings of Steve Ross's wealth and wanted something smaller and more private.

Invariably, Ross got his way. Within a week of the move, however, Burden would be gone. Divorce proceedings were instigated. Within months, Ross would be back in the arms of Courtney Sale.

Having lost another wife, Ross would also lose his best friend soon after. On 9 February 1981, Jay Emmett, Steve Ross's closest friend and confidant, pleaded guilty to a racketeering charge and, as part of a plea bargain, agreed to co-operate with the authorities as the investigation into the Westchester Theater continued. To his horror, that co-operation would entail his endeavouring to tape a telephone call with Steve Ross – now the US Attorney General's prime target – in which he would have to persuade his friend to incriminate himself. It was something that Emmett just couldn't do and Ross would eventually emerge from the investigation unscathed.

Although Emmett did not have to surrender his Warner stock (said to be worth around $7 million), it was the end of his career at the company and, more significantly, the end of his friendship with Steve Ross. After his guilty plea (and a suspended sentence) Jay Emmett resigned from WCI and 'The Two Musketeers', as Mark Ross calls them, would never speak again. 'When Jay left, the glue was gone. The place was never the same,' says Norman Samnick.

The continuing Westchester investigation took the gloss off another stratospheric set of results for Atari. With the nation's video game arcades now taking an astonishing $5 billion annually, and public interest in space exploration reignited by the inaugural flight of the space shuttle Columbia, Atari had cemented its position as the market leader with the release of another hit game, 'Asteroids'. Picking up where Space Invaders had left off, Asteroids was an updated version of an earlier game developed by Nolan Bushnell called 'Computer Space' and capitalized on the public's voracious appetite for virtual intergalactic warfare.

By now, the video arcade had hammered the final nail in pinball's coffin and was fast usurping the movie theatre as the place for young people to spend their time and, crucially, their money. Everywhere you looked there were video games. From Safeways to Sears, from pizza parlours to hotel lobbies, kids would turn up with their quarters and forego that second

Coke in favour of another shot at defending the earth from alien aggressors. If you were good, you could make that quarter last half an hour. If you weren't, you could still hang around and watch some other kid top that high score. In Beaumont, Texas, for example, one David Jeanise broke the record for the 'Asteroids' high score by racking up 22,254,110 points in a game that lasted 36 hours and 29 minutes at the town's Rainbow Roller Rink. As one Atari official said, 'One of the secrets of the success of our games is that the most gnomish kid can play and become a champion. You don't have to be a big athlete or a good dancer. And every kid knows he can beat his parents.'

Despite less than impressive years from the movie and record divisions and the downturn in the economy, the success of Atari – it had now amassed annual profits close to $300 million – had helped double the value of Warner's stock to $61 a share and analysts were suggesting that Atari was now arguably bigger than its parent company. Towards the end of the year, Atari head Raymond Kassar reported to the budget meeting of WCI and declared that, if their projections were right, Atari would be pulling in revenues of $6 billion per annum by 1986. While Steve Ross and the board were delighted with the forecast, they couldn't have been as happy as Raymond Kassar, who would take home a $6 million bonus for his endeavours.

The success of Atari was in direct contrast to the fortunes of the NASL. With clubs haemorrhaging cash and fans in their thousands finding other ways to spend their time, the league roster was cut from twenty-four to twenty teams, as the franchises at Houston, Memphis, Rochester and Detroit folded. Moreover, FIFA had also run out of patience with the NASL's tinkering with the laws and had threatened the USSF with expulsion unless they reverted to the same rules that every other affiliated association used. That meant the end to the 35-yard line and the NASL's unique interpretation of the offside rule. Failure to comply and the NASL would be deemed an outlaw league and therefore unable to trade with those leagues around the world still associated to FIFA. With no option but to conform, the NASL reluctantly agreed to discontinue the 35-yard line rule at the end of the 1981 season. 'I still believe that the 35-yard line made for a more attack-minded game,' says Phil Woosnam today, 'but you can't really argue with FIFA.'

The Cosmos, meanwhile, had embarked on another of its marathon pre-season expeditions. This time, it was nine-game tour of South America taking in Argentina, Chile, Uruguay, Brazil and ending with a stop-off in Mexico on the way home. Like it or not, since Pelé joined in 1975 the Cosmos had become soccer's version of the Harlem Globetrotters. In that time, it had been on two, sometimes three tours a year, visited six continents and played in front of crowds usually far in excess of those it would attract back home.

Not only did its tours give a welcome opportunity for some of the younger players to experience playing against established teams in front of real football crowds that fought, swore and threw things on the pitch, but they also generated considerable amounts of revenue for the club, something it badly needed. In that time, it had beaten some of the leading names in world football such as Santos of Brazil, Roma of Italy and FC Cologne of Germany but it had also been humbled by a long list of teams whose names it would rather forget. That, according to Ahmet Ertegun, was part and parcel of being the Cosmos. 'Playing in a different country every three days in front of packed stadiums may mean an embarrassing loss on occasion,' he told *The New York Times*. 'Our eventual goal is to be the best team in the world, and the way to get there is to play anywhere against the best at any time. We've never shied away from anyone.'

While the results on the tour were typically erratic, the fans still turned out in numbers to see the Cosmos. In one six-day period, the Cosmos beat Penerol of Uruguay 4–3, lost 3–1 to São Paulo of Brazil and then defeated the Paraguayan national team 5–2. The total attendance for those three games alone exceeded 135,000. Proof, if it were needed, that even if the NASL was flagging, the Cosmos was still box office.

A few suspect results, though, were the least of the club's concerns, and trouble, never far behind the Cosmos, caught up with the team in Chile. After a 1–0 defeat at the hands of Colo Colo in Santiago, Carlos Alberto decided to take a flight to his home in Rio de Janeiro, Brazil, to meet up with parents and take part in the annual Mardi Gras carnival. Unfortunately, he didn't tell the coach.

It would be the final spat between Carlos Alberto and Weisweiler. When Carlos Alberto finally returned to the team, Weisweiler handed him an indefinite suspension without pay for his unscheduled sojourn, despite the Brazilian's insistence that Steve Ross had approved the trip.

Back in Manhattan, Carlos Alberto called a press conference on the roof terrace of his apartment on the Upper East Side to announce that he was leaving the Cosmos. Tearfully, he told reporters that the only reason he was going was because of the continuing difficulties he was experiencing with coach Weisweiler. After being dropped for the Soccer Bowl and then being suspended for his trip to Rio, the sweeper had decided that, at thirty-six years old and having been the NASL's best defender for the last three years, he no longer needed the kind of treatment he felt he was receiving. 'The Cosmos gave me two options,' he said. 'One was to retire with pay for the last year of my contract, and the other was to find a team for myself.' A few weeks later and with a number of clubs keen to sign him, Carlos Alberto did just that, securing a three-year deal with the California Surf.

The loss of a player as influential as Carlos Alberto may have finished teams with less strength in depth and less backing than the Cosmos, but the New Yorkers had an embarrassment of alternatives to fill the void. Not only did they have Jeff Durgan in the heart of their defence, they had several players who could play the sweeper role if required. On the trip to South America, for example, Weisweiler took the opportunity of Carlos Alberto's absence to experiment with a variety of players in his position, including Vladislav Bogicevic and the defender they had just re-acquired from the Washington Diplomats, Bob Iarusci. 'I was in Acapulco on holiday and Giorgio happened to be there too. Chinaglia had the penthouse at Warner's Las Brisas resort and I was in one of the hotels on the strip. Anyway, he found out that I was in town and called me... before I knew it he was on the phone to the general manager at the Cosmos and getting me transferred back.'

Both Bogicevic and Iarusci would perform admirably in the sweeper's role, but neither would ever be Carlos Alberto. While the likes of Neeskens, Cabanas, Van der Elst and even an ageing Chinaglia were all still capable of dictating matches in the NASL, they were manifestly not the kind of name players who would fill the swathes of empty seats at Giants Stadium. With no Pelé, Beckenbauer or Carlos Alberto, the Cosmos had become a team without an A-list soccer star and that, with attendances heading in the wrong direction, was a problem.

Even the second Trans-Atlantic Challenge Cup and games against Scotland's Glasgow Celtic, England's Southampton (featuring Kevin Keegan) and the Seattle Sounders failed to charm the crowds back to Meadowlands. Again, the Cosmos went undefeated but this time relinquished its title to Seattle on goals scored.

Crowds or no crowds, Giorgio Chinaglia still wasn't happy. If he wasn't bemoaning the lack of flair in the side or taking pot shots at the coach, he was finding the most inconsequential things to complain about. An hour before the kick-off of the evening game in Montreal, for example, he was seen stomping around the locker room like a grizzly with a migraine. Somebody, it transpired, had forgotten to pack his favourite jockstrap and the replacement they had found for him wasn't up to his usual high standards. It was time to call on Joe Manfredi again. 'You know Giorgio,' smiles Manfredi, 'got to get what he wants, and when he wants it.'

With the players changed and ready to take the field to warm up, Manfredi dived into a cab and demanded to be taken straight to the nearest sports store. He arrived just as the security guard was closing the doors. After some gentle persuasion and desperate name-dropping, Manfredi was allowed in and press-ganged the nearest sales assistant into helping him in his search for a jockstrap. 'She thought I was crazy,' laughs Manfredi.

Manfredi returned to the Olympic Stadium brandishing the jockstrap like Neville Chamberlain and his piece of paper. He arrived to find the locker room empty, except for the lone figure of Giorgio Chinaglia, sat in the corner. 'Giorgio would not go on the field,' he continues. 'Everybody went on the field to warm up, Giorgio didn't go. He was waiting for the jockstrap.'

The dearth of star talent at the Cosmos didn't detract from its results. As usual, the team breezed into the play-offs as Eastern Division champions with a 23–9 regular season record.

Superficially, that record looked solid enough but there was mounting concern that the team was running out of steam at a crucial part of the season. Going into the play-offs, the Cosmos had lost four of its last six games, and in the last eight matches, Giorgio Chinaglia had found the net just three times. For almost any other striker in the league, it would have been a perfectly adequate return, but for Chinaglia, whose goal a game ratio was incomparable, it represented something approaching a slump.

Needless to say, it wasn't his fault. Instead, Chinaglia laid the blame squarely at the feet of Hennes Weisweiler and, in doing so, fired the first shots in a feud with the coach that would make his previous quarrels with Gordon Bradley, Ken Furphy and Eddie Firmani look like a minor misunder- standing. 'I'm complaining about the style of play,' said the Cosmos captain. 'We should attack more. This guy is very conservative. We won only one game comfortably all year.' The fact that he had started referring to Weisweiler as 'this guy' was a sure sign that the once harmonious relationship between coach and captain was as good as over.

Talking to the *The New York Times*, Weisweiler conceded that the bond had been broken, although he considered Chinaglia's persistent interference in team selection and tactics, not to mention his lack of goals in the tail end of the regular season, as the primary factors in their dispute. 'I am the chief of this team. You cannot do this with me,' he insisted. 'That is how my friendship with Chinaglia started to go to bad.'

Having witnessed the treatment Carlos Alberto had received at the hands of Weisweiler, Chinaglia was concerned that he too would soon be asking the players on the bench to squeeze up. He was, after all, thirty-four years old and what pace he once possessed was now disappearing. Indeed, rumours would circulate that Chinaglia's place in the Cosmos starting line-up was no longer guaranteed and that Weisweiler was considering relegating the NASL's all-time record goalscorer to the bench. Not so, said Weisweiler. 'I never threatened to bench Giorgio because I know that the great scorers sometimes go into slumps. But Giorgio is thirty-five years old next year. Maybe he knows I am tough enough to bench him if he does not score.'

It certainly sounded like a threat. As the Cosmos progressed to another Soccer Bowl final – Chinaglia scoring six times in five play-off games – the feud between coach and player simmered and distracted press and fans alike away from the fact that for the first time since Pelé's final year, the average attendance for the Cosmos's home games had dipped under 35,000. The second leg of the semi-final against Fort Lauderdale revealed the scale of the decline. In 1977, the same match-up had drawn over 77,000 fans to Giants Stadium for the play-off game. Now, just 31,112 showed up.

The contrast with US pro-football could not have been more striking. As attendances across the NASL plummeted, the NFL had also capitalized on growing disillusionment with baseball – a mid-season players' strike had found little support among fans – and registered an all-time record attendance average of 60,000 fans per game.

That said, close to 37,000 would turn up in the driving rain to see the season showpiece at the Exhibition Stadium in Toronto, where the Cosmos's opponents would be the Chicago Sting, coached by the former USA international Willy Roy. As a city, Chicago had been without a championship in any sport for over eighteen years. The last had been the National Football League title won by the Chicago Bears in 1963. The Cosmos, in comparison, had grown accustomed to winning and any season without the Soccer Bowl trophy could only ever be deemed a failure.

It would be a closely fought contest but one that didn't really live up to its pre-match billing. While the Sting had already beaten the Cosmos twice in the regular season, this was their first appearance in the Soccer Bowl. After ninety minutes of play, though, the teams were level, both having failed to score. The Sting, aggressive and resolute, had taken the game to the reigning champions but had been kept at bay by the Cosmos keeper, Hubert Birkenmeier. The Cosmos, meanwhile, had been conservative and reserved. There was only a Giorgio Chinaglia scissors kick that came remotely close to breaching the defences of the Sting.

A tie at the final whistle meant another shootout. Even in the shootout, goals would once more be at a premium. With only Vladislav Bogicevic managing to convert his attempt for the Cosmos, it was left to the Sting's American midfielder Rudy Glenn to wrap up Chicago's first NASL title and condemn the Cosmos to its first Soccer Bowl defeat in four appearances. 'I think Chicago wanted it more, and they took it,' Giorgio Chinaglia said impassively after the game.

The Cosmos's Dutch defender Wim Rijsbergen was less gracious in defeat. 'If they were the better team they should have finished first in the regular season,' he said, referring to the Cosmos's five-point advantage over the Sting after thirty-two games. 'I grant you they beat us twice in the regular season, but if they were truly better they shouldn't have to go to a shootout here tonight.'

For Bob Iarusci, it was especially difficult to take. Not only was he playing in his hometown in front of his friends and family, he also had to suffer the ignominy of missing the decisive shootout attempt. 'I was the last guy that night. It was pouring rain and everybody had missed. And we had Julio César Romero, [Johan] Neeskens, [Roberto] Cabanas and François Van der Elst and they all refused to take the shot.

The coach said, "Will you take it?" and I said, "Yeah, I don't care." So I took it, the goalkeeper made a really good save and that was it... The hometown boy could have made good, but I didn't.'

With the game over and the Cosmos now only holding the title of former NASL champions, the gloves came off between Giorgio Chinaglia and Hennes Weisweiler. Incensed at the way the team was being handled and the manner in which it had succumbed in the Soccer Bowl, Chinaglia vowed not to go on the post-season tours to Canada and Europe if Weisweiler was still in charge of the Cosmos. 'There's no way I can do that,' he said. 'I have to look in the mirror.'

Chinaglia's objections were myriad. Under Weisweiler, he believed that the Cosmos had betrayed its tradition of eye-catching soccer in favour of more conservative and precautionary strategies. The coach, Chinaglia said, had 'never tried to make the game more entertaining'. Moreover, the striker believed that unlike him his heart wasn't really in American soccer, maintaining that he seemed to show no great interest in developing soccer on a wider scale. He had a point. Since arriving in the States, Weisweiler hadn't given a single clinic, nor made one public appearance on behalf of the team or, for that matter, attended any of the monthly meetings of the two Cosmos fan clubs.

It was a view reinforced by Julio Mazzei. 'Here your job as coach is 40 per cent on the field, 60 per cent off the field. You must meet the press, soccer clubs, scout players, sell the game. One time I had three hundred coaches for a clinic, and Hennes said he didn't have the time to meet people like that.'

For all Chinaglia's concerns, Weisweiler actually did have more important things to worry about. At sixty-one, he had just become a father for the first time and he was still in demand as a coach back home. 'I have no reason to quit. No,

☻ Once in a Lifetime

never. I have one more year on my contract,' he insisted. 'Jobs are not a problem for me. I have clubs in Germany waiting for me. I am not afraid of that I can get along with Giorgio Chinaglia. All we have to do is give a little.'

That, clearly, wasn't going to happen. As long as Giorgio Chinaglia continued to be so close to Steve Ross, there was little chance that any coach, regardless of reputation or record, would be given preferential treatment over the chairman of the board's chosen one. Indeed, Ross had already sounded Chinaglia out about taking over as general manager of the Cosmos when his playing days were over. For a coach like Weisweiler, who had never really endeared himself to the New York fans, either with his brand of football or with his personality, there was only ever going to be one outcome.

While a truce was called for the post-season tour – Chinaglia eventually relented because he had 'an obligation to his team-mates' – it was clear that Weisweiler was now living on bor-rowed time. Since Chinaglia's arrival at the club in 1976, no coach had survived such a public dispute with the Italian and Chinaglia wasn't about to start giving way now. The only remaining question was whether the club could afford the $350,000 pay-off that terminating Weisweiler's contract would entail.

To his credit, Weisweiler persevered, making the best of an unenviable position. All the time, Weisweiler talked down the rift with his leading striker, publicly welcoming Chinaglia's renewed commitment to the team and looking forward to reclaiming the NASL title the following season.

The tour came and went, with the usual maddening mix of notable victories and comical defeats (the 7–1 thumping against Lille of France was the most perplexing). Weisweiler remained dignified throughout, never doing anything that might jeopardize the compensation package that was surely

210

coming his way. It was as if he was just waiting for the cheque to arrive.

Another man who was covering himself was Steve Ross. As Raymond Kassar announced plans to merge Atari's many offices in Sunnyvale, California into one fifty-acre, $300 million 'Atari Campus', the chairman of the Warner board was busy making plans to protect himself in the event of Atari's lifespan being shorter than analysts the world over expected.

As the financial world fawned over the rocket ship that was Atari, Ross initiated a process that would see 360,000 of his Warner shares transferred to a family partnership, a move that would not only protect him from any reversal in Atari's fortunes but also assist WCI in reducing their tax burden.

It was a typically judicious move from Ross. Throughout his time as the head of Warner, Ross had never owned more than 1 per cent of the company, thereby sparing himself any of the entrepreneurial risk that other executives took while still allowing him to claim handsome remuneration packages. In 1981, for instance, Ross took a salary and bonus package of $3.2 million and a further $7.4 million from exercising a variety of other bonus schemes. It was proof that while his dalliance with the Cosmos had perhaps fostered an image of a big-spending sports nut with scant regard for budgets, the reality was that he was still one of the smartest operators in town.

CHAPTER 13

DANCING IN THE DARK

Hennes Weisweiler became the former Cosmos coach on 16 February 1982. The club cited a 'divergence of views as far as the immediate future' of the team was concerned as the principal reason for the West German's departure.

In a three-paragraph statement, the Cosmos said that Nesuhi Ertegun, the chairman of the board, had returned from several meetings with Weisweiler in Europe and that those meetings had concluded that there were irreparable differences between the club and the coach. The statement also said that Weisweiler 'indicated his desire to follow the games of the German National Team', which was playing in Spain in the World Cup Finals, and that the Cosmos was now actively looking for a new coach with international credentials. 'Quite frankly,' said the general manager, Tom Werblin, 'I don't know who that is.'

While reports linked Weisweiler's assistant, the former Cosmos goalkeeper and coach of its indoor side, Erol Yasin, to the vacant position, it would be Professor Julio Mazzei who would once again step forward to fill the gap on an interim basis. 'I don't want to feel like Bob Lemon,' said Mazzei, referring to the ever-changing position of the New York Yankees' manager. 'I just hope the Cosmos will give me the opportunity to reach the championship game.'

The former Cosmos goalkeeper Shep Messing once said

that it was virtually impossible for young American players to get a break in the NASL because 'experience was spelled European'. Finally, though, after years of being overlooked in favour of expensive and often inadequate imports, a crop of talented Americans and Canadians were beginning to make a name for themselves in the NASL, beneficiaries not only of the league's development programmes for North American players but also of the declining salaries on offer to foreign players.

The inescapable conclusion, however, was that, for all the progress being made by the homegrown talent, the NASL was now in freefall. By the start of the new season, just fourteen teams had posted their bond with the NASL, as the franchises at Calgary, California, Los Angeles, Minnesota and Washington all fell by the wayside. Lamar Hunt's Dallas Tornado, the last remaining survivor of the original NASL line-up, would also fold before the season commenced.

The only silver lining, for the Cosmos at least, was that with the passing of the California Surf came the news that Carlos Alberto was now a free agent. Despite interest from the New Jersey Rockets in the flourishing Major Indoor Soccer League, the veteran Brazilian had answered a call from Professor Mazzei, who convinced him that he could still be a key player for the Cosmos, despite his advancing years. 'The way Carlos Alberto read the game, he's better at five kilometres an hour than someone who can run a hundred kilometres an hour,' said the coach. 'Every time I look at him play I think of Charles Mingus, the late musician. Mingus said to make easy situations complicated, it's easy – to make complicated situations simple takes creativity. That's Carlos Alberto.'

With Weisweiler gone and his old friend back at the helm, it hadn't taken much persuasion to lure Carlos Alberto back to New York for a final season. Initially, his contract only required him to be a member of the Cosmos's team in the NASL's winter indoor league, but as the outdoor season approached it made sense to take the Brazilian back into the fold of the outdoor team.

The existence of two national indoor leagues, especially the MISL, had proved problematic for the main NASL outdoor league. Since Earl Foreman started the six-a-side MISL in 1977, it had prospered into a product quite unlike its struggling counterpart, growing from the six original teams to fourteen just six seasons later. With healthy crowds, a glut of goals, laser beam light shows and more dancing girls than Broadway, it had billed itself as the 'human pinball game' and was a markedly different contest to the outdoor version of soccer.

Although the NASL had experimented with indoor leagues since 1979-80, the Cosmos had never taken part, but with younger players needing the experience and more established players needing the workout, the club decided to throw its hat in the ring for the 1981-82 season.

Now, more than ever, a presence in the indoor league seemed to make some kind of sense, primarily because a new television network, ESPN, were carrying the NASL's indoor games. Indeed, without ESPN, nobody apart from the 13,000 fans who turned up at the Byrne Meadowlands Arena would have been able to see Giorgio Chinaglia score a record-equalling seven goals in a 14–10 win over the Chicago Sting.

Despite the presence of the NASL's flagship franchise in the competition, there was still a sense that the indoor games were nothing more than a warm-up for the outdoor season. The problem was that nobody could say with any authority just what kind of season that was going to be. It was that uncertainty which prompted a radical change in the hierarchy of the NASL. On 25 June 1982 it was announced that the millionaire businessman J. Howard Samuels had been appointed its president and CEO, and while Woosnam would retain his title as commissioner, he would from here on answer to Samuels.

Introducing Samuels to the media, Chicago Sting owner Lee Stern was confident that the man nicknamed 'Harry the Horse' for his work in establishing the state's Off Track Betting programme could provide the impetus needed to revive the NASL. 'Our new man,' beamed Stern, 'is the man who's going to lead soccer to the pinnacle.'

It was a comment born out of optimism rather than any belief that the situation could be salvaged, but in the circumstances Howard Samuels did seem a pretty good bet. Certainly he had the pedigree. As a lieutenant-colonel in General Patton's Third Army he had helped liberate the concentration camp at Buchenwald during the Second World War. He had also been an aide to Presidents Kennedy, Johnson and Carter, marched in Selma, Alabama, with Martin Luther King and twice run to be Governor of New York.

Something as trivial as single-handedly rescuing the NASL should have been a breeze for Samuels, but when he was given access to the full horror of the NASL accounts, all he could say was 'These guys are crazy!' Later, he would conclude that the NASL was 'a major league operating with a minor league income'.

Lack of money wasn't merely the preoccupation of the Cosmos and the NASL. Across America, the general public was feeling the downturn in the economy that had resulted in the nation's biggest depression in the post-war period. Unemployment had reached 10.6 per cent (the highest level since 1940) and interest rates had soared into double digits. With a cloud hanging over the country, it was hardly surprising that anyone with spare cash at the end of the week wasn't going to use it to watch the NASL. Moreover, young Americans had much better ways to spend their time as well as their money. By the end of the year, some twenty million people across the States had caught genital herpes.

In New York, and in the South Bronx especially, there was a new street sub-culture developing, based around the growing interest in rap music, break-dancing and graffiti art. Increasingly, rap groups were breaking away from conventional lyrics based around good times and girls to address the real problems in the ghettos. It was a thriving scene best encapsulated in Grandmaster Flash and The Furious Five's epic single 'The Message'.

This was also the age of a new radicalism. Whereas the political demonstrations of the 1960s and 1970s had often ended with police baton charges, the new decade had seen more peaceful protests, with riot gear and teargas a thing of the past. In June, for instance, a nuclear disarmament rally attracted a record 750,000 people to Central Park's Great Lawn, the biggest political rally in American history. The fact that the demonstration concluded with a free concert by James Taylor, Jackson Browne and Bruce Springsteen may also have bolstered the turnout.

Despite the parlous state of the economy, there was still one area in which people were spending their disposable income. After 1981, a succession of big films had hit the nation's movie theatres. *Tootsie*, *Conan the Barbarian* and *Rocky III* all recorded impressive box office returns. None, though, was bigger than *E.T. – The Extra-Terrestrial*, Steven Spielberg's tale of an alien who lands on earth.

The allure of such a popular film proved irresistible to Steve Ross. Prior to *E.T.*, Atari had never paid more than $1 million to license a game. Moreover, they had never made a computer game based on a movie. Ross, however, was convinced the box office success of *E.T.* and the rude health of Atari was a match made in commercial heaven, and over the course of a weekend at Ross's home in East Hampton he struck a deal with his close friend and the film's director, Steven Spielberg, to make a game out of the film. The price, extraordinarily, was $23 million.

The rationale behind Ross riding roughshod over the Atari management and offering Spielberg such a handsome price for the rights did, however, make some sense. As well as buying the name and logo of the most successful movie of all time, it also served as a signal of intent to Spielberg, a director he had long courted for Warner's movie division but who was tied to a long-term contract with their rivals Universal.

Raymond Kassar and his team of executives at Atari were aghast. While the price itself was enough to make them think that Steve Ross had abandoned the kind of astute deal-making that had defined his career, it was the timescale of the game's production that caused most alarm. One of Spielberg's conditions was that the game had to be ready and in the shops for Christmas. The deal was agreed in July and the game had to be designed and marketed in just four weeks and not the minimum of six months to which Atari was accustomed.

But if any company could pull it off it was Atari, which, by this time, had hit stratospheric heights of commercial success. By 1982, the company was producing more than half of WCI's $4 billion revenues and over 65 per cent of its profits and the Atari bosses were intent on enjoying the good times. When Raymond Kassar announced that Atari's sales in 1981 had passed the $1 billion mark he decided to hold the company's annual sales meeting not in some luxury Californian resort as had become the norm but in Monte Carlo, at the famous Hotel de Paris. Money, it seemed, really was no object. Hardly surprising, then, that over the course of 1981 and 1982 Atari passed on at least $100 million of its profits to shore up less successful parts of the Warner stable.

Faced with the challenge of enticing fans back to their games, the Cosmos moved to re-sign one of the players from its golden era – Steve Hunt. The English winger had returned to the UK at the end of 1978 to try and prove himself in the First Division with Coventry City and earn himself a shot at Ron Greenwood's England team. Now, with the English season over, the Cosmos had pitched in with a $100,000 offer to take him back to New York, with an option for Coventry to buy him back for the same price at the end of the NASL season in September 1982.

On and off the field Hunt was a changed man. In his first spell at the club, he was a young, newly married man with a mop of blond hair and, as Pelé discovered, a quickfire temper. Now, however, Hunt had returned as a father of two, with a more mature outlook and significantly less hair. 'The return of Steve Hunt is the most generous gift to our fans and the team,' announced the club's president, Ahmet Ertegun. 'His return to the Cosmos is one of the historic moments in our club because he is an electric and popular player.'

Hunt, meanwhile, was only too happy to return. 'I missed New York enormously when I got home. I realized what it was all about, what New York was all about and what I'd been part of,' he says. '[When I returned to England] [i]t was Coventry that I went to and no disrespect, but it wasn't the New York Cosmos.'

The move for Steve Hunt smacked of desperation. While the honest toil and creative spark that the Englishman could provide would be of undoubted benefit to the Cosmos, it was going to take more than a familiar face from yesteryear to turn things round at Giants Stadium. Another player who had returned to the club for a second spell was the Canadian defender, Bob Iarusci. 'I could sense that things weren't the same anymore. Franz Beckenbauer was about to leave and everything was going to be redimensioned because Warner were going to put less money into the club,' he says. 'Then they came to me and wanted to cut my salary. You know, I'd played on four championship teams, I was an All-Star and this is what it had come to… So I finished the season and then took an offer from Ron Newman at San Diego.'

In mid-July, the team returned from the longest NASL trip in their history but nobody noticed. Any self-respecting soccer fan was watching the World Cup Finals in Spain. It would be a memorable competition. Northern Ireland beat the hosts 1–0, England's Bryan Robson scored the fastest-ever World Cup goal, Kuwait walked off the pitch against France after a row with the referee, and the second-round game between Italy and Brazil was one of the most thrilling games in World Cup history.

Having edged past Brazil 3–2, Italy, with their striker Paulo Rossi at the height of his powers, would progress to the final, winning the tournament with a convincing 3–1 victory over West Germany. It was a contest notable not merely because it was the *Azzurri*'s third triumph in the competition but for the ABC commentator Jim McKay's faux pas during the game. When Italy scored their second goal, McKay momentarily forgot which sport he was covering. 'Italy,' he announced, 'leads fourteen to nothing!'

The fortnight away had done little for the Cosmos's league standing – it lost three out of its four games – and even less for team spirit. After three consecutive defeats at San Jose, Vancouver and Edmonton, the Cosmos arrived in Chicago for another game against the Sting. While it would win 2–1 and avoid recording its worst run of results since 1974, it was an incident in the match that made the headlines. And, as ever, it was Giorgio Chinaglia at the centre of events.

With only moments of the game remaining, the Cosmos broke out from defence, catching the Sting flat-footed. With a two on one advantage, the Paraguayan midfielder Julio César Romero bore down on goal, and rather than squaring the ball to the unmarked Chinaglia went for goal himself. When Romero missed the chance, Chinaglia saw red and raced across the field to admonish his team-mate. Never one to back down, the diminutive Paraguayan squared up to the veteran striker. After the final whistle, the two clashed again in the locker room, but as punches were about to be thrown, Julio Mazzei separated the players and an uneasy peace was restored. 'Everything is in the past and all forgotten,' said Romero later.

While the idea that two Cosmos players could come to blows was hardly news, the notion that Chinaglia, who at thirty-five years old had scored only twice in ten games, still cared so much was astonishing. Whatever his critics said about him, there was no doubting that Giorgio Chinaglia loved the game as much as ever.

The win against the Sting gave Mazzei some much-needed breathing space. Prior to the game, the Cosmos board had demanded a meeting with the coach to discuss his future but with Nesuhi Ertegun away on business the meeting failed to materialize, much to Mazzei's relief. 'It looks like they don't want to talk to me,' he told reporters after the game, 'and that's a good sign.'

With his rumoured dismissal averted, Mazzei rode his luck and guided the team through to August with seven con- secutive wins. It was a run based largely around Chinaglia's return to goalscoring form and the partnerships he had forged with the American internationals Hernan 'Chico' Borja and, to a lesser extent, Steve Moyers, who, like Carlos Alberto, had moved to New York in the California Surf fire sale. And, as was the norm, the Cosmos made the end-of-season play-offs at a canter.

While noticeably slower and less involved in games, Chinaglia was still as prolific as ever inside the penalty area. His winner in the semi-final game against the San Diego Sockers was typical of his new, languid approach to the game. Having done nothing apart from what the San Diego keeper Volkmar Gross would later describe as 'putting people to sleep', Chinaglia received the ball on the edge of the box, shifted the ball from his left to his right side and then flashed the ball past Gross for a sudden-death overtime winner. 'He's an endangered species,' said coach Mazzei after the match. 'His kind are disappearing.'

For their third consecutive Soccer Bowl (and their fifth in six seasons), the Cosmos would be pitted against the Seattle Sounders, a rerun of the 1977 championship game. As usual, the club pulled out all the stops to make the event a memorable one. There was one plane for the playing staff and the management, and another of United Airlines' DC–8s for the wives, girlfriends and the Cosmos girls. Upon arrival in San Diego, the players were taken to one hotel, the women to another. 'It took two or three Soccer Bowls, but we're finally getting this down pat,' explained Mark Brickley, the director of publicity for the Cosmos. 'We've learned the wives and guests must stay at a different hotel than the players, and the cheerleaders must stay isolated somewhere else.'

The game itself would be a close affair, but noticeably lacking in any of the passion or atmosphere enjoyed by other Soccer Bowl games. In the previous seven Soccer Bowls, there had always been some factor, be it a gleaming new stadium or a hometown team, to help generate public interest. Now, with the game held thousands of miles from Seattle *and* New York, just 22,634 fans turned up for the event – the lowest crowd for a championship game since 1975. When NASL's Howard Samuels learned of the attendance, he called it 'a disaster'.

On a soggy Saturday evening in San Diego, the Cosmos's fifth NASL title would come courtesy of a single goal from Giorgio Chinaglia. Later, in a champagne-drenched locker room, the Italian announced proudly that 'We [the Cosmos] *are* soccer in America.'

It had taken another summer in the States but Steve Hunt, even with another Soccer Bowl commemorative ring, had also realized that outside the vacuum that the Cosmos existed in there was little future for him in the NASL. While it had been good to spend some time catching up with old friends and revisiting some of the sites of the Cosmos's halcyon days, it was clear that the league was now a shadow of its former self. 'It wasn't the same,' he says. 'Pelé had gone, and the crowds and the magic went with him.'

CHAPTER 14

NO SURRENDER

Steve Ross married again in October 1982. Despite the unseemly manner in which he had left Courtney Sale for Amanda Burden, Ross had remained close to his former girlfriend and in a lavish reception at the Grand Ballroom of the Plaza Hotel the thirty-five-year-old Sale would become the third Mrs Ross. Over three hundred guests attended the day, including Cary Grant, Steven Spielberg and Frank Sinatra. The music was arranged by Quincy Jones.

The ceremony over, Ross and his bride headed off to Italy on honeymoon. When he returned to Manhattan three weeks later, the Warner chairman walked headlong into the biggest crisis of his career. Atari, for so long the family member that had cosseted WCI, had hit trouble. 'E.T.' the game looked and played as though it had been knocked up in a few weeks (which, of course, it had) and of the four million copies that Atari shipped, some 3.5 million were returned. The problem, as Raymond Kassar later reflected, was that *E.T.* 'was a lovely, sweet movie, and kids like to kill things'.

The miserable failure of 'E.T.' followed several other setbacks for Atari. Not only had the home version of 'Pac-Man' been uninspiring, but their long-awaited new console, the 5200, had all manner of problems, primarily because existing Atari 2600 cartridges were incompatible with the new machine. There was also increased competition from companies like Coleco, whose ColecoVision boasted the most impressive sound and graphics of any home console to date.

For a company grown used almost to printing its own money, the costly errors had now mounted up to such an alarming extent that Atari was forced to revise its projections for the fourth quarter of 1982. First, on 17 November, they were cut by $81 million, then, on 7 December, by an additional $53 million. The following day WCI issued a statement announcing that its profits for 1982 would be significantly lower than the 50 per cent rise they had anticipated, blaming the fall on its consumer electronics division: Atari.

Overnight, the value of Atari and Warner stock plummeted, as nervy shareholders bailed out. It seemed, though, that Steve Ross had foreseen some kind of crash. From late August through to early November, he had sold 479,000 shares in the company for more than $21 million. He was sitting pretty.

If anyone could save Atari, it certainly wasn't Giorgio Chinaglia. But as the computer firm reeled from crisis to crisis – it would soon be losing more than $1 million a day – the Cosmos's skipper was dispatched to Europe to promote the computer company. While the idea that a burly Italian with a short fuse could bully people into buying Atari might have seemed like a good idea, Chinaglia lacked the basic salesman skills. 'It didn't work,' he concludes.

During the Italian leg of his trip, Chinaglia paid a visit to his old club, Lazio, and took the opportunity to train with the team, much to the delight of the 10,000 fans who had heard of the prodigal son's return. While he was there, the club president, Gian Casoni, broached the idea of Chinaglia returning to the Stadio Olimpico as Lazio's chief executive. He even offered him a six-year contract worth £200,000 a year.

Intrigued, Chinaglia returned to the States and promised to think about it.

Back in the USA, storms were ripping their way across the Midwest. Twenty-two people would die and over $600 million worth of damage would be caused by the freak weather conditions. Storm clouds were gathering over the NASL too. Having seen at first hand the gloomy manner in which the previous season had concluded, Howard Samuels was determined to impose himself in his first full season in charge of the NASL. He introduced a glut of new directives for the franchises designed to not only stimulate interest in the league but, more importantly, prevent any more clubs from going to the wall. Consequently, roster sizes would be cut from a maximum of twenty-eight players to just nineteen and a salary cap was agreed with the NASL Players' Association. 'Band-Aids for a haemorrhaging league,' was soccer commentator Paul Gardner's assessment of the changes.

Perhaps the most significant change enacted by Samuels, however, was his introduction of a new team in the NASL – Team America. While it sounded like some elite squad of superheroes, Team America featured only American or naturalized American players and was actually the US national soccer team in another guise. Under a deal worked out with the United States Soccer Federation, a maximum of three American players from each NASL side could join Team America, provided they came through coach Alkis Panagoulias's trials. Once the tryouts had taken place, the Cosmos would lose Jeff Durgan (who would be named as captain), Chico Borja and, after Rick Davis had opted to stay at Giants Stadium, Boris Bandov to the Washington-based franchise. The compensation to the Cosmos for taking three of its best players would be just $50,000 per man.

The rationale behind Team America joining the NASL was that by giving the United States national side a chance of playing better-quality opposition on a more regular basis, not only would the team itself fare better in international competition but it would significantly increase the chance of that elusive all-American soccer superstar finally emerging.

The strength of the US national team was also of primary importance as the USSF had made a last-minute bid to stage the 1986 World Cup Finals. Having initially awarded the tournament to Colombia, FIFA had found itself without a host when the event was expanded from sixteen to twenty-four teams, and the South Americans decided they could no longer accommodate the tournament.

Colombia's withdrawal (and Brazil's subsequent refusal to stage the competition on economic grounds) left just three countries in the running for the quadrennial event – Mexico, Canada and the United States. In a 92-page presentation to FIFA, the USSF projected gate receipts of $40 million for the month-long tournament and crowds for the first round of matches between 35,000 and 50,000. It boasted about record numbers of American youngsters playing the game and the fillip that hosting such a prestigious event would give the game in the US. Not surprisingly, it failed to mention multimillion dollar losses, folding franchises and falling crowds in the NASL.

If anything could breathe life into the NASL, it was the World Cup Finals. With it, there was a chance that America would finally take to its heart what the rest of the planet knew to be the greatest game of all. Certainly, a future without it didn't bear thinking about. The USSF president, Gene Edwards, was confident they could host the world's biggest soccer tournament, declaring the States to be a 'big events country', and adding, 'There is no greater sports stage on earth.'

Back at Giants Stadium, Professor Julio Mazzei had finally been offered the full-time coach's job, a position he readily accepted. It was the least the man described by Nesuhi Ertegun as 'an actor, a comedian, [and] a philosopher' deserved. However, with attendances falling and public interest waning, Mazzei was forced to assemble a squad with neither the choice nor the financial backing that previous Cosmos coaches had enjoyed.

Despite the imposition of reduced roster sizes and the loss of three more of his most important players, the crucial advantage that Mazzei held over previous incumbents was that his affable personality and unabashed passion for the game far outweighed any doubts the Cosmos board may have had over his lack of professional qualifications and his ability to work within increasingly stringent boundaries. When Mazzei asked the Cosmos board for the backing to buy three new players, for example, his request was denied. 'The board,' he reflected, 'had other priorities.'

While the club had tried to look for a coach of international renown, Mazzei's relationship with his players and the esteem in which he was held gave him an edge in his bid to fill the coach's position. The fact that Mazzei had won the Soccer Bowl seemed to be the clinching factor. 'The Professor has done a great job,' said general manager Tom Werblin. 'He is a Brazilian, but he is a New Yorker as much as you and I.'

Unlike Hennes Weisweiler before him, Mazzei had thrown himself into American life with gusto and, like his friend Pelé, considered it a personal crusade to take the game of soccer not merely to the average American but to the world more generally. 'I gave a clinic in Guadalajara, Mexico, for 45,000 people, maybe the biggest clinic in history,' he once said. 'I love to spread this game.'

As a youngster in Brazil, Mazzei had been a promising soccer player but a cheekbone injury had curtailed his career. With football no longer a possibility, he had instead turned to academia, earning a degree from the University of São Paulo before going on to conduct postgraduate work at Michigan State and the University of Paris. In 1962, he had returned to Brazil to teach physical education where he then became affiliated to the Palmeiras club in São Paulo. Soon after, he moved to Santos, where he would befriend Pelé and the two would embark on their missionary campaign to convince soccer-less nations about what they were missing.

Mazzei's ceaseless enthusiasm was one of the principal reasons (after money, obviously) why Carlos Alberto had decided to return to New York and why Giorgio Chinaglia would decline Lazio's offer of the job of chief executive for one more crack at the NASL.

Indeed, with Mazzei at the helm, it didn't take much persuasion to lure one other old boy back to the Big Apple. Having signed a five-year promotional contract with Warner, Franz Beckenbauer had ended his stint with SV Hamburg in the German Bundesliga in the summer of 1982, but even at his farewell game the Cosmos goalkeeper Hubert Birkenmeier was there to badger him about a return to the NASL. Eventually, after further gentle coercion and a successful post-season tour to the Far East with the club, 'The Kaiser', now thirty-seven, gave in and signed on for another season with the Cosmos.

Any sense that the good times were returning to the Cosmos and to the NASL was soon quashed, though, by the news that the USSF had failed in their bid to bring the 1986 World Cup Finals to the United States. Despite some last-gasp intervention by their World Cup Organizing Committee chairman, Henry Kissinger (who had enlisted none other than President Ronald

Reagan as the honorary chairman of the American delegation), the USSF's impressive presentation featuring Pelé and Beckenbauer counted for nothing at FIFA's meeting in Stockholm, Sweden. Instead, it would be a hastily assembled ten-page document from the Mexican Football Association that helped win them a unanimous decision from FIFA's twenty-one-member executive committee. Canada, said FIFA, lacked the requisite number of stadiums for the event while the United States government had not provided sufficient logistical guarantees. The fact that the International Olympic Committee was more than happy to host the following year's Olympic Games in Los Angeles mattered little, it seemed.

Both the USSF and their Canadian counterparts had suspected that their efforts would be in vain when FIFA didn't even bother to send inspecting delegations to visit as they did in Mexico.

After the decision, Henry Kissinger described his first attempt at soccer diplomacy as 'dismally unsuccessful', and later questioned the fairness of FIFA's decision. 'The politics of soccer,' he sighed, 'make me nostalgic for the politics of the Middle East.'

Nostalgia was also at the heart of Giorgio Chinaglia's decision to look to Rome for a new diversion. When he was just twenty-three years old and making a name for himself at Lazio, Chinaglia had barged into the president's office with a cheque in his hand, demanding to invest in the club and be made a vice-president. Although he was denied on that occasion, Chinaglia had never given up the idea of one day becoming the owner of a club, and having rejected the offer of a job earlier in the year, the Cosmos captain's long-distance love affair with Lazio had finally become too much to resist.

In May, he was approached by a consortium of five Italian-American businessmen, based in New Jersey, and asked whether he would front a bid to acquire the Rome club. Mysteriously, neither Chinaglia nor his manager, Peppe Pinton, revealed the identities of the businessmen concerned. All they would say is that they were involved in real estate and travel.

Within three weeks of the story breaking, Giorgio Chinaglia would be installed as the new president and part-owner of the only other soccer club in his life. When asked whether he could combine playing for the Cosmos and helping to run Lazio, Chinaglia, the man who would be voted Lazio's 'Player of the Century', merely shrugged and said, 'Why not? The Cosmos play in the summer and Lazio in the winter.'

Today, both Chinaglia and his erstwhile manager claim credit for closing the deal to purchase Lazio. 'I negotiated successfully the acquisition of Lazio, on my own with several investors, and I sort of handed that over to Giorgio Chinaglia, to his surprise,' claims Pinton. 'He asked me, "How did you do it?" and I said "Just get on the podium and we'll announce you as the president of Lazio."'

Not quite, says Chinaglia. 'Well,' he says. 'Mr Pinton must be a multi-billionaire.'

Despite widespread concern that his move into ownership would adversely affect his form for the Cosmos, Chinaglia took the long-haul commuting in his stride. In June, for example, he played in an exhibition game against SV Hamburg just hours after stepping off a plane from Rome. Typically, he scored twice in a 7–2 rout of the reigning European Champions. He would also play a significant part in the Cosmos regaining its Trans-Atlantic Challenge Cup, scoring three times in games against Fiorentina of Italy, São Paulo of Brazil and the NASL's Seattle Sounders.

What would affect his form, however, was the first serious injury of his illustrious career. During a game against the new

Team America franchise, Chinaglia pulled his left hamstring so severely that he would be out of action for nearly two months. While not the kind of problem to end a playing career, it would nevertheless be serious enough to end Chinaglia's incredible run of 222 consecutive games for the Cosmos. Moreover, it was the first real sign that although Chinaglia could still talk the talk better than anyone else in the game, he was becoming increasingly incapable of walking the walk.

The game against Team America, however, would have greater significance than Chinaglia's injury worries. The previous day, the former Cosmos coach Hennes Weisweiler had suffered a heart attack at his home near Zurich, Switzerland and died. He was sixty-three. Before the match, the players held a minute's silence for the West German and then wore black armbands throughout the game at Giants Stadium.

Phil Woosnam should have seen it coming. A little over a year since the appointment of Howard Samuels as president and CEO of the NASL, Woosnam's job as commissioner was abolished. Under the restructuring, the Welshman would retain a position as a 'special adviser', but as most of the commissioner's duties would now be passed on to Samuels himself, it was unclear exactly how much special advising Woosnam would ever be required to carry out. 'I'm proud of what we did with the NASL,' says Woosnam today. 'To come as far we did in such a relatively short time was a real achievement, especially when you're up against so many obstacles.'

Howard Samuels's determination to drag the NASL out of its torpor was admirable but ultimately futile. In just three years, the league had halved in size and now, with only twelve franchises, two-thirds of the clubs would be guaranteed a place in the play-offs. It also meant that over the course of a season each team would now play each other up to four times. Consequently, the sense of occasion among supporters that accompanied the big match days of the late seventies had vanished amid a widespread feeling of apathy.

For example, the Cosmos's opponents in the first round of the play-offs were the Montreal Manic. Despite finishing last in the Eastern Division some seventy points adrift of the Cosmos's winning total and having lost each of their four meetings with the New Yorkers, they still sneaked into the play-offs by virtue of their better overall record than Tampa, Seattle, San Diego and the woeful Team America, who lost twenty of their thirty games and scored just thirty-three goals.

With everyone anticipating a mismatch, just 17,202 fans showed up for the first game of a best-of-three series at Giants Stadium. It didn't happen. The Manic, courtesy of two goals from their Northern Irish midfielder, Brian Quinn, emerged from the game with a 4–2 victory. While surprising, the defeat still wasn't expected to cost the Cosmos its place in the next round of the play-offs. But it would. In the second game, the Cosmos dominated proceedings in regulation time, but a combination of wasteful finishing by Giorgio Chinaglia and some exceptional goalkeeping by the Manic's Ed Gettemejer saw the match end goalless.

Seven attempts into the subsequent shootout and with only Rick Davis and Julio César Romero finding the net for the Cosmos, Mazzei's men were facing an embarrassing exit. It was left to the Manic's Dragan Vujovic to settle the tie, and while the Yugoslav striker would score, the referee, Peter Johnson, initially disallowed the goal as the ball had crossed the line after the time limit of five seconds. As a relieved

Cosmos squad gave thanks for their good fortune, though, Johnson consulted with one of his linesmen, who informed him that Vujovic's goal was good.

The Cosmos had been knocked out in characteristically controversial circumstances. Just as Steve Ross had threatened to take his players off the field seven years earlier against the Tampa Bay Rowdies, now general manager Tom Werblin took it upon himself first to berate the match officials about their decision and then telephone the league president, Howard Samuels, and lodge an official complaint about Vujovic's winning kick. Both acts of straw-clutching would come to nothing.

Whereas Pelé and Beckenbauer had departed the NASL as Soccer Bowl winners, Giorgio Chinaglia had been denied a final triumph. Instead, he left the NASL after an unsatisfactory defeat, a missed shootout attempt and with everyone around him complaining that the Cosmos had been cheated. For once, though, Chinaglia was unusually restrained on the subject, shrugging, 'We must believe in destiny.'

For all his posturing, there could be no doubt that Giorgio Chinaglia's goalscoring record in the NASL was phenomenal. In his 213 regular season games he had plundered 193 goals, while in forty-three play-off games he had scored a further fifty. It remains a record that nobody in the modern professional game can claim. 'I just wanted to score goals,' Chinaglia says today nonchalantly. 'I didn't care who played beside me really, I never did, that's why sometimes I wasn't liked but I don't care about that.'

His close friend and team-mate of five years Bob Iarusci rates Chinaglia among the very best the game has seen. 'I can honestly say that I can't recall a time when he went more than two games without scoring a goal,' he says. 'And he scored against everybody. It's one thing to score in league games [in the NASL] but another to go to Montevideo and score three against Nacional or go to Buenos Aires and score against Boca Juniors. I think he and Gerd Muller were the greatest I've ever seen... he was a machine.'

Life at Sunnyvale, meanwhile, was anything but sunny. As the summer of 1983 turned to autumn, Atari's CEO, Raymond Kassar, was fired. Having been the darling of investors in 1981 and 1982, Atari had seen all the gains in their share price wiped out. Moreover, almost 2,000 Atari staff had either lost their jobs or had their positions redeployed overseas.

Concerned that there seemed to be no sign of a reversal in the fortunes of either his electronics division or the stock price of Warner, Steve Ross intervened and took personal charge of a management shake-up at Atari that saw Kassar replaced by James J. Morgan, formerly executive vice-president of marketing at the tobacco company Philip Morris.

It was a frantic time for Ross. Not only was he doing his utmost to reignite Atari in an intensely competitive market but WCI was about to record a $418 million post-tax loss after twelve straight profitable years. Indeed, Warner's plight was such that it had now been targeted by the Australian media magnate Rupert Murdoch, who had purchased 6.7 per cent of the company with a view to a takeover bid. In time, a battle-scarred Ross would manage to hold Murdoch at bay but only by selling 20 per cent of WCI to Chris-Craft Industries, a New York conglomerate headed by the billionaire investor Herb Siegel.

There was also the headache that was the Cosmos. After he had endured the twin trials of Atari and Westchester, Ross's pet project had long since lost its lustre and dropped down his list of priorities. Unlike the golden days of 1977, by 1983 there were no celebrities at the Cosmos games. No pop stars or politicians, no actors or artists. As such, there was now very little PR capital to be gained from the matches, and given the perilous financial state of Warner, the Cosmos had become another debt they could patently do without.

As part of his plan to offload non-core divisions of Warner (and in a bid to make the club a more attractive proposition for potential buyers), Ross once more turned to Rafael de la Sierra to help turn the Cosmos around. As the team's executive vice-president, the Cuban architect had played a fundamental role in the success of the Cosmos during the championship years of 1977 and 1978 but had resigned from the club to co-ordinate the many international branches of the Warner stable. Now Steve Ross brought him back as the new club chairman with a remit to give the Cosmos a much-needed facelift.

The restructuring that followed – 'back to basics' was de la Sierra's description – was as dramatic as it was swift. Out went the Erteguns, who stepped down from the board but retained honorary titles within the organization; a new, smaller board was appointed consisting of de la Sierra, Warner special consultant Robert Morgado, Warner senior vice-president Alberto Cribiore, and the president of Atlantic records, Sheldon Vogel. Tom Werblin left his position as general manager to concentrate on marketing (nobody replaced him as general manager), while Giorgio Chinaglia's agent, Peppe Pinton, who had worked closely with de la Sierra in setting up the successful Soccer Camps of America scheme, was given greater authority in the running of the club.

On the playing side, de la Sierra would also introduce severe salary restrictions for players and, significantly, Julio Mazzei would be jettisoned to make way for the return of the Cosmos's most successful coach, Eddie Firmani. 'I work for a company that doesn't accept excuses,' reflected Mazzei, who was given a consultancy role within the club.

As Rafael de la Sierra's new broom swept through Giants Stadium, there was even a rumour that a certain forty-three-year-old Brazilian player was going to be making a return to the Cosmos side. 'He is now Edson Arantes do Nascimento,' said de la Sierra, calling Pelé by his real name. 'Let him stay that way.'

As the new season hobbled into life, the NASL resembled a league that was merely passing time until someone put it out of its misery. Howard Samuels was still grappling to save it, although tampering with the NASL was becoming increasingly difficult for the New York millionaire. In truth, because there were now only nine teams in the league, there was actually precious little to tamper with. The Montreal Manic, who had morphed into a *de facto* Team Canada, folded because the largely French city of Montreal had never really considered itself Canadian and nobody wanted to see them play; the Seattle Sounders soon followed and Team America, Samuels's ambitious new concept, had fallen flat. Despite a respectable average attendance of around 13,000, the USSF still had reservations about their national team playing in a failing club league and when a potentially lucrative marketing deal for the team was rejected it signalled the end of Team America.

And yet it could have been much worse. Fort Lauderdale, for instance, had moved its operation to Minnesota just to stay afloat and Tulsa was only saved from bankruptcy when a local radio disc jockey launched a fund-raising campaign and raised $65,000 from supporters to keep the team from folding.

Despite only limited progess, Howard Samuels remained positive, convinced that the NASL could survive and prosper. 'We've got the most dynamic sport in the country from a participating standpoint, and we've got the greatest economic failure from a financial standpoint,' he said.

Certainly, there was some evidence to suggest that if those franchises that still existed could just keep their heads above water – the Cosmos included – then there was a chance that the NASL could begin what would be a very long road to recovery. The league's debts had been cut, down from the $40 million it lost in 1980 to a reported $25 million in 1983, league expenses had been slashed and a new three-year collective bargaining agreement had been reached with the players that would see a gradual reduction in salaries and the creation of a salary cap of $825,000 per team per year.

Predictably, the latter initiative met with widespread condemnation. While the accord had undoubtedly helped to save the league from collapse, it had stopped short of what league management considered to be a key demand: that all those NASL players earning more than $40,000 a year take 15 per cent salary cuts. Instead, each team agreed to cut its payroll by 10 per cent for each of the three years of the agreement.

Of all the clubs still operating in the NASL, the agreement would hit the Cosmos the hardest. With an annual players' payroll of $1.7 million – comfortably the highest in the league – there was a clutch of players at the Cosmos who would fall foul of Howard Samuels's cost-cutting. Four of them – Hubert Birkenmeier, Jeff Durgan, Angelo DiBernardo and Steve Moyers – would be summoned before Rafael de la Sierra and told that if they didn't accept the wage cut there was every chance they would be released. Although there were other team members who earned more – Johan Neeskens, Vladislav Bogicevic and Roberto Cabanas to name but three – the quartet were selected because they were the top earners whose contracts had not yet been guaranteed by the club, which meant that if the need arose, they could be dispensed with little or no legal redress. What made the players even more incensed, however, was that they, unlike some of the higher earners, actually played football for twelve months a year because of their involvement in the indoor season as well.

It would be the start of a series of fierce contractual disputes between the playing staff and the club's management. Jeff Durgan, now the club captain, was asked to take a 20 per cent reduction, as were the striker Steve Moyers and the goalkeeper Hubert Birkenmeier. Angelo DiBernardo, meanwhile, had the perfect plan B should the Cosmos carry out its threat to trade them. 'Maybe we can all play for Lazio,' he shrugged.

As the NASL limped on and players and agents and lawyers got to grips with the new salary legislation, American football continued to boom, claiming the title of the undisputed number one game in the USA. The 1984 Super Bowl between the Los Angeles Raiders and the Washington Redskins, for example, was watched by 71 per cent of the country. The Soccer Bowl wasn't.

Contractual disputes were cast aside, albeit temporarily, when the Cosmos made its latest stab at bringing back the good old days to Giants Stadium. On 5 May, the team played an exhibition match against the club's alumni. All the old guard turned up, expect for Giorgio Chinaglia, who was busy with Lazio in Italy; Werner Roth, Siggy Stritzl, Terry Garbett, Bobby Smith, Shep Messing, Francisco Marinho, Franz Beckenbauer, Carlos Alberto – even Randy Horton got the call. 'I played before the so-called glory days, when players made $2,000 a season,' says the Bermudan striker. 'But the Cosmos made me feel like I had been a big part of it.'

And, at the end of the introductions as always, came Pelé, now forty-three, who ran out to a standing ovation from the 32,653 crowd (comfortably the biggest attendance of the year at Giants), blowing kisses to everyone and looking exactly as he had the day he retired.

While the current Cosmos won the game 6–2, the very fact that the loudest cheers of the evening were reserved for the former players suggested nostalgia was the only real future the Cosmos had, especially as most of the ageing ex-players were still showed flashes of talent far beyond what any of the current crop of players could ever aspire to. Franz Beckenbauer, for example, was looking fitter and fresher approaching thirty-nine than players young enough to call him dad. So much so, in fact, that soon afterwards the Cosmos would make another audacious offer to lure him out of his latest retirement. This time, though, there was no persuading 'The Kaiser', who confessed that he was now 'better at skiing than soccer'.

CHAPTER 15

WRECK ON THE HIGHWAY

As June melted into July, it was game over for Atari. Having cut staff levels to 1,100 employees in June 1984 – down from more than 7,000 a year earlier – Steve Ross all but gave the company away a month later in a deal brokered by the Cosmos board member Alberto Cribiore. The recipient was Jack Tramiel, the former chief executive of rival computer firm Commodore International Ltd, which gave Warner $240 million in long-term notes and warrants for a 32 per cent stake in his new computer venture.

Atari would not be the only Warner company off-loaded by Ross. Soon after, Franklin Mint, Warner Cosmetics and Panavision were all sold. By 1985, a total of ten of Warner's ventures would be sold or closed. Inevitably, the Cosmos would be one of them.

The years of celebrities, superstars and sell-outs at Giants Stadium now seemed like a distant memory. Even Bugs Bunny had split, hanging up his carrots to shack up with a Cosmos Girl.

For players like Rick Davis, whose first season on the team was alongside Pelé, it was now an entirely different club. 'It was like everyone was hanging out in the middle of a ghost town,' he recalls.

On 27 July, WCI announced that it had concluded a deal to sell a controlling interest in the Cosmos to none other than its former centre-forward, Giorgio Chinaglia. Although the details of the sale were not disclosed, it transpired that like Atari, Warner would receive no cash payment for the sale. Instead, Chinaglia and his team of investors would acquire their 60 per cent share in return for providing a reported $1.5 million of working capital.

Under the deal, the Cosmos would become a partnership with Chinaglia as manager and general partner and Warner as a limited partner. It was another perceptive, essentially risk-free, piece of dealing by Steve Ross. Not only had he appeared to free Warner of another bothersome debt, but he had maintained some interest in the club in the unlikely event of the new owners turning the sorry situation around.

In a statement announcing the sale, Steve Ross said Giorgio Chinaglia's return to the Cosmos was 'an exciting moment for the team and for soccer in America', adding that 'Giorgio has proven himself as a leader both on and off the field, as his great success running the Lazio club in Italy attests and I look forward to a mutually rewarding partnership in the years to come.'

For his part, Chinaglia seemed intent on saving his former club, even though his experience of running a professional soccer club to date consisted of sitting in an office at one of Europe's most famous stadiums, at a club where the average gate was over 66,000 and where support was ingrained in local history.

Now, as president of the Cosmos, his concerns were on an entirely different level. Instead of wondering if there were enough seats to accommodate the legions of die-hard fans who would turn up if there was a game every day of the week, he would be preoccupied with ways and means of attracting more than 8,000 to games at a ghostly Giants Stadium. Still, it wasn't a task he was going to shirk. 'It is with enthusiasm and an appreciation of the challenges that lie ahead that I return,' he told the press. 'I have great confidence in our ability to rejuvenate soccer on a professional basis in America, and I can think of no better opportunity to accomplish this than with the Cosmos.'

Today, however, Giorgio Chinaglia recognizes that taking on a venture as fragile as the Cosmos, especially in 1984 when the NASL was fading fast, was not merely imprudent but verging on the senseless. It was a costly decision, later compounded by his outright purchase of Lazio, which then fell from the heights of Serie A to the sorry depths of Serie B, taking Chinaglia's millions with them. 'I made a big mistake because of my ego,' he says matter-of-factly. 'I went and bought my own team back. And needless to say I lost a lot of money.'

Not everyone agrees with Chinaglia's version of events. 'Peppe Pinton... confirmed to me that Giorgio never owned a thing,' insists Clive Toye. 'It was passed to him to manage but Warner Communications owned the franchise throughout.'

Come the summer and the eyes of the world were on Los Angeles for the Olympic Games. Across the planet, viewers stayed up to watch the most spectacular (and perhaps the most surreal) opening ceremony in the games' history. There was a flood of cheerleaders, scores of marching bands, a spaceman on a jet-powered back-pack, a bank of eighty-four pianists all playing George Gershwin's *Rhapsody in Blue* and, at the end of it all, Ronald Reagan declaring the games open.

Despite the revenge boycott of the Russian team, the event was a huge cultural and commerical success. First, there were the record-breaking feats of the twenty-three-year-old American athlete Carl Lewis, who having taken gold medals in the 100m, 200m, the long jump and the 4 × 100m relay, emulated the achievements of Jesse Owens in Berlin in 1936. Moreover, with a return of $223 million, the Los Angeles games became the first in over fifty years to turn a profit.

What made the success of the Olympics all the more galling for Gene Edwards and the USSF, was that having missed out on hosting the 1986 World Cup Finals, they now had to sit idly by and watch as a record 101,970 fans packed the Pasadena Rose Bowl to watch the final of the Olympic soccer tournament. In fact, when the games ended, soccer would prove to have been most popular event of all, with 1,422,000 fans turning up for the matches, over 300,000 more than for the traditional favourite, the track and field events.

It also put the declining crowds of the NASL in some kind of perspective. For the majority of the franchises still trying to make a go of things, a five-figure turnout was now a cause for celebration. Remarkably, though, the biggest crowd of the season was at Minnesota's Metrodome, where a crowd of 52,621 turned up for the game against Tampa Bay. Ordinarily, the Strikers struggled to get a crowd of more than 10,000. That the Beach Boys were playing live immediately after the final whistle may have been a factor in the high attendance.

When the Olympic flame was extinguished in August, it was clear that the crowds for the games' soccer tournament would not translate into an upturn in the attendances for the NASL. The fact that the Cosmos, for so long the league's best supported and most recognizable team, would miss out on the play-offs for the first time since 1975 would also make the NASL even less attractive. 'There were fewer teams in the league and we were back to playing the same sides maybe four times a season,' explains Angelo DiBernardo. 'That's not what the fans want to see. They want to see big name players and not the same opposition every couple of weeks.'

⚽

On 26 October, the league president, suffered a fatal heart attack in his Manhattan apartment, aged sixty-four. The league's general counsel, Mark Bienstock, said that J. Howard Samuels had been a man with 'an extraordinary array of traits... His forthrightness with the media, his perseverance in addressing problems of individual clubs and his devotion to the sport were indisputable.'

Significantly, no immediate move was made by the NASL to replace Samuels, suggesting that everyone knew that the game was all but up. 'Right now,' said Clive Toye, the Toronto Blizzard president, 'there is no need whatsoever to employ anyone to take Howard's position on a full-time basis.'

Certainly, the players knew that the end was in sight. 'When you are used to playing in front of an average of 47,000, it's difficult to get as excited when only 10,000 are turning up,' says DiBernardo. 'The problem is that the fans pick up on that and if they're not happy, they won't come again.'

Lifeless and leaderless, the NASL soldiered on without any clear idea of where it was going. At least, it was business as usual at the Cosmos, who decided to sack Eddie Firmani once more. Six or seven years earlier, his departure would have provided lead stories for the sports pages of New York's dailies. Now, though, the event, like the NASL, went largely unnoticed.

Firmani had just watched his Cosmos indoor team slide to a 7–4 defeat to the Cleveland Force at the Byrne Meadowland Arena, East Rutherford when he was summoned to the trainer's room to meet with the president, Chinaglia, and the new executive vice-president, Peppe Pinton. There, Pinton informed the coach that his services were no longer required and that his assistant, Hubert Birkenmeier, would take over on an 'interim basis'.

Eddie Firmani's reaction to his latest sacking suggested not only that he knew it was inevitable, but that his heart was no longer in the club or even the game itself. 'I have no animosity whatsoever against the Cosmos,' said Firmani, who confirmed that he would be seeking compensation for the year remaining on his contract. 'They made the decision and it's fine by me. The club is Mr Chinaglia's and he does what he wants.'

Peppe Pinton, however, was feeling less than generous. 'He owes us a play-off, maybe a championship, that he didn't make,' he replied. 'He should give us back his pay.'

Hubert Birkenmeier's appointment as Cosmos coach wasn't the only interim position filled in the dying days of 1984. Soon after, Giorgio Chinaglia's old adversary, Clive Toye, would step into the role made vacant by Howard Samuels's passing, although it was unclear what he could do to salvage the situation.

The Cosmos now had to decide which version of the game it was going to play. Having prevaricated for months about joining the indoor set-up, the Cosmos had eventually entered the fray but soon found that the MISL's version of the indoor game, played in ice hockey arenas (minus the ice), differed markedly from the indoor game that the NASL had tried to implement. Once described by the MISL founder, Earl Foreman, as 'human pinball', it featured American football-style time-outs and was a faster, more frenetic alternative to the indoor game the Cosmos had played. It was also broken into four periods, partly for television and partly because it was so physically demanding,

That lack of familiarity would be evident from the outset. Having lost twenty-two of their thirty three games in the MISL, gates once more began to dwindle. Those low attendances, coupled with a minuscule marketing budget, meant further trouble for the Cosmos. Without the means to attract new players, yet alone supporters, Giorgio Chinaglia was beginning to rely increasingly on college players like Darryl Gee and Mike Fox, not because he had realized the value of having young Americans in the team, but because they were cheap.

He could not win. As inexperienced players found themselves in the starting line-up, the standard of play at the Cosmos dropped precipitously. The more the standard fell, the fewer fans turned up.

Each time the Cosmos opened up the 19,000-seat Meadowland Arena for a home game it cost it $25,000. That meant drawing a crowd of at least 8,000 just to break even. Its average crowd, however, was half that figure. Add an inflated payroll (perhaps the only constant in the history of the Cosmos) and the withdrawal of commercial sponsors such as Minolta and the Metropolitan Life Insurance Company, and the debts soared, reaching a reported $1.5 million. Even the sight of Giorgio Chinaglia once more pulling on his boots for the Cosmos had failed to make a difference. Something had to give.

On 22 February 1985, Peppe Pinton announced that the Cosmos would withdraw from Major Indoor Soccer League. In retrospect, the Cosmos should have known better as two other New York indoor franchises, the Rockets and the Arrows, had already folded. 'We have no obligation if the fans don't support us,' said Pinton. 'If you sell ice cream and nobody buys ice cream, there is no sense in going to the corner and ringing your bell all day.'

Though logical, the departure of the Cosmos provoked an angry response from some MISL franchise owners who felt they had done what they could to accommodate the New York club, only for the Cosmos to walk away when the losses started to bite. One such owner was the Chicago Sting's Lee Stern. 'Giorgio Chinaglia told me personally many months ago that they [the Cosmos] could not survive without indoor soccer. We worked to get them in,' he said. 'There is no Cosmos as far as we're concerned. All it means is a word in the dictionary referring to astronomy.'

Three weeks later, it was the NASL's turn to consider its options. Having watched the Cosmos call time on its indoor operation with the MISL, league president Clive Toye called Cosmos president Giorgio Chinaglia to the NASL's office on Broadway to see if he had any intention of posting the $150,000 letter of credit required for his team to take their place in the NASL 1985 campaign. He didn't. 'In accordance with the NASL constitution, a hearing was held,' recalls Toye. 'Charges were made against the Cosmos and Chinaglia threatened to throw the league's lawyer out of the window. Charming man, as always.'

Without the necessary funds and, perhaps, the will to find them, Chinaglia had forced the hand of Toye and the NASL. A vote was taken and the Cosmos, so long the life and soul of the NASL party, was expelled from the league on 13 March 1985. It left just two outdoor franchises in the NASL – Minnesota and Toronto – and that, even in the warped world of American soccer, could never be construed as a 'league'. Without the Cosmos, the game of soccer, said the *Chicago Tribune*, was no longer the sport of the 1980s but 'the sport of the 2080s'. The *Los Angeles Times*, meanwhile, reported that 'the Cosmos are a team without a league and, perhaps, without a future'. Even the *Financial Times* in London chipped in, reporting 'how a U.S. soccer strategy came unstuck'.

For Giorgio Chinaglia and Peppe Pinton, that future meant exploiting what little credibility the club still had in the world game and arranging some exhibition games against international opposition. In years gone by, such matches had always proved to be a crowd-puller at Giants Stadium, providing a genuine test for the team as well as a much-needed injection of revenue.

There would also be discussions on taking what was left of the Cosmos into one of the smaller, semi-professional leagues, like the Italian-American league in New Jersey, an organization that now boasted the Brooklyn car dealer Joe Manfredi as its president. It would come to nothing.

With the Cosmos now reduced to a not so distant memory, the interest in the remaining clubs waned. With the New Yorkers in the league's roster, there was always a chance that the NASL could pull through and find its true place in the hearts of American sports fans. Without them, there were just a few soccer teams, none of which had the necessary backing or the star quality to shoulder the burden of taking soccer to the States. A fortnight after the Cosmos's expulsion, on 28 March 1985, the North American Soccer League suspended operations.

Predictably, the passing of the NASL met with the kind of general indifference that had typified the last years of its life. For those who did care, the post-mortem was long and often brutal. Some felt the problems stemmed from the league's rapid expansion in 1978 from eighteen to twenty-four teams; others laid the blame on the over-reliance on scores of only average foreign players who came to the States to wring a few more dollars out of their dwindling careers at the expense of developing young American players.

'They cost people bloody fortunes,' says Clive Toye. 'The owners didn't understand that if Pelé was worth $2.8 million, that Gerd Müller [Fort Lauderdale] wasn't worth $1.5 million or even $100,000. In the later days, rosters were full of overpaid, overweight non-superstars.'

For many observers, though, the principal reason for the demise of the game in the States lay in the lap of the Cosmos, suggesting that the beginning of the end didn't start with the loss of the ABC television deal or the failure to land the 1986 World Cup Finals, but the day when a beaming Brazilian ran out on to a painted pitch at Randall's Island and changed American soccer for ever. In short, it was all the fault of the Cosmos.

When the boom in US soccer began in 1975, driven by Warner's bankroll, it prompted the kind of spending that most franchises could ill afford. As mammoth crowds arrived at Giants Stadium and the latest A-list soccer star put pen to paper for the Cosmos, other owners felt duty-bound to supply the same star quality for their supporters, signing up players who didn't warrant salaries anywhere near those commanded by Pelé or Beckenbauer.

The truth was that what occurred at the Cosmos bore little relation to what was happening at franchises around the country. After all, if soccer was going to work anywhere in America it was going to be in New York, a huge, vibrant city with an ethnically diverse population, many of whom came from backgrounds with a long-standing interest in the game itself. The likelihood of a franchise in, say, Minnesota or Edmonton ever being able to boast the same pulling power was slender. With the death of the NASL, the Cosmos was left to rely on a series of exhibition games arranged earlier in the year to save them from heading the same way as countless other forgotten franchises. Even that was far from simple. Without an affiliation to a recognized league, the games would not receive official FIFA sanction and the number of teams willing to flout FIFA regulations to play the Cosmos soon dried up.

When fewer than than 9,000 showed for the Father's Day defeat against Chinaglia's other team, Lazio, it seemed as though the writing was on the wall. In Europe they called exhibition games 'friendlies' but, invariably, the Cosmos friendlies were anything but friendly. The Lazio game was no different. Under pounding rain, the game descended into an ugly, violent tussle – Chinaglia likened it to 'a bullfight' – and it would end with a mass brawl, six yellow cards and two red ones.

After the match, Chinaglia reflected on the meagre attendance and concluded that the club was 'fighting a losing proposition'. It was an understatement. Without the munificence of Warner and the support of the public, the Cosmos budget had shrunk from super-sized to shoestring. Coach Ray Klivecka and Peppe Pinton had not been paid for nine months, the players' pay cheques had bounced, the club was struggling to meet its rent and Joe Manfredi had long since taken back the keys to his Toyotas. Crucially, too, the collective will to continue had all but disappeared. 'Money,' said Pinton 'is the bottom line, and we don't have it.'

The day after the Lazio game, Peppe Pinton tendered his resignation, just as Giorgio Chinaglia was flying across the Atlantic to keep an eye on the money pit that was Lazio. Speaking to the press, he said that the fate of the team was no longer in his hands. From now on, he said, the team's future was 'strictly an ownership decision'.

The ownership wasted no time in deciding. Four days after the Lazio game, they disconnected the phone in the Cosmos office.

EPILOGUE

ONLY IN AMERICA

On 20 December 1991, Steve Ross died. He was sixty-five. Beset by prostate cancer, he had checked himself into a Los Angeles hospital as 'George Bailey', the name of James Stewart's character in Frank Capra's film *It's a Wonderful Life*. It was his idea of a joke, a last-ditch appeal to be given another chance on earth. For once, though, Ross didn't get his way.

After the demise of the Cosmos, Ross's Warner empire had grown prodigiously, culminating in a $14 billion merger with Time Inc. in 1989. The deal had created the world's largest media and entertainment company, encompassing *Sports Illustrated*, *People* and *Time* magazines; the Warner Bros. movie studio; the Warner, Atlantic, Asylum and Elektra record labels; Warner Books; DC Comics, and Home Box Office and a host of America's biggest cable television channels. By the time of his death, Ross was drawing a salary and bonuses of $78.2 million. 'If you're not a risk-taker,' he once said, 'you should get the hell out of business.'

The truth was, when it came to the New York Cosmos there really wasn't much of a risk to speak of, especially once Ross had greenlit the decision to pay for Pelé. Even at the outset, Ross and his investors had eradicated any personal risk by transferring the club's ownership to Warner Communications, which could afford to bankroll the club.

As with McDonald's opening a restaurant in Moscow, the Cosmos concept was driven not by profit but by perception. It was, as Mark Ross reveals, a means to an end. 'Over time, he [Steve Ross] considered it a very good business idea in that the Cosmos could take the Warner Communications name into parts of the world that it hadn't gotten to before.'

The Cosmos was perhaps the ultimate act of commercial arrogance, a moment in time when sport and money, Steve Ross's favourite things, collided head on. Here, after all, was a nation that had, for the most part, never given soccer a second thought, even though the rest of the world clutched it to its heart. 'That was Steve Ross's idea: "Let's buy it. Let's bring it here. And if we show it to people they will like it and they will come back, and then it will grow and we'll really be on to something"', explains Lawrie Mifflin, Cosmos correspondent at the *New York Daily News*.

While it was a fine idea in principle, the mistake in Ross's plan to take soccer to Apple Pie America was that it made no concession to developing the game at any level other than that of the choppers and cheerleaders at Giants Stadium. It was like building a house and starting with the light fittings.

Clearly, the responsibility for putting in place a structure that guaranteed a steady flow of young, talented American players rested not solely with the Cosmos but with the NASL as a whole. While importing a mass of supremely talented players from other countries was commendable, the failure to divert the necessary resources to first improve the collegiate soccer system and then develop the American players who emerged from it would prove costly. Who knows what may have developed if the NASL had happened upon their own Joe Namath or Reggie Jackson?

Thirty years after Pelé ran out on a painted pitch at Downing Stadium, it is hard to escape the feeling that, for all its success, the Cosmos phenomenon was never really anything other than a victory of marketing muscle and conspicuous expenditure over any understanding or love of the game.

When the team and the NASL peaked in 1977 and 1978, it had seemed as if America had finally capitulated to soccer. For a couple of seasons, the Cosmos really was *the* news and its exploits managed to dislodge the Mets and Yankees, the Knicks and the Giants, from the back pages. No longer was soccer the game that papers sent the junior hacks to cover. No longer was it that foreign game for commies and fairies. Even when the Yankees, carried by the bat of Reggie Jackson, beat the Los Angeles Dodgers in the World Series in 1977, they still had to share the spotlight with the Cosmos.

For all its achievements on the field, though, the Cosmos never made a profit. For fourteen seasons it was the most successful and, by some distance, the most visible franchise in the North American Soccer League. No other club, regardless of the profile or salaries of their imported players or the designs they may have harboured on emulating their New York counterparts, came close to capturing the imagination of the American public in quite the same way as the Cosmos. But then no other team could afford Pelé.

With a company like Warner behind them and a chairman as wholehearted as Steve Ross, the Cosmos was always going to be in a league of its own. But just as the financial clout of English Premiership club Chelsea under the Russian billionaire Roman Abramovich has fundamentally changed the landscape of contemporary English football, so it was that the Cosmos under Steve Ross could buy whichever player it wanted, whenever it wanted, to the detriment of the rest of the competition.

While it was a position that any other franchise would have gladly accepted, it nevertheless caused resentment among the other NASL teams, even though a visit from the Cosmos would always put thousands on the gate. On one hand, they were feted for raising the profile of soccer to unprecedented heights in the States. On the other, they were slated for being the team that killed the NASL. Terry Hanson, the vice-president of the Atlanta Chiefs, perhaps summed it up best when he concluded that the Cosmos 'were the best and the worst thing that happened to this league'.

That, though, is just a natural consequence of professional sport, where there will always be a hierarchy, in which some teams dominate and others merely aspire. When the NASL's pre-eminent members, the Cosmos, transformed a dormant league with the signing of just one player, every other franchise in the fragile NASL felt obliged to deliver the same standard of players to their supporters, irrespective of ability to cover the costs. Other clubs, keen to keep pace, traded poorly, enlisting foreign players who ill deserved their salaries and, sometimes, their reputations.

When Giorgio Chinaglia purchased his controlling stake, he did so amid high hopes that his reputation and his tireless promotional effort would breathe much-needed life into the club. It didn't work. Without the expertise or the capital to back up his rhetoric, Chinaglia, who had returned to the Cosmos as a saviour, was left to administer the last rites. Certainly, those at the heart of the NASL, notably Clive Toye, believe that Chinaglia's role in the demise of the club was crucial. 'Giorgio had a malign influence on the Comsos,' he contends. 'I would say he was almost single-handedly responsible for the death of the Cosmos.'

To all intents and purposes, the Cosmos was the North American Soccer League. It was the flagship franchise and the cornerstone, the showcase and the cabaret. With Pelé on board, the Cosmos brought instant credibility to a league widely derided as substandard and irrelevant. It succeeded in introducing the game of soccer to a new generation of New Yorkers, who had been spoilt on the success of the Knicks, the Mets and the Jets. As Shep Messing maintains, 'they laid the foundation for every single kid that plays soccer in this country now.'

But it was more than that. Despite their failure, the Cosmos managed to foist soccer on to a nation that had long resisted. Today, you can travel from coast to coast and find soccer games and soccer fans. Walk into many bars in New York on a Saturday morning and there'll be the English Premiership on the television. Look a bit harder and you'll find live football from Mexico and Argentina, Italy and Spain. Even the commercials have kids kicking soccer balls around. There really is no avoiding it. 'People like me,' says Gordon Bradley, 'don't have to explain what it is anymore.'

Clearly, the truth is that Americans *do* get soccer; it has simply taken them longer to first embrace the game and then discover their own indigenous form of it. Today, there are over twenty million registered players in the country; America has a national team ranked in the top ten in the world; it has successfully hosted the World Cup Finals; and it can boast a women's team that have won their World Cup; and a professional league, the Major League Soccer (MLS), which seems to have learned from some of the mistakes of the many previous efforts and, despite a question mark over the standard, is developing a competition based largely around homegrown players. To call soccer 'un-American', especially in the twenty-first century, makes no sense at all. 'I think more utter rubbish has been written and talked about American soccer both inside America and particularly in the UK than any other single subject ever devised by man,' argues Clive Toye.

Today, two decades after their demise, there are Cosmos websites and chat rooms, supporters clubs and forums, yet there is no Cosmos as such. There are campaigns to relaunch the team and get them back in the MLS but there are also lingering disputes over who actually owns the name. The commonly held belief is that the rights are owned by Giorgio Chinaglia's erstwhile manager, Peppe Pinton, who says he acquired the rights as a 'mark of a respect for Steve Ross'.

Not so, laughs Jay Emmett. 'I'll sue him in every court in the land... he may have been a big player in the pizza parlour but he was never a big player in the Cosmos.'

David Hirshey, meanwhile, regards the current situation as 'surreal', adding that Pinton owning the Cosmos 'would be like Gazza's great friend Jimmy Five Bellies running the Spurs'.

On Sunday, 21 July 1991, there was a reunion match at Giants Stadium to commemorate the twentieth anniversary of the birth of the New York Cosmos. With the exception of Franz Beckenbauer and Giorgio Chinaglia, virtually all of the legendary Cosmos players made an appearance. Hubert Birkenmeier, Werner Roth, Shep Messing, Steve Hunt, Johan Neeskens, Rick Davis, Jeff Durgan – all pulled the shirt on for one more time. The two teams were even coached by Julio Mazzei and Gordon Bradley. Pelé was there too, but, for once, he didn't play. Instead the fifty-year-old took a half-time salute to the strains of the Barbra Streisand song *The Way We Were*.

It would be an emotional night, as another of the Cosmos alumni, Vladislav 'Bogie' Bogicevic, explained. 'This was being home again, born again. So many memories, so many great memories. You just try to think about what happened, sometimes, and I feel I think I should almost cry. People cheering, the national anthem, players, fans. Who knows, maybe one day it will come again – maybe.'

Harold the Chimp was unavailable for comment.

Index